B.S.A.V.A

MANUAL OF PARROTS BUDGERIGARS
AND OTHER
PSITTACINE BIRDS

Edited by

Colin J. Price
M.A., Vet.M.B., M.R.C.V.S.

Published by
British Small Animal
Veterinary Association
5 St. Georges Terrace
Cheltenham
Glos. GL50 3PT

Printed by KCO, Worthing
West Sussex

Published 1988

ISBN 0 905214 07 2

CONTENTS

CONTENTS

ACKNOWLEDGEMENTS

It is a pleasure to acknowledge the willing support of the contributors to this manual. In all areas of its activity, the BSAVA is dependent on the enthusiasm of those who give their time and expertise so generously; without them, the Association would cease to function. This is nowhere more apparent than in the publication of the Association's manuals and the support of all those who have contributed to this book is acknowledged with gratitude.

From inception to publication, Brian Coles has been a wise and supportive adviser. Martin Lawton and John Cooper stepped in when others broke their promises and Martin Lawton helped with the dreadful job of indexing.

Michael Gorton Design are responsible for the layout and graphics of all the Association's manuals. Their skill and helpfulness are gratefully acknowledged.

COLIN PRICE

FOREWORD

I am delighted to have been asked to write the foreword to the Manual of Parrots, Budgerigars and other Psittacine Birds, the latest in the series of B.S.A.V.A. Manuals. The Exotic Pets Manual, which included a chapter on the care of cagebirds, has been a tremendous success and has confirmed the important role played in small animal practice today of the care of species other than cats and dogs.

But more was needed. It has long been the policy of the B.S.A.V.A. to provide suitable publications where there are gaps in the literature. Fortunately, the knowledge about cagebirds has been increasing all the time and with it the necessary authorities available to impart this knowledge in written form. So, in May 1986, the decision was made to publish a Manual of Parrots, Budgerigars and other Psittacine Birds.

Of necessity, the practicing veterinary surgeon must be involved in the care of these fascinating birds and must also be prepared to give authoritative advice on all aspects of their health and welfare. Parrot owners have tended to think that veterinary surgeons know very little about psittacine birds. Indeed whilst veterinary surgeons might have an interest in psittacine birds, in the absence of a satisfactory text book many have felt that their care was less than adequate. This Manual will provide all the necessary information for them to manage, handle, diagnose and treat these birds to a very high standard.

The Editor, Colin Price and his team of ten veterinary and three non-veterinary authors, are to be congratulated on bringing to fruition, in less than two years since inception, this publication which I am sure will become a familiar and much used addition to the range of B.S.A.V.A. Manuals on the practice bookshelves.

PETER H. BEYNON, B.V.Sc., M.R.C.V.S.
President B.S.A.V.A.

Chapter 1

HANDLING AND CLINICAL EXAMINATION

W. T. Turner B.Vet.Med., M.R.C.V.S.

The clinical examination of the sick psittacine, especially one of the smaller varieties, budgerigar *(Melopsittacus undulatus)* or Lovebird *(Agapornis Spp.)* is frequently more meaningful if the immediate environment can also be examined. Therefore, clients should be instructed to transport the sick bird in its cage whenever possible. It is worthwhile arranging appointments for sick avian species at the quietest consulting times. This is especially important in the case of birds with suspected respiratory problems.

Clients should be advised not to clean the cage in order that droppings and seed husks may be observed. They should be advised to empty the water containers although these can be replaced, if necessary, in order to prevent the escape of the inmate.

It is essential that the cage is covered to minimise stress and retain warmth. Any swings should be removed or tied to one side of the cage. High perches should be removed or lowered. Very sick or nervous birds should, as far as practicable, be segregated from other animals waiting for examination and will settle down quickly if placed in a quiet room with subdued lighting.

HISTORY

The value of comprehensive case histories cannot be over-emphasised. Clinical examination is often reduced or foregone either to reduce the stress on the subject or as a consequence of the difficulty of handling some of the larger psittacines. Careful history taking and evaluation of the cage environment can often reveal as much as, if not more than, the physical examination itself.

In order that no vital parts of the history are omitted during the consultation, it is worthwhile using a questionnaire which can be answered by the owner (with or without the help of the nurse/receptionist) before the bird and cage are examined. (See example on page 8). This form should include static data, i.e., name and address of owner, type of bird, age, colour, sex (if known). The owner's description of the type of bird often, with the subsequent examination of the cage, gives an insight into the knowledge of the owner in respect of his pet. Also, it mitigates to some extent the possible embarrassment of being confronted with an owner who expects the veterinary surgeon to be able to immediately identify any captive bird presented. The form illustrated serves as an example and this can be expanded or contracted according to the individual practitioner's interest in avian medicine.

With a very sick bird, evaluation of a proper history together with observation of the bird, the cage and contents, may lead to a diagnosis without the stress of handling.

Avian History Form

Owner's Name and Address

....

....

....
.... Telephone No. ....

Type of Bird .... Age .... Sex ....

Colour .... Name ....

Please answer as many questions as possible:

When acquired ....

Source, e.g. Petshop, Friend, Breeder, Unknown ....

Do you keep other birds? ....

Do you keep other pets? ....

Has the bird been ill before? ....

What is the problem now? ....

How long has it been present? ....

Have you introduced any new birds recently? ....

Or any different seed or medicines? ....

Is the bird confined in a cage or allowed to fly freely? ....

Has there been any change in environment? ....

Is appetite normal? ....

What diet do you feed? ....

Any abnormal appetite? ....

Do you give any supplements, vitamins, minerals, tonics etc? .....

Has drinking increased or decreased? ....

Please tick either yes or no to the following questions:

	Yes	No		Yes	No
Normal activity	☐	☐	Lameness	☐	☐
Normal flying	☐	☐	Spending more time on floor of cage	☐	☐
Normal walking	☐	☐	Ruffled appearance	☐	☐
Normal perching	☐	☐	Tail bobbing	☐	☐

EXAMINATION OF THE CAGE AND CONTENTS

The state of the cage and its contents will reveal much regarding the standard of husbandry as well as the relationship between the client and the bird. This is more salient in the case of smaller birds, when the cage may be filled with toys and treats whereas with the larger parrots, cages are relatively smaller and therefore less liable to be overcrowded with ancillary objects. Nevertheless, an obvious accumulation of dried faeces on the bottom of the cage with dirty food and water containers indicates a poor standard of caring whereas a clean cage, overfilled with toys and ancillaries may indicate a caring relationship but a lack of knowledge of basic requirements.

Steiner and Davies (1981) suggest a check list for the examination of a cage. The most important points to note are:

(a) The presence of toys or mirrors which influence regurgitation especially in the male budgerigar.

(b) Are the perches made from dowelling of the same diameter (which can exacerbate foot pad problems) or have branches been used? Is sandpaper fitted around perches?

(c) Is there any evidence of regurgitation of seed? Seed covered with sticky saliva often adheres to the bars of the cage and also perches, toys etc., but may not be apparent on superficial inspection.

(d) The droppings should be closely observed. 'Nerves', due to the trip to the veterinary surgeon, may have induced some diarrhoea or other abnormal droppings. These should be disregarded and previously voided but fresh faeces observed. Normal faeces consist of white urates or uric acid surrounded by dark faecal material. The consistency of the droppings varies with the species. In the budgerigar and small grass parakeets it is quite compact, but in larger species it is more bulky and in lorikeets almost liquid. Always determine how long it has been since the cage was cleaned. If droppings appear sparse consider abdominal obstruction and/or constipation. If there appears to be an abnormal amount of urates present (more than half the total volume of the droppings) consider renal problems or an increase in catabolism due to a wasting condition. Light coloured bulky, waxy-looking faecal material may indicate undigested fat or starch due to pancreatic insufficiency or liver dysfunction. Psittacine birds with infectious bowel problems often present bulky, fluid faeces containing mucus and/or blood and occasionally undigested seed or grit. Abnormal faecal material should be investigated further in the laboratory.

(e) The food containers and surrounding area should be checked to establish if the bird has been eating the seed or merely dehusking it. Also, the nature of the food offered should be noted.

(f) If the bird has been presented with a history of trauma, the cage should be checked carefully for any projections, broken bars etc.

(g) The perch edges should be examined for any evidence of mites. This is particularly important in the case of birds which are scratching or feather picking. A magnifying glass or otoscope (auroscope) with the speculum removed may be useful when checking for ectoparasites both in the cage and on the bird. However, ectoparasites are not usually a problem in birds caged individually.

OBSERVATION OF THE BIRD

Macaws, Amazons and African Grey parrots are especially vocal in strange surroundings and when handled. Owners should be warned of this at the outset and offered the opportunity to leave the consulting room.

The larger parrots are sometimes brought in without their cage and it is useful to have a portable perch available. Insist that the owner 'perches' the bird in order that it can be observed on 'neutral ground' and not on the owner's shoulder especially before attempting physical examination.

Whether within or without a cage, observe the bird for several minutes. Note posture, attitude and any abnormal movements. Will the bird perch? Is it conserving heat by ruffling? Is it lame? The bird should be observed for muscle tremor which may indicate latent hypocalcaemia, poisoning or pruritis.

Abnormal positioning of the wings may indicate neoplasia, metabolic bone disease or a fracture. Note the eyes; are they closed or half closed? Excessive lacrimatation is often a sign of terminal disease in birds the size of an African Grey parrot or larger. What is the respiration rate? Is it enhanced? Are there any respiratory sounds? Is the bird tail bobbing?

Psittacines, like all birds, are subject to predator attack in the wild. Sick birds therefore 'guard' their condition for as long as possible and frequently appear virtually normal in initial presentation. Therefore, it is important to spend some time examining the cage contents and discussing the case with the owner to note any change in the bird's demeanor as it settles down and becomes accustomed to the new environment.

Any evidence of feather loss should be noted. Is the bird feather picking and if so is it generalised or restricted to a specific area? Has there been an excessive moult? Evidence of feather disease can be easily observed without handling the bird as can evidence of infection with *Cnemidocoptes Spp.*

EXPANSION OF THE HISTORY

At this stage the initial history and the static data can be usefully expanded. Basic questions should be directed at establishing the origin of the bird, length of time in present owner's possession, type of housing, feeding and general caring arrangements. For example, is it a solitary bird or are others present within the household? Is it left for long periods when the owner is absent etc?

Careful questioning to evaluate the owner's opinion of the bird's condition is often helpful. At the same time any changes in diet, water consumption and environment can be established. The owner should be questioned about changes which may have stressed the bird such as the presence of builders or the introduction of a new pet. Has the bird received previous medication either by the owner or another veterinarian? Has this been successful? Owners are initially reluctant to volunteer such information and the few minutes needed for the bird to settle down in the environment of the consulting room can be used to obtain this very useful background information.

Equally important is the information relating to origin and length of ownership. The possibility of illegal importation should be considered. Newly acquired birds, particularly those of uncertain origin, are much more likely to have been exposed to sources of infection than a bird long in the owner's possession and perhaps enjoying solitary status.

EXAMINATION OF THE BIRD

Before attempting to capture a bird or to handle it in any way the owners should be warned of the risks involved especially if the bird is sick, as the stress may be fatal. At the same time, it should be explained that a complete physical examination cannot be performed without handling but where necessary this will be kept to a minimum.

Before attempting to capture the bird, several points should be borne in mind.

HANDLING HINTS

1. The psittacine beak is often referred to as the 'third appendage'. Severe damage can be inflicted particularly by the beak but also by the claws even when handling quite small birds.

2. The bite from the budgerigar is often considerably more severe than expected from the size of bird.

3. Lovebirds, in the author's experience, seldom bite if handled gently. Hen cockatiels can bite quite severely but seldom do so with the same aggression as the hen budgerigar unless very frightened.

4. Any restraint that restricts movement of the sternum will severely compromise respiration. This can kill any bird, particularly those suffering from respiratory disease. If the bird is chased before capture the increased muscular activity will result in considerable heat production. This will not be dissipated when restrained and can result in panting, hyperthermia and collapse.

5. A bird thrashing around its cage can easily injure itself; fractures are not uncommon and feathers are easily damaged.

6. All psittacines are much calmer in subdued light or even total darkness. Some birds appear blind

to red or blue lights. Examination in a dark room using a red or blue filter may reduce stress and facilitate catching and handling.

Protection from beaks and claws obviously has to be employed when capturing and restraining any psittacine bird, irrespective of size. The form of protection will obviously depend upon individual choice but it should be noted that birds the size of the African Grey parrot and larger can inflict severe bites through even quite thick leather gloves.

The only gloves employed by the author are surgical gloves for the capture of budgerigars. Leather gloves tend to restrict finger movements resulting in roughness of movement and possible injury to the bird but for the inexperienced practitioner handling a large parrot they may be essential to avoid injury.

The primary aim during capture should be to secure the head and immobilise the beak. At the same time wing flapping must be prevented. A cloth or paper towel serves as a visual barrier to the bird which can be forced into a corner of the cage. The aim is to grasp the bird from behind with the thumb and forefinger on either side of the temporomandibular joint. A cluttered cage should be cleared in order that this manoeuvre can be carried out with the minimum of hindrance. It is sometimes useful to remove all the perches in order that free access can be gained although with larger parrots it is preferable to restrain the bird while perched using several thicknesses of cloth towel.

The cloth towel can be introduced through the small door opening with ease but the removal of the bird, plus towel, presents problems. It is, therefore, sometimes preferable to turn the cage gently on its side and approach the bird through the bottom opening once the sand-tray has been removed. Again this procedure should be carried out in semi-darkness or in red light.

Handling of the larger parrots, particularly cockatoos and macaws is dangerous both for the veterinary surgeon and the owner if attempted from the owner's person.

RESTRAINT

The technique of restraint is basically the same in all psittacines irrespective of size. A finger and thumb are placed around the bird's neck in order to immobilise the mandible. With small birds the size of the budgerigar, a finger can be placed over the legs and the bird rested in the palm of the hand. The sternum is then left unrestricted. (See illustration).

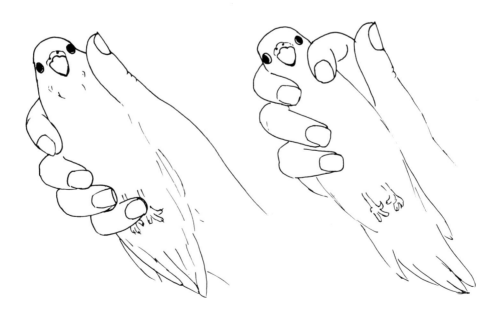

With larger birds a two handed technique is the preferable and for this reason entering the cage via the base is often the easiest approach. Alternatively, the owner may be able to remove the bird from its cage and, while distracting it, a towel can be thrown over the bird and the mandible grasped in one hand and the wings and legs restrained with the other. This manoevre should be carried out in subdued lighting and as calmly and deliberately as possible.

The most difficult psittacine to capture is the large, intelligent parrot that soon becomes aware of the technique and promptly falls on to its back, screaming all the while. The best capture technique for such a bird is to use several thicknesses of towel, attempting to hold the legs and move up towards the mandible, feeling gently through the towel until this can be immobilised with the other hand. Once out of the cage the larger parrots should be held close to the body or wrapped in the towel, in order that wing flapping is prevented. An assistant may be necessary with larger birds in order that the veterinary surgeon can carry out the full physical examination.

Owners sometimes insist on handling birds themselves and it is wise to warn them that even the most placid bird will bite if frightened and that most birds are frightened in a veterinary environment.

Very occasionally a quiet bird such as one of the macaws can be examined without any restraint provided the veterinary surgeon is patient, moves quietly and slowly and is confident in his movements. At the other extreme, some birds are so difficult to handle that sedation may be necessary to carry out a thorough clinical examination. (See chapter 2).

WHAT TO DO IF YOU ARE BITTEN

The immediate reaction is to try to prise the mandible apart but this in most cases only leads to further injury, often for both bird and veterinary surgeons. Tips to remember are:

1.   Blowing in the bird's face.

2.   Spin it round.

3.   Cease to hold the bird.

One of these usually results in release.

THE PHYSICAL EXAMINATION

The physical examination should be conducted in a systematic fashion. A description of the system in print probably takes longer to read than the actual examination. Once the bird has been captured and the veterinary surgeon has acquired some experience and confidence in avian examination, bare hands should be used in order that the strength, vitality and general demeanor of the bird may be accurately gauged.

Respiratory rate and the degree of alertness or otherwise, should be monitored constantly during handling.

WEIGHING

An accurate weight for the bird should be recorded during the examination. Whether this is done at the commencement of the physical examination or just prior to release depends on the difficulty of capture of the bird and its general condition. For methods of weighing, see Chapter 2.

EXAMINATION OF THE HEAD

In the more vocal species examination of the mouth is relatively simple since the bird will still be screaming and the mouth will be open; otherwise the beak can be opened with a pair of Spencer Wells or similar type forceps. Care is necessary to prevent damage to the beak.

Any smell indicative of pus or abscessation within the mouth should be noted. The most obvious lesions are caseous abscesses involving the tongue or choana but tumours are occasionally seen, (see Plate 18:3).

The beak should be checked for any abnormalities, cnemidocoptic mange, overgrowth, malocclusion etc., (see Plates 10:2, 12:3). The beak should also be carefully examined for signs of 'Psittacine Beak and Feather Disease' which may include splits in the horn, fractures, flaking, lack of normal sheath or increased keratin, (see Plate 10:1).

The colour of the cere should be noted. In budgerigars this is the site of sexual dimorphism, blue in the adult male and brown in the hen. Changes can also indicate hormone alterations associated with normal breeding conditions or with hormone-secreting gonadal tumours in male birds.

Neoplasms such as carcinomata, sarcomata and osteosarcomata often cause distortion of the beak and must be differentiated from bacterial, viral and fungal granulomata.

The nostrils and eyes should be checked for discharges. Is the nictitating membrane prominent? Are there any clinical signs of periorbital swelling? Epiphora, causing matting of surrounding feathers and/or conjunctivitis sometimes indicates an infectious problem, either systemic or local.

The eyes should be carefully examined for cataracts which are not uncommon in aged parrots, (see Plate 5:5.). Intra-ocular haemorrhage is suggestive of trauma.

A pupillary light reflex is difficult to evoke in the normal bird as it is under voluntary control. So if the response is rapid this indicates C.N.S. damage.

Next, the external auditory canal should be examined. Discharges cause moulting and discolouration of the feathers just behind the eye. It should be remembered that there is no pinna in the bird.

The feathers round the head are examined for evidence of dried mucus which is an indication of recent vomiting particularly in the budgerigar. The skin of the head may reveal evidence of bruising which can indicate recent trauma, e.g. flying into windows, mirrors etc.

THE NECK

In small birds translumination of the neck will illuminate the trachea in silhouette and foreign bodies, mites etc. can sometimes be detected.

The crop must be palpated. Impaction is a common condition and dilation can occur, especially in budgerigars, as a result of thyroid hyperplasia.

FEATHERS

The bird should be examined thoroughly for evidence of feather abnormalities.

By holding the feathers up to the light, ectoparasites may be seen.

Stress lines occur where the barbules fail to hook together due to malformation and lead to structural weakness, (see Plate 18:1).

Colour breaks are bands of abnormal colour, for example, a yellow band on a blue feather.

Damaged or soiled feathers may indicate inadequate housing or poor hygiene. Broken feathers may indicate trauma.

With cockatoos, the powder down feathers of the rump and thigh and also the crest should be examined for evidence of 'Psittacine Beak and Feather Disease'. In later stages of the disease most of the covert feathers are affected and become deformed often with club shaped bases and are prematurely shed, (see Plate 10:1).

Feather cysts are not common in psittacines but should be noted if present, (see Plate 5:2).

If the bird is feather picking, the feathers of the head remain in good condition, (see Plate 19:1). Another clue is that feather pickers often start by chewing feathers and this can be detected by careful examination.

If a bird is being bullied, the feathers of the head may also be involved and, in fact, the base of the skull is the most common site for such attacks.

Self-mutilation of just one site is suggestive of an underlying problem such as neoplasm.

The prepatagium (wing web) should be carefully examined as the feathers are less dense in this area allowing closer examination of the skin.

THE WINGS

In larger birds, adroit manipulation is often necessary to avoid injury when extending the wings.

It should be noted whether or not the bird has been pinioned.

The humerus, radius, ulna and manus should be palpated carefully. Neoplasms and fractures can be difficult to differentiate without radiography.

LEGS
The legs should be palpated to detect any distortion from the normal shape. Joints should be palpated and manipulated to assess the range of movement.

FEET
The skin of the legs and feet should also be examined for evidence of cnemidocoptic mange or bumble foot.

The nails should be normal in appearance, not overgrown or deformed.

Occasionally budgerigars and small psittacines exhibit necrosis of the digits due to vascular constriction as a result of encircling foreign material — hair, synthetic nesting material etc. Larger psittacines kept in outside aviaries may show evidence of frostbite.

The digits should be palpated for evidence of fractures, dislocations, arthritis or gout.

THE PECTORAL AREA
By palpatating this area it can be assessed whether the muscle mass is normal or the bird has 'gone light', i.e. is thin or emaciated.

This area is a common site for superficial tumours particularly lipomata in budgerigars.

Auscultation can be carried out on larger parrots but its value is limited in birds smaller than an African Grey parrot.

ABDOMINAL PALPATION
Using the index finger, with or without the thumb depending on the size of the bird, abdominal palpation can be carried out.

Liver enlargement is easily detected as is egg retention. If abdominal distension is present, it should be possible to assess whether it is fluid in nature or of more solid consistency. Tumours may be palpable.

VENT
Soiled vent feathers may indicate gastro-intestinal disease.

The vent should be checked for evidence of prolapse. Care must be taken to differentiate between impaction, a prolapse and a tumour of the cloaca.

The condition of the surrounding skin should be noted. Soiled and broken feathers should be removed from the area.

Some parrots lack a preen gland but the area dorsal to the vent should nevertheless be carefully examined since this is a common site of tumour formation. Squamous cell carcinomata are common in this site, (see Plate 5:3); adenomata and abscesses are also seen, particularly in budgerigars, and must be differentiated.

REFERENCES

ARNALL, L. and KEYMER, I. F. (1975). Bird Diseases. Bailliere Tindall, London.

COOPER, J. E. et al (1985). Eds. BSAVA, Manual of Exotic Pets.

COLES, B. H. (1985). Avian Medicine and Surgery. Blackwell, Oxford.

ENSLEY, P. (1979). Caged Bird Medicine and Husbandry. Vet. Clinics Nth. America **9** 499.

HARRISON, G. J. and HARRISON, L. R. (1986). Clinical Avian Medicine and Surgery. W. B. Saunders, Philadelphia.

LAFEBER, T. J. (1971). Physical Examination, Laboratory and Medication Techniques and Hospitalisation Procedures for the Common Parakeet and Canary. Vet. Therapy (IV) 357.

KING, A. S., McLELLAND, J. (1984). Birds — Their Structure and Function. Bailliere Tindall, Eastbourne.

PETRAK, ML. (1982). Ed. Diseases of Cage and Aviary Birds 2nd Edition. Lea and Febiger, Philadelpia.

SOIFER, F. K. Physical Examination and Medication of Cage Birds. Vet. Clinics Nrth. America, **3**2, p.143.

STEINER, C. V. and DAVIS, R. B. (1981). Caged Bird Medicine. Iowa State University Press, Ames.

TURNER, W. T. (1985). First Aid for Cage Birds. In Practice 7.76.

TURNER. T. (1985). Cage Birds in BSAVA Manual of Exotic Pets. p. 106.

Chapter 2

ANAESTHESIA

B. H. Coles B.V.Sc., M.R.C.V.S.

LOCAL ANAESTHETICS

Local anaesthetics, particularly those of the procaine group, should be used with care because of their toxicity. Dosage should be calculated carefully and administration can be facilitated by dilution.

There is considerable variation in the pain threshold over the various parts of the avian body. Wounds to the crop and over the pectoral muscle can often be sutured in the fully conscious bird without any apparent discomfort. However, the skin around the eyes, cere and cloaca and over the legs is extremely sensitive and general anaesthesia is required for surgical procedures in these areas.

THE ASSESSMENT OF THE PATIENT PRIOR TO GENERAL ANAESTHESIA

All parrots must be carefully assessed by a thorough clinical examination before induction of anaesthesia because the bird's condition will affect the risk and may influence the choice of anaesthetic.

Age

Atheroma and arteriosclerosis of the main blood vessels are not uncommon in aged parrots and are undetectable in the living bird.

Fitness

A bird kept in a cage for most of its life is unlikely to be as fit as one which inhabits an aviary.

Respiratory System

Chronic respiratory disease is common in parrots but usually the air sac system is the part of the anatomy which is affected. Unless this is grossly diseased so that the passage of air is severely restricted or the rate of respiration during anaesthesia is allowed to become very depressed, then the anaesthetic risk is not greatly increased. However, if any part of the bronchial system is diseased, and this applies particularly to the syrinx, the anaesthetic risk is increased. It is not uncommon for the syrinx to be partially occluded with exudate from, for instance, an aspergillosis infection resulting in a change in voice. Birds in which obvious rhales can be heard during respiration should be viewed with caution.

Bodily conditions

Excessive thinness or fatness increase the anaesthetic risk. Parrots which have lost a lot of feathering through self plucking or disease are liable to lose a lot of heat during anaesthesia and the necessary precautions should be taken.

Hydration

Birds which have consistently watery faecal droppings or exhibit abnormalities in the white urate portion of the droppings may have impaired renal function. These parrots may not properly excrete some drugs such as ketamine. If dehydration or shock are suspected it is a simple procedure to clip a nail, collect a small amount of blood in a microhaematocrit tube and determine the P.C.V. If this is over 55%, the bird needs rehydrating, if the P.C.V. is below 20%, then the parrot theoretically needs a blood transfusion (see Coles 1985).

Abdomen

Birds with a space occupying lesion of the abdomen or an egg impacted in the oviduct, both of which may be palpated abdominally, will have a reduced air sac capacity. The minute volume will be depressed or respiratory rate may be increased. In either case these birds need special care.

Crop

Birds with a full crop are liable to regurgitate and obstruct the glottis during anaesthesia.

ASPECTS OF AVIAN PHYSIOLOGY WHICH INFLUENCE ANAESTHESIA

Although the avian lung is relatively smaller than its mammalian counterpart, it is a more efficient gas exchanger. It is a fixed volume structure not expanding and contracting with each respiration as does the mammalian lung. The bird's lung is composed of a rigid meshwork of blood and air capillaries, the size of the latter being less than one third the size of the smallest mammalian alveolus. Air flow and blood flow take place at right angles to one another in this laticework. The net result is a gas exchange surface approximately ten times more extensive than in mammals. There is also a high pressure gradient for the exchange of oxygen and carbon dioxide and, what is of importance to the anaesthetist, anaesthetic gases.

The flow of gases through this non-expansible lung is pumped by a system of bellow-like air sacs. These occupy a large part of the volume of the bird's body. The air sacs are almost bloodless and are not part of the gas exchange surface. For a fuller explanation of the avian respiratory system the reader is referred to King and McLelland (1984).

The flow of air through the lung is unidirectional. It is true that inhaled gases pass twice through the lung but they do not follow the same route on both occasions. Little if any absorption takes place as air is drawn through the mesobronchi into the posterior air sacs. Most gas exchange takes place when the gas is expelled from the posterior air sacs back though the matrix of blood and air capillaries in the lung to the anterior air sacs.

Marley and Payne (1960) showed that should the respiratory rate become too depressed during anaesthesia, the level of CO_2 in the lung can, within a short time, build up to dangerous levels with fatal results. These workers showed that even if the rate of respiration appeared normal there was always a gradual build up of carbon dioxide. Many anaesthetics are respiratory depressants. It is therefore important that the anaesthetist should make sure that the flow of oxygen in the anaesthetic circuit is high enough. Flow rates should be at least three times the normal minute volume of the bird. To be on the safe side, flow rates should be approximately 3ml per gram of body weight. Therefore an Amazon parrot weighing 400g needs a flow rate of oxygen of 1200mls. Also the whole anaesthetic circuit should be flushed with oxygen every 5 minutes.

The anaesthetist should take into account that many vaporisers are not accurate at low flow rates. It is therefore far safer to have too high a flow rate rather than one which is too low.

Because of the large internal surface area of the air sacs there is considerable loss of body fluid during anaesthesia, particularly if this is prolonged. If the body cavities are opened for laparotomy or there is blood loss in a patient which is already dehydrated the situation could become critical. Some workers (Smith, 1985) take the precaution of giving a bolus of warm saline intravenously before and after carrying out abdominal surgery on small birds.

Atropine

An injection of atropine at the same time as the anaesthetic may be helpful. Although atropine does, to some extent, help in reducing the excess secretion of mucus, which can be important in birds where there is upper respiratory disease, the drug's most important influence is on the heart. Atropine reduces any tendency to bradycardia through vagal stimulation as a result of handling or of traction on the viscera during laparotomy. Also some anaesthetics produce bradycardia and atropine may help to counteract this effect.

MEASURES TO BE CARRIED OUT TO ENSURE SAFE ANAESTHESIA IN PARROTS

1. Always carry out a careful clinical assessment of the patient prior to anaesthesia.
2. Weigh the bird accurately if an injectable agent is to be used.
3. It is probably safer to give atropine ($0.05 - 0.1$mg/Kg) with the anaesthetic in all cases. The higher dose rates should be used for the smaller birds.
4. If the size of the bird permits, always use an endotracheal tube. This allows more efficient artificial ventilation of the respiratory system should this become necessary.
5. It is safer to have the bird on oxygen whether a gaseous anaesthetic is used or not.
6. It is preferable for the oxygen flow rate to be too high than too low.
7. Flush out the circuit with oxygen every $5 - 10$ minutes to prevent a rise in carbon dioxide levels.
8. Always warm the bird on a heat pad. In an emergency a hot water bottle covered in newspaper will suffice, although a custom made electrical or water circulating pad is better.
9. Do not remove excess feathering from the surgical area or excessively wet the bird during pre-operative cleaning and antisepsis.
10. Keep the plane of anaesthesia as light as possible so that respiration does not become too depressed.
11. If possible position the parrot in sternal or lateral recumbancy during anaesthesia.
12. Withhold food for 12 hours in birds weighing over 1Kg. For birds weighing about 500g, withhold food for 6 hours and for those weighing less, do not withhold food for more than 3 hours.

JUDGING THE DEPTH OF GENERAL ANAESTHESIA

This can be difficult. It is not unusual for a parrot which appears to be anaesthetised to suddenly flap violently if a sensitive part of the integument is stimulated. The clinician will usually assess the state of anaesthesia on the loss of righting reflexes and by the rate, depth and regularity of respiration. Respiratory movements should be deep and regular and the rate should not be less than half that of normal respiration in the conscious bird. Rapid, shallow or intermittent respiration are undesirable.

During moderately deep anaesthesia the eyes are usually closed but the corneal reflex, indicated by movement of the nictitating membrane, should always be present. Response to stimulation by pinching or pricking the cere and the cloaca should be just preceptible or only just abolished. Pinching the feet is unreliable in parrots.

WEIGHING

The bird's weight should never be guessed in order to calculate the dose of an injectable agent. It is essential that it is accurately weighed. Smaller parrots and parakeets are confined in a small cloth bag or elasticated tubular bandage and weighed using a Persola spring balance (obtainable from the British Trust for Ornithology, Tring, Herts). For large parrots, the author prefers to use a large black plastic sac because the bird is less liable to panic being in the dark and also because it will have difficulty biting through a smooth plastic bag. It is also possible to weigh the parrot by placing it in a cardboard box, which is then placed on weighing scales. Whichever container is used care should be taken not to damage tail feathering.

Weighing the cage with and without the parrot may be easier for large parrots if accurate scales are available.

APPROXIMATE AVERAGE WEIGHTS OF THE COMMON SPECIES OF PSITTACINE BIRDS

(All weights refer to anatomically and physiologically normal adult birds)

Scarlet Macaw	1Kg	Jendaya conure	120g
Lesser Sulphur Crested Cockatoo	300g	Budgerigar	30—50g
Greater Sulphur Crested Cockatoo	700g	Lovebird	45—55g
African Grey Parrot	400g	Cockatiel	80g
Amazon Parrot	250—700g	Kakariki	55g
Senegal and Meyer's Parrots	150g	Rosella parakeet	100g
Blue headed pionus	250g	Bourke's parakeet	50g
Dusky headed conure	170g	Turquoisine parakeet	50g

INJECTABLE GENERAL ANAESTHETICS

A variety of drugs have been used successfully for anaesthesia by injection although most have now been discarded for this purpose.

The following are the most useful: —

Alphaxalone — Alphalodone ('Saffan', Glaxovet Ltd)

This drug has been used in parrots by the intravenous, intramuscular and introperitoneal routes. It is only really effective by intravenous injection and because of the small size and fragility of avian veins, its use is only practical in the moderate or large size parrots. When used intravenously a suitable dose is 10—36mg/Kg. Because there is some evidence that this drug may have an adverse effect on the heart it is not safe for use in aged parrots.

**Pentabarbitone Sodium
Thiopentone Sodium
Methohexitone Sodium
Equithesin**

All these drugs can be, and have been, used for avian anaesthesia but none of them are very satisfactory because of their narrow safety margins.

Xylazine ('Rompun', Bayer U.K. Ltd)

When used alone in doses of 10mg/Kg or higher it is not a satisfactory anaesthetic. It has serious affects on the cardiovascular and respiratory systems. Also there is usually violent wing flapping during induction and recovery from anaesthesia. Recovery times are prolonged.

Ketamine

This drug produces a cataleptic state of hypnosis but has no analgesic effect. It is widely used both alone and in combination with other drugs. Mandelker (1973) first used it intramuscularly in budgerigars and other birds at doses ranging from 50—100mg/Kg. The author has used it on many occasions and in one instance used it in a budgerigar at the rate of 50mg/Kg on three consecutive days, without ill effect. There is some evidence that this drug has a depressive effect on the cardiac and respiratory systems. Ketamine is broken down by the liver and excreted through the kidneys, so any disease or malfunction of these organs is liable to prolong recovery.

Ketamine is most useful when used in combination with other drugs such as Acetyl Promazine, Diazepam and Xylazine.

Ketamine and Diazepam

Ketamine 10—40mg/Kg intramuscularly.
Diazepam 1.0—1.5mg/Kg intramuscularly.

This combination has been used in different species of birds by the following workers: Redig & Duke (1976), Forbes (1984) and Lawton (1984).

Turner (1986) uses the related water soluble compound, Midazolam (Hypnovel, Roche Products Ltd.) which can be mixed in the same syringe with the Ketamine. This worker used 50mg/Kg of Ketamine together with 4mg/Kg of the Midazolam. The author prefers to use a dose of 20mg/Kg of Ketamine in combination with 4mg/Kg of Midazolam. Both drugs slightly depress respiration but at the latter dose rate this effect is not very evident. There is usually good sedation, the level of which depends on the dose of ketamine used. Also there is good muscle relaxation. Induction and recovery are smooth.

Ketamine and Acetyl Promazine

This combination has been used by Stunkard & Miller (1974) and Steiner & Davis (1981) and others. It is said to result in a smoother recovery with less tendency to wing flapping than when Ketamine is used alone. The dose used is 0.5—1.0mg/Kg of Acetyl Promazine and 25—50mg Kg of Ketamine intramuscularly.

Ketamine and Xylazine

This is probably the most widely used combination of injectable anaesthetics and would appear to give the most consistently reliable results.

Ketamine 20mg/Kg intramuscularly.
Xylazine 4mg/Kg intramuscularly.

This dose will always produce some level of sedation, usually only light in the smaller species but fairly profound in the larger specimens. If the sedation produced is not sufficient for the procedure envisaged, the anaesthesia can be supplemented with a volatile anaesthetic such as Halothane. Harrison (1984) uses a repeat dose of the Ketamine and Xylazine for prolonged anaesthesia. Doses quoted by different workers have varied from 5mg/Kg to 50mg/Kg for the Ketamine whilst the dose of Xylazine has usually been kept at about one fifth that of the Ketamine (i.e. an equal volume of Ketamine and Xylazine have usually been used). In the writer's experience doses below 15mg/Kg of Ketamine, although they produce some sedation, rarely produce satisfactory anaesthesia in parrots unless the bird is very ill, when it is wiser to use a lower dose.

GENERAL ANAESTHESIA USING VOLATILE ANAESTHETICS

METHODS OF ADMINISTRATION:
A volatile anaesthetic may be used to induce anaesthesia either via a head mask or an anaesthetic chamber.

Anaesthetic Chambers
The anaesthetic gases are carried from the anaesthetic machine to the chamber by a small bore tube.

A custom-made glass box approximately 12''x 8'' can be used as the anaesthetic chamber and is suitable for most sizes of parrots. Alternatively, a portable fish tank which is readily available from many pet shops will also serve this purpose.

Most birds will settle in the box providing there is not a lot of movement in their immediate vicinity and there are no bright lights shining into the box.

This technique is unreliable. It is only suitable for induction of very light anaesthesia and many birds thought to be anaesthetised will flap violently when lifted from the chamber.

The use of a head mask
Anaesthetic gases may be administered via a head mask either to induce anaesthesia or to deepen anaesthesia which has been induced in a chamber.

Holding a struggling bird's head in the mask to induce anaesthesia requires a gentle but firm grip to avoid restriction of movement of the bird's thorax and abdomen.

A variety of objects may be converted for use as face masks. For smaller species the barrels or syringe cases of plastic hypodermic syringes can be adapted. Alternatively, masks can be made by cutting the bases off various sizes of plastic bottles. Standard small animal face masks can be used but transparent plastic has the advantage that the eye of the bird can be seen.

Endotracheal tubes
Once anaesthesia is induced, if the bird is over 200 grammes in weight, an endotracheal tube should be introduced. It is possible, with difficulty, to intubate birds down to 100 grammes in weight but below this weight the thickness of the wall of the tube becomes a factor in obstructing the airway. Small semi-rigid uncuffed plastic tubes, size 2.5mm to 4mm are obtainable from Portex Ltd. Alternatively, a canine urinary catheter can be adapted by cutting the end obliquely at a suitable length and then smoothing the edges in a flame. All endotracheal tubes should be as short as practical and lubricated before insertion.

The tube should fit loosely in the glottis. The glottis in psittacines lies hidden at the root of the bulbous piston-like tongue and to bring it into view, it is necessary to pull the tongue forward a short distance with fine forceps.

Before inserting the tube, it is preferable to anaesthetize the mucous membranes of the glottis and proximal trachea with 1—2 drops of 2% lignocacaine and adrenaline. This can be dripped from the needle of a dental syringe. A zylocaine spray should never be used as the metered dose (10mg) is far too high for any bird and, as there is no adrenaline, systemic absorption is rapid.

The endotracheal tube can be kept in place by a strip of adhesive plaster around the upper or lower beak.

ANAESTHETIC CIRCUIT
Whether a mask or an endotracheal tube is used, the bird should be connected to a ''T'' piece anaesthetic circuit. An Ayre's T-piece is satisfactory for all birds above 400—500 grammes in bodyweight and, in fact, works for all sizes of birds. However, the Bethune ''T'' which has minimum dead space and was designed for use in small laboratory animals, is safer for birds below 500 grammes in weight.

RESPIRATORY MONITOR

An "Imp" audible respiratory monitor can be used with a "T" piece circuit. The monitor will function in all sizes of birds if the sensitive probe is extended into the opening of the head mask or endotracheal tube. If it does not work satisfactorily, particularly in the smaller birds, it is probably because the movement of air in the system is sluggish as a result of respiratory depression. Practically, it is wiser to set the monitor at minimum sensitivity so that it only detects air movement due to respiration.

VOLATILE ANAESTHETIC AGENTS

Ether

This agent has been used in the past by the author and others and is satisfactory. However, it has been superseded by more satisfactory anaesthetics. Induction and recovery are prolonged because ether is very soluble in plasma. Ether is irritant to mucous membranes and therefore not particularly pleasant for the patient. It also suffers from the disadvantage that it is highly inflammable.

Cyclopropane

This anaesthetic has been used in birds other than parrots, mainly by laboratory workers. It is probably quite suitable for the anaesthesia of parrots but is rarely used because it is highly explosive and there are safer volatile anaesthetics available.

Methoxyflurane

This anaesthetic is not particularly volatile and has a high boiling point so that concentrations about 3.5% are difficult to achieve. The agent is also quite soluble in plasma so that induction and recovery times tend to be prolonged (8—10 minutes). It takes longer to change the depth of anaesthesia and a suitable level of anaesthesia is easier to maintain. Because of these factors it is considered to be the safest of volatile anaesthetics and can be administered by the open drip method. However, using the agent in this way without a proper vaporizer is wasteful and expensive. The anaesthetic is a good analgesic and analgesia is said to persist after recovery.

Halothane

This is a potent anaesthetic which has been used in birds of all kinds for many years. It is a safe anaesthetic so long as the anaesthetist understands the peculiarities of the avian respiratory system. The drug is relatively insoluble in plasma so that induction and recovery of anaesthesia are rapid (1—3 minutes). When used for induction a low concentration of 0.5—1% is used initially and gradually increased to 3% or possibly 4% until the required level of anaesthesia is achieved. Some clinicians start with the higher concentration so as to produce a rapid knock-down effect but in the author's opinion this procedure is dangerous. If the bird is struggling large volumes of potent anaesthetic are rapidly inhaled and a surplus builds up in the posterior air sacs. Should apnoea ensue, this excess anaesthetic has to be flushed out by artificial ventilation. In so doing, the gas in the posterior air sacs has to pass across the exchange surface in the lung and further systemic absorption occurs.

In most cases, anaesthesia can be maintained using a concentration of 1.5—3% Halothane. If an injectable anaesthetic agent has been used to induce anaesthesia, then the bird can usually be maintained on 0.5—1.5%.

Although a Boyle's type vaporizer or Trilene bottle can be used for administering the anaesthetic, a 'Tec' vaporizer is preferable. A Mark III or Mark IV Fluotec should be used as the Mark II is not accurate at low rates.

Isoflurane

The author has no experience of this anaesthetic and is indebted to two colleagues, R. S. Jones (1986) and G. J. Harrison (1986) for the following information. At present the compound is licensed by the Federal Drugs Administration for use on horses in the U.S.A. and is marketed as Aerrane but is not yet available for veterinary use in Great Britain. It has obvious advantages and is likely to become important for anaesthesia in avian practice in the future.

Induction and recovery with Isoflurane are very rapid. Also much less of the drug is metabolised (0.3%) in the body compared with Halothane (15—20%) or methoxyflurane (50%) and, because of this, organ toxicity, particularly hepatotoxicity, is very much reduced. This is important in avian anaesthetics where patients are liable to be presented with undiagnosed liver problems.

Harrison (1986) induces anaesthesia with a concentration of 5% in an oxygen flow of 1—2 litres and maintains anaesthesia on a concentration of 2.5 — 3.5% in an oxygen flow of one litre.

The depth of anaesthesia can be very rapidly adjusted and the length of time between apnoea and cardiac arrest is much longer than with Halothane or Methoxyflurane. Recovery from the anaesthetic is usually so rapid that there is much less chance of the bird injuring itself during this period by violent flapping. Its main disadvantage is it is likely to cost approximately six times as much as Halothane.

POSTOPERATIVE RECOVERY
When recovering from the anaesthesia, the bird is wrapped in a paper towel and placed in the bottom of its cage in a warm and preferably dark room. In the case of the large macaws, which sometimes flap violently during recovery, a length of adhesive zinc oxide or masking tape can be lightly wrapped around the wings to produce some restraint. Very small birds, or birds which have been anaesthetised for a prolonged period, should be left to recover in an incubator at 80°F (27°C).

REFERENCES

COLES, B. H. (1985). Avian Medicine and Surgery. pp 104, 111, 175. Blackwell Scientific Pub. Oxford.

FEED, M. R. and KULMAN, W. D. (1977). Intra Pulmonary Carbon-Dioxide Sensitive Receptors: Amphibians to Mammals. Respiratory Function in Birds, Adult and Embryonic. Symposium of the 27th International Congress of Physiological Sciences, Paris. (Ed. J. Piper), pp 30-50 Springer-Verlag, Berlin.

FORBES, N. A. (1984). Avian Anaesthesia. Vet. Record 115 (6), 134.

HARRISON, G. J. (1984). New Aspects of Avian Surgery. Veterinary Clinics of North America, 14 (2), 363-380.

HARRISON, G. J. (1986). Personal communication.

HARRISON, G. J. and HARRISON, L. R. (1986). Clinical Avian Medicine and Surgery. W. B. Saunders, Philadelphia.

JONES, R. S. (1986). Personal communication.

KING, A. S. and MCLELLAND, J. (1984). Birds: Their Structure and Function. pp 64, 140-142, 311-312. Baillière Tindall, London.

LAWTON, M.P.C. (1984). Avian Anaesthesia. Vet. Record, 115 (3), 71.

MANDELKER, L. (1972). Ketamine Hydrochloride as an Anaesthetic for Parakeets. Veterinary Medicine/Small Animal Clinician, 67, 55-56.

MARLEY, E. and PAYNE, J. P. (1964). Halothane Anaesthesia. Proceedings of a B.S.A.V.A./U.F.A.W. Symposium, (Ed. O. Graham-Jones), p 127. Pergamon, Oxford.

REDIG, P. T. and DUKE, G. E. (1976). Intravenously Administered Ketamine and Diazepam for Anaesthesia of Raptors. Journal of the American Veterinary Medical Association, 169, 886-888.

STEINER, C. V. and DAVIS, R. B. (1981). Caged Bird Medicine, p 136. Iowa State University Press, Ames, Iowa.

SMITH, R. E. (1985). Hysterectomy to Relieve Reproductive Disorders in Birds, p 40. Avian/Exotic Practice, Vol. 2 No. 1. Vet. Practice Publishing Co., Santa Barbara.

STUNKARD, J. A. and MILLER, J. C. (1974). An Outline Guide to General Anaesthesia in Exotic Species. Veterinary Medicine/Small Animal Clinician, 69, 1181-1186.

TURNER, W. T. (1986). Personal communication.

Chapter 3   # RADIOGRAPHIC EXAMINATION

B. H. Coles B.V.Sc., M.R.C.V.S.

SEDATION/ANAESTHESIA FOR RADIOGRAPHY

Sedation or light anaesthesia are almost invariably necessary for satisfactory restraint and positioning. Often Halothane alone administered via a head mask is sufficient for short procedures. For longer investigations, which may include endoscopy and blood sampling as well as radiography, an injectable drug given to produce a deeper and longer period of sedation may be required. (See chapter 2).

POSITIONING

In the sedated parrot, the body can be held in position using adhesive tape placed over the wings, legs and neck. If this is attached to a sheet of transparent plastic (Perspex), repeated exposures can be taken, if necessary, on different cassettes.

For routine diagnosis, dorso-ventral and lateral views should be taken. Accurate positioning is essential for the radiograph to be of diagnostic value. In the dorso-ventral projection, the sternum should overly the vertebral column. If it does not, distortions will occur and accurate comparison of the left and right sides of the body is impossible. In the lateral projection, the two hip joints should be superimposed as should be the two shoulder joints; furthermore, the two wings should be equally extended as well as the legs.

FILM, CASSETTES AND EXPOSURE FACTORS

Envelope wrapped non-screen film is used for very small species and in cases where greater detail is required. For larger species, intensifying screens may be required in which case rare-earth screens are preferable. A grid is never necessary.

When using non-screen film the required KV will usually be between 45 and 60 and the mAs between 4 and 6. If the required exposure time results in blurring due to movement, this can be reduced by reducing the film focus distance.

All exposures should be timed to take place at the end of inspiration when the air sacs are at maximum distension. This makes the best use of the natural air contrast of the air sacs filling much of the bird's body. Accurate processing is essential to obtain films of diagnostic quality.

THE USE OF CONTRAST MEDIA

Barium sulphate suspension can be administered using a crop or gavage tube (See chapter 20). It can be given neat or diluted 50:50 with water. In either case it should be given slowly so that there is no chance of the fluid refluxing up the oesophagus and flooding the glottis. A suitable quantity of barium for a small parakeet is 0.5ml and for an Amazon parrot is 2ml. For a large macaw or cockatoo 7—8ml can safely be given. The contrast medium will be in the crop, proventriculus and gizzard within a few minutes and will usually reach the intestine in 30—60 minutes. However, the rate of passage will obviously depend on any drugs such as atropine given before hand and on any pathological condition of the alimentary canal.

The use of barium sulphate in the alimentary canal is most useful in outlining the position of the intestines in relation to the other abdominal organs. Neoplasms of the gonads or kidneys are best delineated by this method.

Barium sulphate or one of the water soluble iodine contrast agents such as meglumine iothalamate ('Conray', May and Baker Ltd.) or sodium diatrizoate ('Hypaque', Sterling Research Laboratories) can be used in the cloaca and rectum to outline these organs.

Occasionally, it can be useful to use air as a contrast agent for the crop.

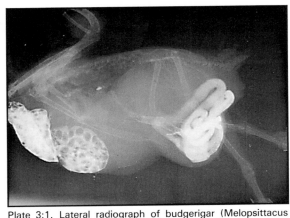

Plate 3:1. Lateral radiograph of budgerigar (Melopsittacus undulatus) showing a large seminoma of the testes, outlined by the displaced barium filled intestine. Note the increased density of the appendicular skeleton probably caused by a rise in oestrogen levels.

BRONCHOGRAPHY

One of the water soluble iodine contrast agents mentioned above can be introduced in the lower trachea to outline the lungs. With the bird under general anaesthesia, the posterior air sacs are first cannulated, in the same way as would be done when carrying out laparoscopy. The metal cannula used with the laparoscope, can be secured in position, or better replaced with a soft plastic cannula or non cuffed endotracheal tube sutured to the body wall. The cannula then acts as a patent airway whilst the trachea is temporarily obstructed. If necessary, this cannula can be connected to the anaesthetic machine to maintain gaseous anaesthesia.

A suitably sized nylon catheter approximately 1mm diameter or 16 gauge (for example, a canine intravenous catheter) is then introduced into the trachea and advanced to a position just proximal to the syrinx. In parrots the position of this structure lies just caudal to the rim of the thoracic inlet formed by the two clavicles or sternoclavicular ligaments. About 1ml of the iodinated contrast agent can then be introduced into the bronchial system. This technique is only suitable for parrots above 300g in weight.

UROGRAPHY AND ANGIOCARDIOGRAPHY

The iodinated water soluble contrast agents can be used intravenously to outline both heart and kidneys. One millilitre of contrast agent can be given to a bird weighing 400g such as an African grey parrot.

THE INTERPRETATION OF THE RADIOGRAPH

When carrying out this task it is best to approach it in a logical manner and to examine each organ system separately. If this is done the observer is less likely to have his or her attention focused on an obvious abnormality and then to not properly evaluate the rest of the radiograph.

Wherever possible, a normal radiograph of the same species should be available for comparison.

When looking at small areas, a magnifying glass or a mask to shield the eyes from a particularly bright underexposed area of the radiograph is useful.

The Respiratory System

In the dorso-ventral projection, some parts of the respiratory system are overlapped by the relatively dense plate of the sternum and its accompanying pectoral muscles and thus obliterated. However, the trachea can be seen lying to the right of the vertebral column and narrowing slightly before it enters the body at the thoracic inlet. If the trachea is seen to be expanded this may confirm that there is some difficulty in breathing. The tracheal rings tend to become calcified in older birds.

The syrinx, which lies just cranial to the base of the heart, is overlayed by the cranial part of the carina of the sternum in the dorso-ventral view. It can, however, be seen in the lateral view where it is isolated by the dark outline of an extension of the clavicular air sac which surrounds it. (Plate 3:4).

Mottling of the shadow of the syrinx accompanied by over-distension of the air sacs together with obvious dypsnoea, is highly suggestive of aspergillosis. However, changes in the shadow of the syrinx are difficult to determine. In some older birds the syrinx can become partially calcified.

The lungs are seen as fine honeycomb-like structures best seen in the lateral view (Plate 3:3). The holes of this honeycomb are formed by the parabronchials which lie approximately along the axis of the X-ray beam. Loss of detail in this meshwork in an otherwise properly exposed radiograph may be caused by increased fluid in the lungs as a result of cardiac incompetance rather than any inflammatory condition of the lung. If the reticular pattern of the lung shadow is very conspicuous this could be an indication of cellular infiltration around the parabronchi and mesobronchi. If the lung shadow becomes merged with that of the heart in the lateral projection and there are areas of increased density in this area, this may be an indication of a severe respiratory infection, often mycotic in origin. Aspergillosis often starts in the region of the stem bronchi which are in this area adjacent to the syrinx but are difficult to distinguish in either dorso-ventral or lateral radiograph.

In both the lateral and particularly in the dorso-ventral view the end projections of the major blood vessels should not be mistaken for granulomata.

The air sac system can be seen better in some parts than others. The cranial thoracic air sac cannot be seen except where it extends into its clavicular diverticulum in the axillary region (Plate 3:2). The abdominal air sacs can readily be seen in both dorso-ventral (Plate 3:2) and lateral views (Plate 3:3). Their apparent size will depend on whether the X-ray exposure was taken during inspiration or expiration and also on the fullness of the alimentary canal and cloaca. When these organs are relatively empty the abdominal air sacs are seen to extend into the caudal part of the body cavity (Plate 3:2).

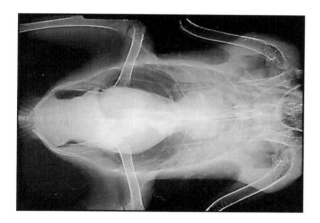

Plate 3:2. Dorso/ventral projection of a Festive Amazon parrot (Amazona festiva). The clavicular extensions of the cranial thoracic air sacs can be seen as can the abdominal air sac extending into the caudal extremity of the body cavity. Just cranial to both hip joints can be seen the outline of the anterior kidney.

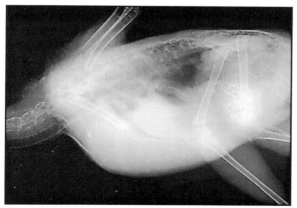

Plate 3:3. Lateral projection of a Blue Fronted Amazon parrot (Amazona aestiva). There is grit retained in the proventriculus due to overloading and impaction of the gizzard.

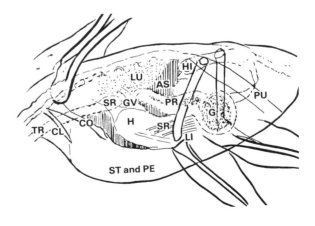

Figure 1

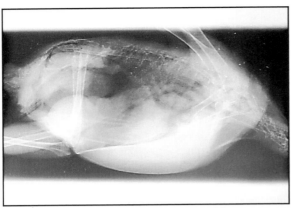

Plate 3:4. Lateral radiograph of a Blue Fronted Amazon parrot (Amazona aestiva). The syrinx can be seen outlined by an extension of the clavicular air sac. Note the thin wedge or air sac tending to separate the heart shadow from the sternal plate due to over extension of the cranial thoracic air sac.

Over-distention of the air sacs due to stenosis caused by a ball valve effect of a mycotic granuloma in the region of the syrinx or primary bronchi, is difficult to assess and is best seen in the lateral projection. In this condition the heart shadow is sometimes completely separated from that of the sternum by an over distention of the cranial thoracic air sac (Plate 3:4). Normally, a thin wedge of air sac can be seen only at the cranial part of the heart shadow where this is adjacent to the sternum.

Asymmetry or distortion of the shadow of the air sacs cannot be truly assessed if the patient has not been properly positioned during the X-ray exposure. Air sac distortion can be caused by the expansion of an adjacent organ or by adhesions between neighbouring tissues (Plate 3:7). Air sacs may become filled with exudate as in the case of ascites when the whole area shows an increased density and an associated loss of clarity. A blurred outline of the air sacs usually indicates infection of these structures (Plates 3:7 and 3:13). An uneven dense mottling of the air sacs is very indicative of advanced aspergillosis, since bacterial air sac infections usually produce a more diffuse shadowing effect. A very fat bird may cause the air sacs to appear to have an increased density and could lead to a false diagnosis. In the female during the breeding season the ova occupy much of the abdominal cavity and obliterate most of the shadow caused by the air sacs. The walls of the air sacs between the thoracic and abdominal air sacs are not usually visible in healthy birds. However, should they be affected with an advanced air sacculitis so that they become thickened by contained exudate, they may then become visible as fine lines which are viewed end-on. This is particularly apparent in the region of the cranial pole of the kidney where the air sac wall may be seen running in a cranial ventral direction between the thoracic and abdominal air sacs.

The Alimentary System

The crop can usually be seen occupying a position at the base of the neck. Its shadow should be assessed for the thickness of the crop wall and whether it is dilated beyond its normal size. An increased size of the crop may be due to the exit of this structure being restricted by, for example, enlargement of the thyroid glands or other space occupying lesion causing compression. Such a condition caused by an intramural carcinoma of the proventriculus is described by Levine (1984). All parts of the digestive system are made more easily visible by using barium contrast. Also the crop can be delineated by negative contrast using air.

The oesophagus is not easily seen in the dorso-ventral view but can be seen in the lateral view where it lies above the trachea.

The proventriculus is best seen in the lateral projection, where it is visible lying dorsal to the heart and liver shadow (Plates 3:3, 3:4, 3:14). This part of the alimentary canal should be assessed for increased density, normal position, dilation and content of the lumen. An increase in density may be due to an inflammatory reaction but it is more likely to be due to hypertrophy of this organ caused by hypovitaminosis A. This sign, taken together with a lack of grit in the gizzard, which is necessary for proper digestion of food, is a good indication of vitamin A deficiency (Plate 3:6). The proventriculus may also be dilated (Plate 3:14) or filled with food or grit because of overloading due to changes in the gizzard or to a paralytic ileus with the bird continuing to eat (Plate 3:3). This may be succeeded by vomiting. Clark (1985) describes a condition in macaws and cockatoos where the proventriculus is so dilated as to occupy most of the thoracoabdominal cavity and other visceral organs are atrophied. This condition is usually accompanied by a history of anorexia, weight loss, lethargy and vomiting. Neoplasms of the proventriculus may also cause an increase in the radiographic shadow. Very occasionally, fine lines lying vertical to the horizontal outline of the organ can be seen and indicate the folds in the proventricular glands.

The gizzard is easily seen in both the dorso-ventral and lateral views when filled with grit. However, even if this structure is not filled with grit, which is sometimes the case even in the apparently normal bird, its dense muscular coat can still usually be defined (Plate 3:4). The normal position of the gizzard in the dorso-ventral view is just to the left of the mid line and with the greater part lying just caudal to a line joining both hip-joints (Plate 3:5). The exact position will vary dependent on whether it is displaced by enlargement of other organs such as ova during the breeding period or by a neoplasm of the gonads or liver. To function normally the gizzard should have a constant volume, and if it is seen to be expanded or enlarged, this is an indication of disease. Atrophy of the gizzard is often associated with an apparent enlargement of the proventriculus. A gizzard containing excessive grit indicates a digestive problem (Plates 3:3 and 3:5). The bird is probably trying to compensate for the lack of tone in the muscular wall of this organ. Occasionally, areas of increased density amongst the grit may indicate metal fragments. A lack of grit in the gizzard leads to a lowered digestibility of food because this is not being adequately ground. In time this will lead to nutritional deficiencies.

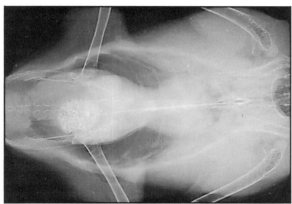

Plate 3:5. Dorso/ventral projection of the same bird as in Plate 3:3. The gizzard contains excessive amounts of grit and this can be seen extending into the proventriculus. Note the duodenum situated opposite the gizzard on the right side of the abdomen and tending to follow the curve of the gizzard.

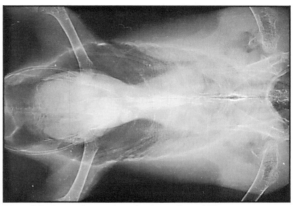

Plate 3:6. Dorso/ventral projection of an African grey parrot (Psittacus erithacus). There is an absence of grit in the gizzard which is likely to result in a Vitamin A and other deficiencies because of improper digestion

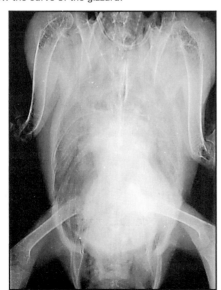

Plate 3:7. Dorso/ventral projection of a Blue and Gold macaw (Ara arraiauna). Adhesions of the heart and viscera to the body wall caused by gross airsacculitis which has also resulted in an overall loss of clarity of the post air sacs. Compare the clavicular and abdominal air sacs in this radiograph with the air sacs shown in Plates 3:2 and 3:5, also compare the heart and liver shadows.

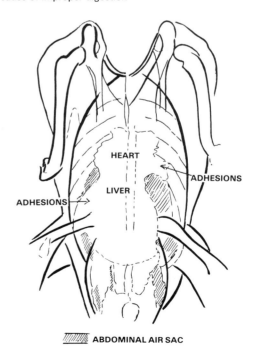

ABDOMINAL AIR SAC

Figure 2.

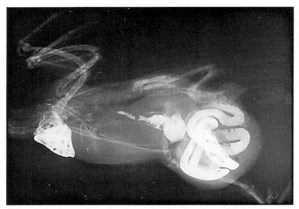

Plate 3:8. Lateral projection of a budgerigar (Melopsittacus undulatus). The intestine filled with barium is shown to be enlarged and contains undigested seed and some gas bubbles. This indicates malfunction of the alimentary canal and possible infection.

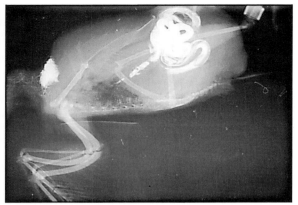

Plate 3:9. Lateral projection of a Love bird (Agapornis fischeri). The barium filled bowel can be seen to contain Ascarid worms.

The intestines can be seen as a diffuse mass occupying the posterior abdomen. The only recognisable part is the duodenal loop which can be identified, in the dorso-ventral projection, lying to the right of the general intestinal mass. The duodenum often stands out better when the abdominal air sac is seen to extend into the posterior abdomen and partially surrounds the intestinal mass (Plate 3:5). If the duodenal loop or any other loop of intestine is prominently dilated and stands out because of an increase in density, this is an indication of parasitic, bacterial or mycotic infection or pancreatitis (Plate 3:14). Ascarid worms can sometimes be individually identified when barium contrast medium is used (Plate 3:9). A ravenous appetite, together with little faecal matter in the droppings and the above radiographic

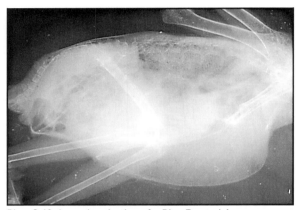

Plate 3:10. Lateral projection of a Blue Fronted Amazon parrot (Amazona aestiva). The intestine occupying the posterior abdomen can be seen to contain an accumulation of gas indicating stasis and bacterial infection.

picture, is a good indication of a heavy infestation of ascarids, even if no worm ova are to be found on faecal examination.

Individual loops of intestines can sometimes be seen to be filled with gas, fluid (see Plate 3:8 and 3:10), grit or seed. Enterolyths containing calcium oxalate have been found in the duodenum of an Umbrella cockatoo (Cacatua alba), Kallias (1984). A build up of gas in any part of the alimentary tract including the intestine is often associated with bacterial infection particularly with *E. coli* (Plates 3:8 and 3:10). Gas in the duodenum may be associated with pancreatitis. Grit in the intestine, particularly if associated with impaction of the gizzard, indicates a rapid turnover of grit due to malfunction of the gizzard.

The Cloaca
The cloaca can be identified occupying the most caudal area of the abdomen and can be observed in both lateral and dorso-ventral projections. The size of this structure will depend on the amount of excreta it contains. If the bird is showing signs of discomfort in this region, the radiograph should be carefully examined for the presence of a calculus in the cloaca. Gas in the cloaca may be an indication of infection when swelling and an increase in density of the cloacal wall may also been seen. Alternatively, gas in the cloaca may indicate infection of the rectum.

The Liver
The shadow of the liver is best identified in the dorsal-ventral projection where its cranial border is outlined by the abdominal air sac. It forms the caudal part of the typical dumbbell or hourglass shadow with the heart forming the cranial part of this shadow (Plates 3:2 and 3:3). Should the waist of this hourglass shadow be indistinguishable this is usually an indication of hepatomegaly. In the dorsol-ventral projection, the

image of the caudal part of the liver is overlayed by that of the gizzard and intestines and consequently cannot be well defined. An apparent enlargement of the liver may be due to an increase in bulk of these latter organs and so can only truly be confirmed if the alimentary canal is filled with barium contrast.

In the lateral projection, the liver is not so easily defined. It lies caudally to the heart shadow and cranially to that of the gizzard and intestines. Ventrally lies the carina of the sternum, whilst dorsally is the proventriculus (Plate 3:3). Again, if these organs are filled with barium, the liver is more easily distinguished. The size of the liver should be assessed together with any increase in the density of the shadow of this organ. An increase in density is most easily decided upon if the liver shadow is compared with that of adjacent tissues; the intestines, for example, should have a comparable density. An increased density is probably a more reliable sign of hepatic disease, such as hepatitis, gout or neoplastic change than is an apparent increase in the size of this structure.

The Heart and Blood Vessels

The image of the heart forms the cranial part of the typical hourglass shadow as seen on the dorso-ventral projection (Plates 3:2 and 3:3). The caudal part of this compound shadow, due to the liver, is rarely separated from that of the heart and if this occurs it probably indicates atrophy of the liver. In the lateral view, the heart can be seen as an eliptical shadow lying dorsal to the sternum and midway along its length. In this projection the heart is separated from the sternum at the cranial part by a thin wedge of the clavicular air sac (Plate 3:3). Should this wedge increase, this indicates an overexpanded air sac system (Plate 3:4). Loss of this wedge indicates cardiac enlargement or increased pericardial fluid. In the lateral projection, the aorta and the left and right brachiocephalic vessels can be seen emerging from the heart. At the curve of the aorta the brachiocephalic trunk can be distinguished and the aorta can sometimes be traced as far as the kidneys. In very old psittacines, some of these vessels may be calcified which may indicate arteriosclerosis. If the shadow of the cranial end of the heart is not well defined when other tissues in the radiograph are easily seen, this usually indicates a problem in or around the primary bronchi such as bronchitis or bronchopneumonia. In the dorso-ventral projection, the large blood vessels leaving the heart are mainly seen in end-on view and can be mistaken for areas of increased density in the lung tissue.

When deciding whether or not the heart is enlarged, comparison with a normal radiograph preferably of the same species, but at least of a bird in the same genus, is helpful. An enlarged heart, taken together with the loss of detail in the honeycomb structure of the lung, is a good indicator of heart disease. Sometimes, an increased density of the heart shadow can be seen and could be due to the deposition of uric acid crystals in the pericardial fluid of a bird afflicted with gout.

The Kidneys

In the dorso-ventral view, the kidneys are overshadowed by the gizzard and intestines but the cranial edges of the kidneys can sometimes be distinguished as areas of increased density (Plate 3:2) particularly in cases of pyelonephritis or renal gout. In the lateral projection, the cranial poles of the kidneys can easily be recognised as they project into the abdominal air sac and often appear slightly denser than the surrounding tissue (Plates 3:3 and 3:4). Enlargement of the kidney shadow may indicate infection or a neoplasm (Plate 3:14). Occasionally, the irregular outline of a kidney tumour can be recognised but usually it is necessary to use barium contrast in the alimentary canal to define the organs more easily. Sometimes a network of fine tubules can be distinguished in the kidney tissues, where these are filled with urate crystals (Plate 3:11). This is not

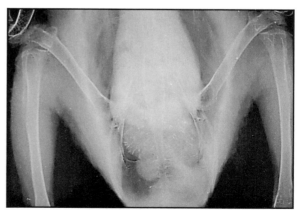

Plate 3:11. Dorso/ventral projection of the posterior body of an African Grey parrot (Psittacus erithacus). A fine network of kidney tubules filled with urate crystals can be seen.

necessarily an indication of gout but may indicate a chronic infection, particularly by *E. coli.*

The Spleen

This is not normally seen in either projection. Very occasionally, it may be recognised on a lateral view as a small round object in the angle formed by the liver and gizzard. If the spleen can be recognised, either because of its increased size or because of its increased density, this usually is an indication of serious infectious disease. If air sacculitis and pulmonary consolidation are also evident this is very suggestive of psittacosis.

The Gonads

These are best seen in the lateral view during the breeding season or when the alimentary canal is filled with barium. In these circumstances the testicles can be distinguished as an oval or round shadow occupying a position either cranially or ventral to the cranial pole of the kidney (Plate 3:3). The ovary occupies a similar position but is less easily defined. Irregularity of the testicular outline does not necessarily indicate neoplasia as it may be caused by fat. The fallopian tube and oviduct are only really distinguishable from the intestines if the latter are filled with barium. An area of increased density dorsal and caudal to the intestinal mass may indicate salpingitis. Occasionally, fragmented egg shell material can be seen in this area (Plate 3:12). An impacted egg is easily recognised radiographically.

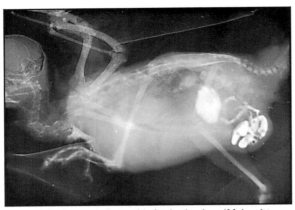

Plate 3:12. Lateral radiograph of a budgerigar (Melopsittacus undulatus). An area of increased density caused by fragmented egg shell material dorsal to the intestineal mass can be seen. This indicates a salpingitis.

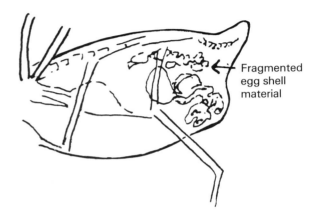

Fragmented egg shell material

Figure 3.

Ascites

If there is a generalised loss of contrasting detail over the whole of the body's organs, in spite of the fact that the exposure of the X-ray film looks correct after an examination of those areas containing the limbs, then this is probably caused by ascites. There is also often an associated distension of the caudal abdomen (Plate 3:13). Ascites has a variety of causes in parrots. It may be due to liver conditions, tuberculosis, ascariasis, *E. coli* infection, salpingitis, egg peritonitis (Plate 3:12) or nephrosis.

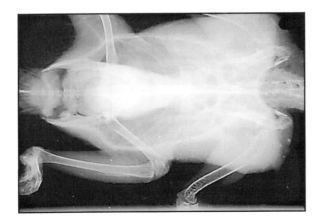

Plate 3:13. Dorso/ventral radiograph of an African Grey parrot (Psittacus erithacus). There is a generalised loss of contrasting detail over the whole of the body's organs indicating gross airsacculitis and ascites.

The Skeleton

The radiographic examination of the skeleton and muscles is discussed in Chapter 12.

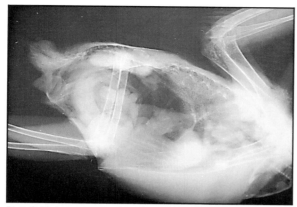

Plate 3:14. Lateral projection of an African Grey parrot (Psittacus erithacus). There is a dilation of the proventriculus due to malfunction of the gizzard or intestine. A large loop of intestine (probably duodenum) shows congestion and the kidney is also markedly congested indicating infection or possible neoplastic change. Compare the size of this proventriculus with that in Plates 3:3 and 3:4.

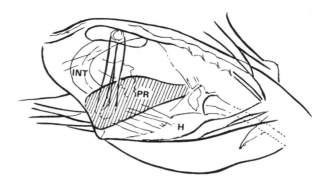

Figure 4.
H. Heart; INT. Intestine, probably the duodenum.
PR. Proventriculus — hatched area.

REFERENCES:

ALTMAN, R. B. (1973). Radiography, Veterinary Clinics of North America (Small Animal Practice 3; 165).

BLACKMORE, D. K. (1982). Diseases of the Reproductive System in: Diseases of Cage and Aviary Birds 2nd Edition (Ed. Petrak, M.L.) Lea and Febiger, Philadelphia.

CLARK, F. D. (1985). Proventricular Dilation Syndrome in large Psittacine Birds: Avian/Exotic Practice Vol. 2 No. 1 p 19-20. Veterinary Publishing Company, Santa Barbara.

COLES, B. H. (1985). Radiography in Avian Medicine and Surgery, pp 35-44. Blackwell Scientific, Oxford.

COOPER, J. E. and KREEL, L. (1976). Radiographic Examination of Birds, Report of a small series. Journal of Small Animal Practice, 17: 199-808.

EVANS, S. M. (1986). Avian Radiography, in: Textbook of Veterinary Diagnostic Radiology (Ed. Thrall, D. E.) W. B. Saunders, Philadelphia.

HASHOLT, J and PETRAK, M. L. (1982). Diseases of the Urinary Tract, in: Disease of Cage and Aviary Birds, 2nd Edition (Ed. M. L. Petrak) Lea and Fabiger, Philadelphia.

KALLIAS, G. V., WHERMAN, S. and STETZER, E. R. (1984). Enterolithiasis in an Umbrella Cockatoo, J.A.V.M.A. pp 1407.

LEE, R. (1984). Radiography: Problems and Reasons for poor quality in practice, Vol. 6 No. 5. Supplement to Vet. Record.

LEVINE, B. S. (1984). Intramural Mass — Gastric Carcinoma in the Proventriculus of a Budgerigar. J.A.V.M.A. pp 912.

MCMILLAN, M. C. (1982). Avian Radiology in Diseases of Cage and Aviary Birds, 2nd Edition (Ed. Petrak, M. L.) pp 320-359. Lea and Febiger, Philadelphia.

MCMILLAN, M. C. (1983). Avian Gastrointestinal Radiology. Compendium of continuing Education, Pract. Vet 5: pp 273.

MCNEEL, S. V. and ZENOBLE, R. D. (1986). Avian Urography. J.A.V.M.A. 178: 366.

RUEBEL, A. (1985). Rontgenunter Suchungen bei inneren Erkankungen bon grossen Psittaziden, Inaugural Dissertation for a Doctorate, University of Zurich.

SILVERMAN, S. (1974). Avian Radiographic Technique and Interpretation in current Veterinary Therapy V (Ed. Kirk, R. W.) W. B. Saunders, Philadelphia.

SILVERMAN, S. (1975). Avian Radiographic Techniques, in: Radiographic Techniques in Small Animal Practice (Ed. Ticer, J. W.) W. B. Saunders, Philadelphia.

T.-W.-FIENNES, R. N. (1982). Diseases of the Cardiovascular System, Blood and Lymphatic System, in: Diseases of Cage and Aviary Birds (Ed. Petrak, M. L.) Lea and Febiger, Philadelphia.

Chapter 4   # CLINICAL HAEMATOLOGY

Christine Hawkey Ph.D.
Frances Gulland M.A., Vet.M.B., M.R.C.V.S.

Clinical haematology is becoming well recognised as a useful aid to differential diagnosis and monitoring of disease in birds (Woerpel and Rosskopff 1984, Hawkey and Samour 1987) and there is accumulating evidence of its value in parrots and other psittacines. This chapter describes methods of obtaining blood samples from these birds, haematological tests which are available and normal reference values for some of the more commonly encountered species of parrots, cockatoos and macaws. Information is also provided on haematological changes associated with certain disease processes. Since clinical experience suggests that the responses of the blood to disease are generally similar in all avian species, some information is included which, although it has not yet been verified in psittacines, is considered to be of potential relevance.

THE BLOOD SAMPLE

Ideally, blood for haematological examination should be of venous origin. The total volume required for a complete blood count is 0.3 ml; this amount can usually be obtained by venepuncture of a cultaneous ulnar vein or of the right jugular vein of most psittacine birds without risk, even in varieties as small as budgerigars and lovebirds. Alternatively, micromethods are available for use on small or debilitated individuals (see below). On all occasions, great care should be taken to minimise haemorrhage and haematoma formation at the puncture site as the amount of blood lost in this way can be greater than the amount removed for testing. There is no evidence that the commonly employed anaesthetic or tranquillising drugs influence the blood picture of psittacine birds.

Samples of venous blood should be delivered without delay into a tube containing anticoagulant, having first removed the needle from the syringe. The anticoagulant of choice is ethylene diamine tetra-acetic acid (EDTA, sequestrene, 1.5 mg/ml blood). Tubes containing the amount of EDTA to prevent clotting in 0.5ml volumes of blood are available commercially (Teklab Ltd.) and are suitable for smaller samples. Blood tests should be carried out within 24 hours of obtaining the sample. If a longer delay is anticipated, blood films should be prepared and air-dried at the time of collection. Films will remain suitable for examination for up to 72 hours without fixation but great care must be taken to avoid exposure to all forms of moisture.

MICROMETHODS: These are based on collecting blood samples directly into micro-collection devices suitable for specific tests. The accuracy of these tests depends on obtaining a free flow of blood, uncontaminated by tissue fluid. This can be achieved by pricking a suitable small vein with a lancet or by inserting a thin walled, 23 gauge hypodermic needle into a vein and collecting blood directly from the needle hub. Sampling from a clipped claw is not recommended since the crushing action used to cut the claw not only increases the risk of sample contamination with tissue fluid but is painful to the bird and can produce permanent damage.

A variety of micro-collection devices is available for direct blood sampling. These include fixed volume microcapillary tubes, micro- and minihaematocrit tubes and Red Cell and White Cell Diluting Pipetted. The Compur 1011 Minicentrifuge (Centronic Sales Ltd.) is of value for measuring the packed cell volume (haematocrit) on very small blood samples but it should be noted that the Compur 1100 Miniphotometer is not suitable for red cell counts or haemoglobin measurement in non-mammals.

35

CLINICAL BIOCHEMISTRY

Little information is available on changes in the biochemical constituents of the plasma related to disease in psittacine birds but normal reference values are available for some species. For the convenience of the clinician, these are summarised in the appendix at the end of this chapter.

GENERAL FEATURES OF THE BLOOD OF HEALTHY PSITTACINE BIRDS

Compared with mammalian blood, the blood of psittacine and other birds differs mainly in the morphology of the red cells, granular leucocytes and thrombocytes. The lymphocytes and monocytes are generally similar to those of mammals (Plates 4:1 and 4:2).

Avian *red cells* are oval and each contains a centrally placed nuclei (Plates 4:1 — 4:9). The cells are relatively fragile and a proportion of them tends to become broken up during the preparation of blood films, so that free nuclei in various stages of disintegration are often seen on the blood film (Plate 4:3). The presence of the nucleus confers a biconvex outline to the cells in section. Probably because of this, rouleaux formation does not occur and the cells show little tendency to sediment. The erythrocyte sedimentation rate (ESR) is not, therefore, a useful clinical test in birds. Immature red cells (erythroblasts) generally appear smaller than mature red cells on stained blood films and can be identified from their bluish or polychromatic cytoplasm and relatively large nucleus (Plate 4:4). The presence of a small number of polychromatic erythroblasts indicates normal erythropoiesis and is usually observed in healthy birds. Immature red cells are more common in young birds and in species of small body size.

The granulocytic leucoctyes equivalent to mammalian neutrophils are known as *heterophils.* When stained with Romanowsky stains, these cells have spiculate, brick-red cytoplasmic granules (Plates 4:5 amd 4:6) and the term 'neutrophil' is inappropriate. The nucleus is normally bilobed. The most significant pathological changes affecting heterophil morphology are reduced nuclear lobulation (left shift, Plate 4:7) and changes in the cytoplasmic granules. The latter include loss of regular spiculate form, reduction in number and/or the presence of extra, round, strongly basophilic granules which vary in size and number (Plate 4:8). These variations are often seen in cases of bacterial or fungal infection.

Because the cytoplasmic granules of normal heterophils are eosinophilic, it can sometimes be difficult to differentiate between heterophils and true eosinophils. In macaws and cockatoos, *eosinophils* can be identified on the strength of their smaller, round, more brightly eosinophilic granules (Plate 4:9) but, in some species of parrots, the eosinophils have atypical, round pale blue granules (Plate 4:10). The *basophils* are smaller cells, characterised by the presence of a variable number of dark purple cytoplasmic granules and an unlobed nucleus (Plate 4:11). All granulocytes have a tendency to lose their cytoplasmic granules in blood films made from stored samples or during inadequate fixation.

Thrombocytes are similar in size or slightly smaller than the lymphocytes and have a darkly-staining, round nucleus and, in carefully collected blood samples, are oval (Plates 4:1 and 4:2). The cytoplasm may contain one or two small basophilic granules. As with mammalian platelets, avian thrombocytes rapidly lose their regular form and tend to aggregate together as soon as the blood is removed from the circulation. It is not unusual to find evidence of these normal physiological changes in blood films from psittacine birds.

LABORATORY TECHNIQUES

The laboratory tests which provide information most valuable for diagnostic purposes are listed in Table 1. The choice is based on tests normally undertaken on mammals but excludes the reticulocyte count and ESR. These are not useful tests in birds, the former because a valid definition of a reticulocyte is not yet available for non-mammals and the latter for reasons already stated. An estimation of fibrinogen is usefully included as a measure of an acute reactive protein response to inflammation.

Techniques are based on those used for mammals but modifications are necessary to take account of the fact that the red cells are relatively large and contain nuclei. In particular, the red cell nuclei interfere with haemoglobin measurement and white cell counts. The methods described below are those which have been found to be feasible and accurate by the authors. A knowledge of mammalian haematological techniques is assumed.

Table 1:
Haematological Tests for use on Psittacine Birds

Test	Abbreviation SI units	Method
Haemoglobin	Hb g/dl	Colourimetry, spectophotometry
Red cell count	RBC x 10^{12}/l	Microscopy/haemocytometer or electronic particle counter
Packed cell volume (haematocrit)	PCV 1/1	Microhaematocrit or minihaematocrit centrifuge
Mean cell volume	MCV fl	Calculated from RBC and PCV
Mean cell haemoglobin	MCH pg	Calculated from Hb and RBC
Mean cell haemoglobin concentration	MCHC g/dl	Calculated from Hb and PCV
White cell count	WBC x 10^{9}/l	Phase contrast microscopy and Cristalite haemocytometer
Differential WBC	%	Stained blood film
Differential WBC	x 10^{9}/l	Calculated from WBC and differential count %
Examination of cell morphology, blood parasites		Stained blood film
Fibrinogen (protein denatured at 56°C)	g/l	Incubation of PCV tubes at 56°C

HAEMOGLOBIN (Hb): The amount of haemoglobin present in a known volume of blood is measured colourimetrically or spectrophotometrically after release from the red cells by haemolysis. In mammals, haemoglobin is usually converted to cyanmethaemoglobin before measurement, by dilution in Drabkins solution. With avian blood, unless akaline Drabkins solution is used, the red cells nuclei remain intact, and the resultant cloudy test solution is unsuitable for spectrophotometry. Since some of the haemoglobin is apparently bound to the red cell nuclei, their removal by centrifugation will give a falsely low result. The problems can be ovecome by using alkaline Drabkins solution or by measuring the haemoglobin as alkaline haematin or oxyhaemoglobin. The latter method is recommended below:

Routine method:
— Wash 20µl EDTA blood into 4.0 ml of 0.4 ml/l ammonia (sp gr 0.88) in a tube with a tightly fitting lid. Mix immediately.
— Against a blank consisting of 0.4 ml/l ammonia, read extinction in a spectrophotometer at 540 nm or in a photoelectric colourimeter fitted with a narrow-band yellow-green filter with maximum transmission near 540 nm (eg: Ilford 625).
— Convert reading to Hb g/dl by reference to a calibration curve prepared from commercially available standards or from dilutions of mammalian blood with a predetermined Hb level.

Micromethod:
— Collect blood directly from a lancet prick or needle hub by means of a 20 µl *Unopipette (Beckton Dickinson). Carefully wipe away any blood contaminating the outside of the Unopipette.
— Place graduated portion of Unopipette into a tube containing 4.0 ml ammonia solution as above and shake tube vigourously until all the blood is released from the capillary into the ammonia solution.
— Determine Hb g/dl as above.

   *Alternatively, use a 20 µl glass pipette fitted with a suction mouthpiece and wash blood directly into 4.0 ml of ammonia solution.

In adult psittacine birds, the normal Hb range is 12.0 — 20.0 g/dl. Lower values are found in immature individuals. Values below 10.0 g/dl in adults are diagnostic of anaemia and values of greater than 21.0 g/dl are generally indicative of dehydration or polycythaemia secondary to respiratory or cardiac disease.

RED CELL COUNT (RBC): Psittacine red cells are larger than those of most mammals and can be counted without difficulty using a microscope and haemocytometer. Alternatively, an electronic particle counter can be employed, providing that it can be adjusted to accommodate the relatively large size of the cells. A Coulter Electronic Particle Counter, Model ZF (Coulter Electronics Ltd.) is suitable in this respect. Diluting fluids for mammalian red cell counts can be used without modification for psittacine birds.

Method using microscopy:
— As for mammals, using a 1/200 dilution of whole blood in formal citrate solution (10 ml of 40% formaldehyde made up to 1 litre with 32 g/l trisodium citrate solution).

Method using a Coulter counter, Model ZF:
— As for mammals, using a 1/50,000 dilution of blood in Isoton 2 (Coulter Electronics Ltd.). The correct threshold (T), aperture current (D) and attenuation (B) settings should be determined for each species according to the manufacturers instructions. For most psittacine birds, the settings are:

$$T = 4$$
$$B = 62 \text{ (or 32 in small birds)}$$
$$D = .707$$

Micromethods:

Microscopy
— Collect 20 μl of blood from a lancet prick or needle hub, by means of a Unopipette or glass pipette as described for Hb estimation. Add to 4.0 ml formal saline solution and mix well. Alternatively, prepare a 1/200 dilution using a Red Cell Diluting Pipette (Arnold Horewell Ltd.), fitted with a suction mouthpiece.
— Fill haemocytometer and process as for mammalian samples.

Electronic counter
— Collect blood with a 40 μl Unopipette, directly from a lancet prick or needle hub. Place Unopipette in a cuvette containing 20 ml of Isoton 2 and proceed as for routine method description above.

The RBC of adult birds varies with species and, as a general rule, is higher in small birds such as budgerigars and lovebirds than in larger varieties. The main value of determining the RBC is to obtain an indication of red cell size by calculation of the MCV (see below). It is not an essential test and can be omitted if the amount of blood available is limited.

PACKED CELL VOLUME (PCV, HAEMATOCRIT): This measurement can be carried out by any of the standard centrifugation methods available for use on mammals. It is not necessary to correct the result for trapped plasma. Results obtained by automated methods are not usually reliable.

Standard microhaematocrit method:
— Fill a non-heparinised* microhaematocrit tube to within 2 cm of the end with well mixed EDTA blood. Seal.
— Centrifuge and read as for mammals.
— Observe plasma for the presence of haemolysis **, lipaemia***, jaundice****, colour pigments****. Note extent of buffy layer as an indication of WBC/thrombocyte number).
-- (Reserve microhaematocrit tube for fibrinogen estimation*)

    * Heparinised microhaematocrit tubes must not be used if it is intended to carry out a subsequent fibrinogen estimation.
   ** Haemolysis is most likely to be a result of poor sampling techniques or prolonged sample storage. Results of PCV and RBC are invalid in badly haemolysed samples.
  *** Indicates excessive consumption of fatty foods, eg: sunflower seeds etc. Invalidates Hb results.
 **** Yellow plasma is often seen in yellow and green budgerigars and should not be mistakenly considered as an indication of jaundice.

Method for use on very small birds: Blood can be collected directly from a lancet prick or needle hub into a heparinised or, if a fibrinogen estimation is to be undertaken, an EDTA (Bilbate Ltd.) microhaematocrit tube. In very small birds, the PCV can be measured using a Computer Minihaematocrit Centrifuge (Centronic Sales Ltd.), which is designed for use with microcapillary tubes holding only 10 μl of blood.

In adult birds, the normal range for PCV is 0.37 — 0.56 1/1. Lower values are found in immature individuals.

In adults, a reduction to below 0.35 1/1 indicates anaemia and values of more than 0.60 are found in dehydration and polycythaemia secondary to respiratory or cardiac disease. In conjunction with the Hb value, the PCV is used to calculate the MCHC and thus has an important role in the identification of hypochromia.

RED CELL ABSOLUTE VALUES: Mean cell volume (MCV), Mean cell haemoglobin (MCH) and Mean cell haemoglobin concentration (MCHC) are calculated by standard formulae as used for mammals (Dacie and Lewis 1984).

The MCV and MCH of psittacine birds show species variation and are generally lower in small birds than in larger varieties. There is an indirect relationship between the MCV and RBC. Knowledge of the MCV can give an indication of the presence of macro- or microcytosis. Microcytosis often occurs in birds with infection or chromic haemorrhage but the significance of macrocytosis is not yet known.

In healthy adult psittacines, the range for MCHC is 30.0 — 39.0 g/dl. Lower values are found in immature birds and sometimes in apparently healthy budgerigars and lovebirds. Values of less than 29.0 g/dl indicate hypochromia.

TOTAL WHITE CELL COUNT (WBC): In mammals, white cells are counted, either microscopically or electrically, after removing the non-nucleated red cells by haemolysis. There is no known haemolysing agent which will remove the nuclei of avian red cells without also removing the white cells. In the presence of red cell nuclei, an accurate electronic white cell count has not yet been proved to be possible. Methods are available for counting white cells indirectly on a stained blood film or directly, using a diluting fluid with differential staining properties (Lucas and Jamroz 1961). In the method described below, white cells are counted directly, using a Cristalite Improved Neubauer haemocytometer (Gelman Hawksley) and phase contrast microscopy. Because of the potential obliteration of the white cells by unlysed red cell nuclei, samples from small birds such as budgerigars and lovebirds, which have relatively high red cell counts, must be tested at a greater dilution than those from parrots, macaws and cockatoos.

Routine method:
— prepare a 1/20 dilution of well mixed EDTA whole blood in ammonium oxalate solution (10 g/l). For budgerigars and other small varieties, use a 1/40 dilution of blood.
— Count white cells as for mammals, but using a Cristalite Improved Neubauer haemocytometer and phase contrast microscopy. White cells are more easily identified if the filled haemocytometer is left undisturbed in a moist atmosphere for 15 minutes before examination.
— If using a 1/40 dilution of blood, multiply answer x2.

Micromethod:
— Collect blood from a lancet prick or needle hub using a 20 μl unopipette.
— Wipe excess blood from outside of tube.
— Place graduated portion of the capillary in a tube containing 0.8 ml of ammonium oxalate solution as above.
— Shake vigorously until all the blood is released into the oxalate solution.
— Count white cells as above.
— Multiply answer x2.

The WBC is used in conjunction with the diffferential white cell count to calculate the absolute number of each white cell type present (i.e. cells x 10^9/l). It is also used for calculating the absolute platelet count.

FIBRINOGEN: Fibrinogen functions mainly as a clottable protein in the blood coagulation process but is also one of the proteins which is increased in infection and other inflammatory conditions. In this respect, a fibrinogen estimation is usefully included in routine haematological investigations on psittacine and other birds as a marker of acute inflammatory disease. The recommended micromethod depends on the differential denaturation of fibrinogen in EDTA plasma at a temperature of 56°C. It can be carried out on the sample that is used for PCV determination and does not, therefore, increase the volume of blood needed. It should be noted that heparin invalidates the results of this test.

Routine method:
— After reading the PCV, incubate the microhaematocrit tube by immersion to above the top of the plasma column in a thermostatically controlled water bath at 56°C for 3 minutes.

— Recentrifuge in a microhaematocrit centrifuge for 5 minutes at 10,000 — 12,000 g to precipitate the denature protein.

— Place the microhaematocrit tube in a modified slide holder (Figure 1). Using a microscope fitted with a measuring eyepiece and a stage micrometer, take micrometer measurements at the interface between the buffy layer and the precipitated protein (A), at the top of the precipitated protein layer (B) and at the top of the plasma column (C) as shown in Figure 1.

$$\text{Then fibrinogen g/l} = \frac{B - A}{C - A} \times 100$$

Micromethod:
— Collect blood directly from a lancet prick or needle hub into an EDTA microhaematocrit tube.

— Proceed as for the routine method.

In psittacine birds, fibrinogen levels of greater than 3.5 g/dl suggest the presence of acute inflammatory disease.

PREPARATION OF FILM:
The morphological characteristics of avian blood cells can be demonstrated successfully with any of the Romanowsky stains formulated for use with mammalian blood. The choice of stain is a matter of personal preference. Optimal staining conditions should be determined for each new batch of stain. As white cell and thrombocyte morphology can be affected by exposure to anticoagulant, films are best prepared before, or as soon as possible after, addition of the blood to EDTA. They can be stored for up to 72 hours without fixation but, during this time, must be protected from exposure to all forms of moisture.

Differential white cell count: On an area of the film where the cells are evenly and thinly spread, classify one hundred consecutive white cells and heterophils, eosinophils, basophils, lymphocytes, monocytes or abnormal leucocytes. Convert to absolute values by reference to the total WBC:

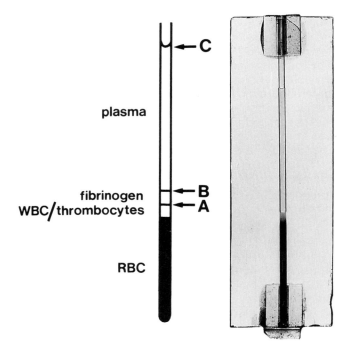

Figure 1: Measurement of fibrinogen

Enlarged drawing of a microhaematocrit tube after incubation and recentrifugation, showing points at which measurements are taken. The photograph on the right shows a microscope slide, also enlarged, modified to hold the tube in place.

e.g. Heterophils x 10⁹/l = (Heterophils %) x (WBC x 10⁹/l x 10

Thrombocyte count: Note the number of thrombocytes seen while observing one hundred consecutive white cells.

Then thrombocytes x 10⁹/l = (Thrombocytes/100WBC) x (WBC x 10⁹/l) x 10

The value of thrombocyte counts in psittacines birds has not yet been assessed. In mammals and in some avian species, there is evidence that increased counts occur in association with bacterial infections. Low counts are most likely to be due to difficulties with sample collection. If this possibility can be excluded or if evidence of haemorrhage is present, thrombocytopenia or disseminated intravascular coagulation should be considered.

PHYSIOLOGICAL FACTORS WHICH INFLUENCE THE BLOOD COUNT

Significant sex differences have not yet been found in the haematological values of psittacine birds. Age-related differences have not been investigated in detail but immature individuals often show some degree of hypochromic anaemia which usually resolves without treatment. There is evidence that stress gives rise to heterophilia and eosinopenia. These factors must be considered when assessing the haematological findings on clinical cases.

INTERPRETATION OF RESULTS

In individual birds which have been subjected to regular haematological monitoring when healthy, abnormalities in the blood count can be identified by direct comparison with previous findings. More often, normal reference values for the species in question are used for this purpose, and suggested reference values for the more commonly encountered psittacine species are provided in an appendix at the end of this chapter.

If species-specific reference values are not available, anaemia, polycythaemia and hypochromia can be confirmed or excluded by application of the general principle that, although the red cell count varies with species, normal values for Hb, PCV and MCHC are constant within fairly narrow limits in all birds. Normal white cell counts show species variation but values outside certain fairly wide limits can be taken as indicative of clinical abnormality. In all instances, observations on cell morphology should be considered in parallel with the quantative findings (Table 2).

Table 2:
Significant Abnormalities in Cell Morphology

Cell Type	Abnormality	Possible significance
Red cells	Hypochromia	Mineral (iron?) deficiency, blood loss, infection (normal in immature individuals)
	Microcytosis	Mineral (iron?) deficiency, blood loss, infection
	Anisocytosis	Increased erythropoiesis
	Poikilocytosis	Increased erythropoiesis, lead poisoning, renal disease, microvascular pathology.
	Polychromasia	Increased erythropoiesis
	Erythroblastosis	Increased erythropoiesis
Heterophils	Band-form or unlobed nuclei (Plate 4:7 & 4:8)	Infection
	Cytoplasmic granules reduced in number and/or irregular in shape (Plate 4:8)	Infection
	Extra basophilic granules present (Plate 4:8)	Infection
Monocytes	Absence of nuclear indentation, excess cytoplasm, vacuolation	Bacterial or fungal infection

Figures are given in Table 3 which provide a guide to the identification of significant abnormalities in psittacine groups. These should not be used if reference values are available for the species in question.

SIGNIFICANT ABNORMAL FINDINGS

Primary haematological diseases are rare in psittacine birds and the most informative haemopathological changes encountered are those secondary to infection, inflammation, red cell loss, dehydration and dietary insufficiency (Table 4). In our experience, the most frequent red cell abnormalities found in these birds are anaemia, often of a hypochromic microcytic type, secondary to infection, and polycythaemia associated with dehydration or respiratory disease. In cases of anaemia, the presence or absence of red cells with polychromatic or basophilic cytoplasm and immature nuclei, gives an indication of the regenerative response of the marrow. A finding of heterophilia (Plate 4:6), often with a proportion of the cells showing reduced nuclear lobulation (Plate 4:7) and/or abnormal cytoplasmic granules (Plate 4:8), is characteristic of bacterial or fungal infections and a raised fibrinogen level confirms this diagnosis in many cases. It should be noted that the understanding of haemopathological responses in psittacine birds is far from complete and some of the causes of abnormal blood findings suggested in Table 4 are based on information extrapolated from other avian species and from mammals. Those concerned with the veterinary care of psittacines (and other birds) should be encouraged to remedy this situation by publishing well documented case reports on their patients whenever possible.

Table 3:
Suggested Normal Ranges in Species for which Haematological Reference Values are not available.

	Parrots	Conures	Macaws	Cockatoos	Small Psittacines
Hb g/dl	12.9—20.0	15.0—20.0	12.0—20.0	12.5—19.4	12.2—20.0
RBC x 10^9/l	2.3—3.7	3.1—4.1	2.6—4.0	2.2—3.9	3.4—5.5
PCV l/l	0.44—0.57	0.43—0.55	0.40—0.57	0.37—0.59	0.45—0.56
MCV fl	148—192	121—153	153—174	136—200	99—142
MCH pg	44—69	41—55	40—65	43—69	28—44
MCHC g/dl	28—39	31—39	28—39	28—39	27—35
Hetero x 10^9/l	1.1—11.6	0.6—10.0	1.8—14.9	0.9—13.3	0.1—4.0
Lymphs x 10^9/l	0.5—3.7	0.6—3.2	0.5—5.5	0.4—3.9	0.4—4.1
Monos x 10^9/l	<0.9	<0.4	<0.6	<0.5	<0.6
Eos x 10^9/l	<0.6	<0.7	<0.6	<0.7	<0.6
Basos x 10^9/l	<0.4	<0.4	<0.4	<0.9	<0.4
Thromb x 10^9/l	5—28	6—28	4—21	3—31	5—25
Fibrinogen g/l	<3.5	<3.5	<3.5	<3.5	<3.0

Table 4:
Clinical Significance of Haematological Abnormalities Identified by Reference to Species-specific Normal Values

Finding	Possible causes
Anaemia	Haemorrhage, haemolysis, marrow supression
Polycythaemia	Secondary to cardiac or pulmonary disease, dehydration
Hypochromia	Nutritional deficiency, infection
Microcytosis	Infection, mineral deficiency
Leucocytosis	Infection, stress, ACTH, cortical hormones
Leucopenia	Folic acid deficiency, degenerative response to infection
Heterophilia	Pyogenic infections, acute and chronic inflammation, mycobacterial infections, severe toxic or traumatic tissue necrosis, stress, ACTH, cortical hormones
Heteropenia	Degenerative response to severe infection, early phase of viral disease, toxic drugs and chemicals, Pacheco's disease.
Lymphocytosis	Chronic viral infection, immune-mediated diseases
Lymphopenia	Stress, some chronic viral diseases
Monocytosis	Some bacterial infections, mycobacterial infection, tissue necrosis, chronic diseases
Eosinophilia	Parasite infestation, allergy, tissue necrosis
Basophilia	Respiratory disease, tissue necrosis
Thrombocytosis	Bacterial infection?
Thrombocytopenia	Poor collection technique, idiopathic?
Hyperfibrinogenaemia	Infection, inflammatory response
Hypofibrinogenaemia	Poor collection technique, liver failure, disseminated intravascular coagulation?

BLOOD PARASITES
The blood parasites of psittacine birds have been well described by Burr (1983). They may be identified by careful examination of stained blood films (Table 5). Since transmission of these parasites has not been recorded within the U.K., their presence is usually considered to be a strong indication that the bird has been imported.

Table 5:
Morphological Characteristics of Intracellular Blood Parasites

Genus	Identification Characteristics	Vector
Haemoproteus (H. handai, H. desseri)	Kidney-shaped, intraerythrocytic gametocytes, usually occupying more than 50% of cell cytoplasm (Plate 4:12).	Midges (Culicoides) louse flies (Hippobosca) etc.
Plasmodium (P. circumflexum, P. relictum, P. vaughnii etc.)	Sausage-shaped intraerythrocytic gametocytes, occupying less than 25% of cell cytoplasm, clusters of small round sporozooites free in plasma.	Mosquitoes
Leucocytozoon	Macro and microgametocytes infecting erythrocytes and lymphoid cells. Infected cells grossly deformed and usually not identifiable.	Blackflies (Simulium), midges etc.
Lankesterella	Mature schizonts in lymphocytes and monocytes	Red mite (Dermanyssus), fowl mite (Ornythonyssus)
Aegyptianella	Signet ring-like structures in red cells	Ticks (Argas persicusi and Ixodes recinus)

The parasites most commonly encountered in psittacine birds are *Haemoproteus* ssp. (Plate 4:12), *Plasmodium* ssp., *Leucocytozoon* spp., *Trypanosoma* spp. and microfilariae (Plate 4:13). *Haemoproteus*, trypanosome and microfilarial infections are usually well tolerated unless the organisms are very numerous or the bird is stressed but *lasmodium* and *Leucocytozoon* infections can cause severe illness and death (Table 6). Other clinically significant parasites, found only rarely, include *Lankesterella, Aegyptianella* and *Toxoplasma.*

Table 6:
Clinical Signs and Suggested Treatment of Blood Parasite Infections
in Psittacine Birds (Modified from Burr, 1983).

Parasite	Clinical and Post Mortem Findings	Suggested Treatment
Plasmodium	Anaemia, anorexia, emaciation, oedema of eyelids, sudden death, serosal haemorrhage, hepatomegaly, splenomegaly	Quinacrine HC1, 250 mg/kg body wt SID, 5 days or chloroquine phosphate PO, 500 mg/kg SID for 5 days
Leucocytozoon	Anaemia, lethargy, emaciation, greenish diarrohoea, hepatomegaly, splenomegaly, cysts in skeletal and cardiac muscle, myocarditis, subcutaneous haemorrhage.	As for plasmodium
Haemoproteus	Usually none. Chronic anaemia in severe infection	If necessary, as for plasmodium
Lankesterella	Gradual onset anaemia, lethargy, emaciation.	Control of vectors, treat bird as for plasmodium
Aegyptionella	Anaemia, fever, lethargy, occasionally jaundice	As for plasmodium, one treatment usually sufficient
Toxoplasma	Torticollis, paralysis, blindness	Sulfaquinoxaline PO, 1 oz/gal water, 5 days or pyrimethamine PO, 0.5 mg/kg, 10 days
Trypanosoma	Rare	Not warranted
Microfilariae	Rare; anaemia, lethargy, emaciation in heavy infections	Levamisole HC1 PO, 20 mg/kg, one dose or fenbendazole PO, 25 mg/kg, one dose.

REFERENCES AND FURTHER READING

BURR, E. W. (1983). Parasites of psittacines blood. Modern Avian Practice, April, 1983, 333-335.

CLUBB, S. L. and CRAMM, D. (1981). Blood parasites of psittacine birds. A survey of the prevalence of *Haemoproteus,* microfilaria and trypanosomes. Annual Proceedings of the American Association of Zoo Veterinarians, Seattle, Washington, 1981, pp32—37.

CAMPBELL, T. W. and DEIN, F. J. (1984). Avian Haematology. Veterinary Clinics of North America: Small Animal Practice. 14:233-248.

DACIE, J. V. and LEWIS, S. M. (1984). *Practical Haematology,* Sixth Edition, Churchill Livingstone, Edinburgh, London, Melbourne and New York.

GODWIN, J. S., JACOBSON, E. R. and GASKIN, J. M. (1982). Effects of Pacheco's parrot disease on haemotologic and blood chemistry values of quaker parrots *(Myopsitta monachus).* Journal of Zoo Animal Medicine, 13:127—132.

HAWKEY, C. M., HART, M. G. and KNIGHT, J. A. (1982). Haematological findings in healthy and sick African grey parrots *(Psittacus erithacus).* Veterinary Record 111:580—582.

HAWKEY, C. M. and SAMOUR, H. J. (1987). The value of clinical haematology in exotic birds. In *Disorders of exotic animals.* Eds D. E. Jacobson and G. Kolias. Contemporary Issues in Small Animal Practice. Churchill livingstone, New York, 1987.

LUCAS, A. J. and JAMROZ, C. (1961). *Atlas of Avian Haematology,* U.S.D.A. Monograph No 25, Washington D.C.

RAPHAEL, B. L. (1980). Haematology and blood chemistries of macaws. Annual Proceedings, American Association of Zoo Veterinarians., 1980. pp 97—98.

ROSSKOPF, W. J. and WOERPLE, R. W. (1982). The use of haematologic testing procedures in caged bird medicine: An introduction. California Veterinarian, 36:19—22.

ROSSKOPF, W. J., WOERPLE, R. W., ROSSKOPF, G. and VAN DE WATER, D. (1982). Haematologic and blood chemistry values for commonly kept cockatoos. California Veterinarian, 36:9—15.

ROSSKOPF, W. J., WOERPLE, R. W., ROSSKOPF, G. and VAN DE WATER, D. (1982) Haematological and blood chemistry values for common conure species. Californian Veterinarian, 36:32—34.

ROSSKOPF, W. J., WOERPLE, R. W., ROSSKOPF, G. and VAN DE WATER, D. (1982) Haematological and blood biochemistry values for the African grey parrot and the Timneh grey parrot. California Veterinarian, 36:37—40.

ROSSKOPF, W. J., WOERPLE, R. W., ROSSKOPF, G. and VAN DE WATER, D. (1982) Haematological and blood chemistry values from the cockateil. Californian Veterinarian, 36:41—43.

TANGREDI, B. P. (1981). Heterophilia and left shift associated with fatal diseases in four psittacine birds: Yellow-collared macaw *(Ara auricollis),* yellow-naped Amazon *(Amazona ochrocephala auropalliata),* yellow-crowned Amazon (Amazona ochrocephala ochrocephala), blue and gold macaw *(Ara ararauna)* Journal of Zoo Animal Medicine, 12:13—16.

WOERPLE, R. W. and ROSSKOPF, W. J. (1984). Clinical Experience with Avian Laboratory Diagnostics. Veterinary Clinics of North America: Small Animal Practice. 14:249—286.

Appendix 1:
Suggested Haematological Reference Ranges for Amazon Parrots
(*Amazona* ssp.)

	Blue-fronted Amazon *A.aestiva*	Orange-winged Amazon *A.amazonica*	Yellow-billed Amazon *A.collaria*	Mealy Amazon *A.farinosa*	Lilac-crowned Amazon *A.finchi*	Yellow-fronted Amazon *A.ochrocephala*
Hb g/dl	14.4—20.0	15.0—18.0	16.7—18.8	14.9—16.7	17.0—20.0	13.5—17.5
RBC x 10^{12}/l	2.6—3.3	2.6—3.3	2.6—3.1	2.7—3.2	3.2—3.7	2.3—3.1
PCV l/l	0.44—0.54	0.45—0.50	0.45—0.52	0.48—0.55	0.49—0.57	0.45—0.50
MCV fl	158—175	148—190	153—175	168—181	149—162	158—178
MCH pg	44.7—66.0	48.6—68.9	56.3—64.2	52.5—55.6	54.1—59.2	47.3—57.6
MCHC g/dl	29.6—39.0	28.6—35.8	34.0—38.0	30.6—32.0	34.6—37.6	29.0—37.2
WBC x 10^9/l	2.3—8.1	2.7—7.9	3.5—7.7	3.5—9.7	2.1—6.2	1.5—11.6
Hetero x 10^9/l	1.5—6.2	1.7—7.0	1.6—5.1	1.5—7.0	1.0—4.0	0.6—8.0
Lymph x 10^9/l	0.6—2.8	0.5—3.3	1.5—2.2	1.2—3.7	1.0—2.1	0.8—3.7
Mono x 10^9/l	0.0—0.1	0.0—0.1	0.0—0.8	0.0—0.1	0.0—0.1	0.0--0.1
Eo x 10^9/l	0.0—0.3	0.0—0.3	0.0—0.5	0.0—0.4	0.0—0.4	0.0—0.4
Baso x 10^9/l	0.0—0.2	0.0—0.4	0.0—0.1	0.0—0.2	0.0—0.1	0.0—0.2
Thromb x 10^9/l	5—24	8—21	9—26	11—17	17—28	11—22
Fibrinogen g/l	1.0—3.1	1.1—2.6	1.0—2.8	1.1—2.4	1.1—2.0	1.0—2.0

Appendix 2:
Suggested Haematological Reference Ranges for Budgerigars and Lovebirds

	Budgerigar *Melopsittacus undulatus*	Fischer's Lovebird *Agapornis fischeri*
Hb g/dl	13.8—16.8	12.2—20.0
RBC x 10^{12}/l	4.4—5.5	3.4—5.3
PCV l/l	0.48—0.58	0.45—0.60
MCV fl	99—116	107—142
MCH pg	28.2—34.7	28.6—43.9
MCHC g/dl	27.5—31.5	26.0—34.5
WBC x 10^9/l	1.0—7.7	0.6—7.1
Hetero x 10^9/l	0.4—5.0	0.2—4.9
Lymph x 10^9/l	0.4—2.2	0.9—4.1
Mono x 10^9/l	0.0—0.1	0.0—0.3
Eo x 10^9/l	0.0—0.4	0.0—0.3
Baso x 10^9/l	0.0—0.5	0.0—0.4
Thromb x 10^9/l	6—24	5—25
Fibrinogen g/l	1.0—2.5	0.9—2.3

Appendix 3:
Suggested Haematological Reference Ranges for Cockatoos (*Cacatua* ssp.)

	Lesser Sulphur-crested Cockatoo (*C.sulphurea*)	Greater Sulphur-crested Cockatoo (*C.galerita*)	Bare-eyed Cockatoo (*C.sanguinea*)	Blue-eyed Cockatoo (*C.ophthalmica*)	Moluccan Cockatoo (*C.Moluccensis*)	Roseate Cockatoo (Galah) (*C.roseicapillus*)
Hb g/dl	12.6—16.9	13.8—17.1	15.4—19.0	12.5—16.9	13.0—15.5	14.0—19.0
RBC x 10^{12}/l	2.2—3.2	2.4—3.4	2.5—3.5	2.3—2.8	2.3—2.6	3.1—3.9
PCV l/l	0.38—0.50	0.41—0.50	0.47—0.59	0.37—0.43	0.37—0.45	0.48—0.59
MCV fl	150—186	145—187	181—200	152—167	159—195	136—164
MCH pg	48.6—67.3	53.8—60.6	56.6—63.1	52.5—64.8	49.5—66.7	43.5—51.3
MCHC g/dl	32.5—38.0	33.3—37.6	29.0—37.0	33.3—39.0	29.8—35.0	29.0—33.9
WBC x 10^9/l	3.5—11.0	1.4—10.0	4.2—11.0	2.0—3.6	4.0—12.4	1.6—3.1
Hetero x 10^9/l	2.6—8.0	1.1—6.6	2.8—10.6	0.9—1.7	2.5—10.0	0.6—9.2
Lymph x 10^9/l	0.4—3.3	1.0—3.6	0.5—3.9	0.8—1.8	0.8—1.8	0.5—2.0
Mono x 10^9/l	0.0—0.1	0.0—0.2	0.0—0.5	0.0—0.2	0.0—0.3	0.0—0.1
Eo x 10^9/l	0.0—0.5	0.0—0.2	0.0—0.7	0.0—0.4	0.0—0.4	0.0—0.2
Baso x 10^9/l	0.0—0.5	0.0—0.9	0.0—0.8	0.0—0.1	0.0—0.2	0.0—0.8
Thromb x 10^9/l	17—30	7—24	5—24	4—17	5—22	4—31
Fibrinogen g/l	0.9—2.0	0.9—2.0	1.5—2.8	1.1—2.6	0.9—2.2	0.8—3.5

Appendix 4:
Suggested Haematological Reference Ranges for Conures

	Golden Conure *Aratinga guarouba*	Patagonian Conure *Cyanoliseus patagonus*	Slender-billed Conure *Enicognathus leptorhynchus*
Hb g/dl	17.0—20.0	17.0—19.0	16.6—18.5
RBC x 10^{12}/l	3.0—4.0	3.6—4.1	3.2—4.1
PCV l/l	0.47—0.55	0.45—0.50	0.43—0.52
MCV fl	138—149	121—129	126—153
MCH pg	49.9—55.4	41.7—50.0	44.6—54.2
MCHC g/dl	33.4—38.0	34.2—38.5	34.4—38.2
WBC x 10^9/l	2.4—12.0	4.2—11.0	2.0—10.5
Hetero x 10^9/l	1.2—10.0	2.9—9.8	0.6—7.0
Lymph x 10^9/l	1.2—2.4	0.7—1.8	1.3—3.2
Mono x 10^9/l	1.0—0.1	0.0—0.1	0.0—0.1
Eo x 10^9/l	0.0—0.3	0.0—0.6	0.0—0.6
Baso x 10^9/l	0.0—0.1	0.0—0.1	0.0—0.1
Thromb x 10^9/l	9—25	11—28	6—17
Fibrinogen g/l	1.9—3.4	1.0—2.2	0.7—1.8

Appendix 5:
Suggested Haematological Reference Ranges for African Grey Parrots

	African Grey Parrot *Psittacus erithacus*
Hb g/dl	14.2 — 17.1
RBC x 10 ^{12}/l	3.0 — 3.6
PCV l/l	0.43 — 0.51
MCV fl	137 — 155
MCH pg	41.9 — 52.8
MCHC g/dl	28.9 — 34.0
WBC x 10 ^{9}/l	3.3 — 10.3
Hetero x 10 ^{9}/l	1.8 — 7.4
Lymph x 10 ^{9}/l	0.7 — 2.2
Mono x 10 ^{9}/l	0.0 — 0.2
Eo x 10 ^{9}/l	0.0 — 0.4
Baso x 10 ^{9}/l	0.0 — 0.8
Thromb x 10 ^{9}/l	11 — 42
Fibrinogen g/l	1.5 — 3.0

Appendix 6:
Suggested Haematological Reference Ranges for Keas

	Kea *Nestor notabilis*
Hb g/dl	11.0 — 17.0
RBC x 10 ^{12}/l	2.3 — 3.1
PCV l/l	0.35 — 0.46
MCV fl	137 — 185
MCH pg	41.6 — 68.2
MCHC g/dl	30.4 — 36.7
WBC x 10 ^{9}/l	12.1 — 22.6
Hetero x 10 ^{9}/l	9.4 — 20.1
Lymph x 10 ^{9}/l	1.2 — 2.7
Mono x 10 ^{9}/l	0.0 — 0.1
Eo x 10 ^{9}/l	0.0 — 0.5
Baso x 10 ^{9}/l	0.0 — 0.4
Thromb x 10 ^{9}/l	11 — 22
Fibrinogen g/l	1.0 — 2.0

Appendix 7:
Suggested Haematological Reference Values for Macaws

	Blue & Yellow Macaw *Ara ararauna*	Scarlet Macaw *Ara macao*	Green-winged Macaw *Ara chloroptera*	Red-fronted Macaw *Ara rubrogenys*	Military Macaw *Ara militaris*	Yellow-collared Macaw *Ara auricollis*	Chestnut-fronted (severe) Macaw *Ara severe*	Buffon's Macaw *Ara ambigua*	Hyacinthine Macaw *Andorhynchus hyacinthinus*
Hb g/dl	12.0 — 20.0	14.7 — 18.4	14.5 — 18.8	13.8 — 19.6	15.4 — 18.0	16.6 — 19.2	15.6 — 17.1	14.9 — 16.2	13.5 — 17.7
RBC x 10 ^{12}/l	2.8 — 3.5	2.7 — 3.6	2.8 — 3.5	2.6 — 3.5	2.7 — 3.1	3.2 — 3.8	3.1 — 4.1	2.8 — 3.4	2.9 — 3.4
PCV l/l	0.40 — 0.52	0.46 — 0.51	0.41 — 0.56	0.41 — 0.51	0.44 — 0.50	0.49 — 0.52	0.45 — 0.53	0.42 — 0.50	0.43 — 0.53
MCV fl	128 — 166	130 — 166	142 — 171	133 — 146	154 — 161	133 — 149	124 — 156	150 — 156	139 — 156
MCH pg	40.0 — 64.7	41.5 — 64.2	43.1 — 59.6	40.6 — 59.6	55.2 — 58.1	47.9 — 53.8	39.2 — 55.2	53.0 — 54.0	45.1 — 55.1
MCHC g/dl	29.6 — 39.0	31.6 — 38.5	28.7 — 38.3	29.4 — 38.4	34.6 — 37.0	32.8 — 36.9	31.6 — 35.6	34.4 — 35.5	30.1 — 37.3
WBC x 10 ^{9}/l	3.5 — 15.4	6.4 — 15.4	4.4 — 12.3	3.0 — 7.2	12.6 — 17.8	5.0 — 14.5	4.2 — 10.2	8.6 — 12.5	5.6 — 12.6
Hetero x 10 ^{9}/l	2.3 — 8.0	4.2 — 12.9	2.8 — 11.1	1.9 — 6.1	10.4 — 15.0	4.0 — 9.4	3.0 — 6.8	6.6 — 10.8	4.4 — 9.7
Lymph x 10 ^{9}/l	1.1 — 3.2	0.9 — 3.3	1.2 — 5.2	1.0 — 2.5	0.7 — 2.9	0.9 — 4.8	0.6 — 3.6	1.5 — 1.8	0.8 — 2.9
Mono x 10 ^{9}/l	0.0 — 0.1	0.0 — 0.1	0.0 — 0.3	0.0 — 0.1	0.0 — 0.1	0.0 — 0.3	0.0 — 0.5	0.0 — 0.1	0.0 — 0.1
Eo x 10 ^{9}/l	0.0 — 0.4	0.0 — 0.4	0.0 — 0.4	0.0 — 0.4	0.0 — 0.4	0.0 — 0.4	0.0 — 0.5	0.0 — 1.0	0.0 — 0.4
Baso x 10 ^{9}/l	0.0 — 0.1	0.0 — 0.8	0.0 — 0.2	0.0 — 0.2	0.0 — 0.0	0.0 — 0.1	0.0 — 0.2	0.0 — 0.1	0.0 — 0.3
Thromb x 10 ^{9}/l	11 — 29	6 — 34	8 — 30	7 — 28	20 — 30	10 — 20	10 — 20	20 — 25	7 — 29
Fibrinogen g/l	1.0 — 3.2	1.0 — 2.8	1.0 — 3.2	1.3 — 3.8	1.0 — 1.6	1.0 — 2.0	0.8 — 2.1	2.0 — 3.0	1.3 — 2.5

Appendix 8:
Suggested Normal Plasma Biochemical Values for Psittacine Birds (Zoological Society of London)

Component		Mean + SD	Observed range
Plasma urea	mmol/l	0.6 + 0.3	0.1 — 1.0
Creatinine	μmol/l	49.4 + 25.3	20.0 — 94.0
Bicarbonate	mmol/l	13.5 + 4.7	4.0 — 20
Chloride	mmol/l	113.4 + 4.2	107 — 120
Sodium	mmol/l	146.2 + 3.2	141 — 152
Potassium	mmol/l	2.86 + 1.15	1.10 — 4.60
Total protein	g/l	31.1 + 4.7	21.0 — 36.0
Albumin	g/l	14.9 + 2.0	12.0 — 18.0
Globuilin	g/l	16.2 + 5.0	4.0 — 22.0
Calcium	mmol/l	1.88 + 0.30	1.16 — 2.11
Inorganic phosphate	mmol/l	1.03 + 0.58	0.14 — 2.14
Alkaline phosphatase	IU/l	224.2 + 163.5	42 — 479
Total bilirubin	μmol/l	2.2 + 1.8	0.0 — 6.0
Conjugated bilirubin	μmol/l	0.6 + 0.7	0.0 — 0.2
Alanine transaminase	IU/l	30.6 + 25.1	6.0 — 84.0
Y-glutamyl transaminase	IU/l*	2.8 + 3.9	0.0 — 10.0
Aspartate transaminase	IU/l*	163.0 + 61.0	92.0 — 270.0
Urate	μmol/l	400.9 + 177.9	63.0 — 596.0
Iron	μmol/l	14.4 + 8.0	7.2 — 32.8

* at 37 C

Appendix 9:
Suggested Normal Clinical Biochemistry Values for Psittacine Birds (Woerpel and Rosskopf, 1984)

		Amazon Parrot	Grey Parrot	Budgerigar	Cockatoos	Cockateils	Conures	Lovebirds	Macaws
Total protein	g/dl	3.0—5.0	3.0—5.0	2.5—4.5	2.5—5.5	2.2—5.0	2.5—4.5	2.2—5.1	3.0—5.0
Glucose	mg/dl	220—350	190—350	200—400	190—350	200—450	200—350	200—400	200—350
Calcium	mg/dl	8.0—13.0	8.0—13.0		8.0—11.0	8.5—13.0	8.0—15.0	9.0—15.0	9.0—13.0
SGOT	IU/l	130—350	100—350	150—350	125—350	100—350	125—350	100—350	100—280
LDH	IU/l	160—420	150—450	150—450	225—650	125—450	125—420	100—350	75—425
Creatinine	mg/dl	0.1—0.4	0.1—0.4	0.1—0.4	0.1—0.4	0.1—0.4	0.1—0.5	0.1—0.4	0.1—0.5
Uric Acid	mg/dl	2.0—10.0	4.0—10.0	4.0—14.0	3.5—11.0	3.5—11.0	2.5—10.5	3.0—11.0	2.5—11.5
Potassium	mEq/l	3.0—4.5	2.6—4.2	—4.5	2.5—4.5	2.5—4.5	3.4—5.0	2.5—3.5	2.4—4.5
Sodium	mEq/l	136—152	134—152	135—155	131—157	132—150	134—148	137—150	136—155
T4	μg/dl	0.05—2.0	0.3—2.0	2.5—4.5	1.5—5.5	0.7—2.4	0.25—0.9	0.2—1.9	1.0—4.0

Chapter 5 # SURGERY

B. H. Coles B.V.Sc, M.R.C.V.S.

PRE-OPERATIVE CONSIDERATIONS

a) Clinical examination

Before commencing any surgical procedure on a parrot there are a number of factors that it is wise to take into account. Firstly, a thorough clinical examination should be performed so that an appraisal can be made of the bird's ability to withstand the stress of anaesthesia and surgery. It should be considered whether the bird is obese or too thin. The carina of the sternum should be palpated and if this is markedly prominent it may be better, if practical, to postpone surgery until the parrot can be got into better physical condition. Some assessment of the parrot's nutritional state can be gained by measuring the serum total protein and P.C.V. The P.C.V. can be quickly determined using blood from a cut toe nail drawn into a microhaematocrit tube. After centrifugation, the tube can be broken in half and the serum blown onto a refractometer face to obtain the total protein value. This should be between 25g/1 and 30g/1 and certainly not below 20g/1. A blood glucose estimation should be carried out prior to surgery on all parrots which are obviously ill. This is easily performed in practice using one of the stick methods. Blood glucose should not be below 180g/1 and if it is, 5% glucose saline should be given. In some species of parrot the normal blood glucose is at least 200g/1.

Alternatively, birds which feel heavy when handled may be obese and, if time allows, it may be prudent to slim the bird before attempting surgery. How this can safely be achieved is discussed later when considering lipomata. Obese birds often have livers infiltrated with fat which impairs normal function and leads to an elevation in liver enzymes. These can be assessed on small quantities of blood, using an autoanalyser. SGOT (AST) is normally 150 − 350 i.u./l for most species and γ GT should not exceed 20 i.u./l. The serum cholesterol level could also be measured and should not exceed 2g/1. For more information reference should be made to the tables on page 48. Birds with faulty liver function often have clotting defects, so that at the time when blood is collected for biochemistry an assessment of clotting time can be obtained. If a drop of blood is placed on a microscope slide and gently rocked, clotting should occur within one minute. Also, if direct pressure is applied to the site of venous puncture seepage of blood should not be unusually prolonged. If clotting time is prolonged, an injection of vitamin K (0.2 − 2.5mg/Kg) prior to surgery would be in order.

Another important part of clinical assessment is to make some judgement of the state of the respiratory system. Apart from any obvious nasal discharge, dypsnoea or a change in the voice may indicate an abnormality of the respiratory system. Some evaluation of the respiratory system can be gained during initial handling of the bird. During this period the rate of respiration will rise but after being returned to the cage this should return to normal within 3 − 5 minutes.

b) Withholding food prior to surgery

There is some difference of opinion amongst authors as to whether food should be withdrawn from a bird before surgery. Certainly, if a parrot has a full crop just before the induction of anaesthesia there is a risk of regurgitation and aspiration of food material. This can, of course, be prevented by using an endotracheal tube or plugging the oesophagus with moist cotton wool. In the author's opinion, it is a wise precaution to withhold food from the majority of parrots for 3 − 6 hours prior to surgery. For those birds below 100 grams in body weight, food should not be taken away for more than one hour. In those cases where it is proposed to carry out surgery on the alimentary canal, parrots can be fasted for up to 6 hours except in the case of the smallest birds below 100 grams in weight.

c) Heat loss and preparation of the surgical area.

There is little doubt that a fall of several degrees in body temperature can take place during surgery. This is particularly important for the smaller species since hypothermia is a contributory factor in shock and cardial failure. For this reason, the area of body surface prepared for the surgical incision should be kept to a minimum. Feathers need to be gently plucked so that the germinal layer of the feather follicle is not damaged. If cut, the feather does not grow again until the bird's next moult. Feathers in the growing stage ('in the blood') may bleed slightly when plucked. Once cleared of feathers, cleaning and antisepsis of this area should be kept to a minimum. A swab dampened with a quaternary ammonium antiseptic or a povidone iodine solution can be used. Excess fluid should not be allowed to drain down in the surrounding areas and soak the bird. Alcoholic solutions are best not used since their latent heat of vaporisation contributes to a lowering of body temperature. An exception to this rule can be made around the joints or fracture sites where the use of an alcoholic antiseptic may help to make the underlying tissues stand out more clearly.

During surgery the bird should be placed on a heat pad. The author uses an electrically heated pad which gives a surface temperature of 30°C but Harrison (1986) prefers to use a circulating water blanket. In an emergency a hot water bottle wrapped in paper towelling could be used, providing the surface temperature is no more than 35°C. Whichever method is used, it is safer to protect the patient from direct contact with the heat source using a sheet of polythene bubble wrap commonly used as packaging material. Hyperthermia leading to hyperventilation should be avoided because this can result in the washing out of carbon dioxide and respiratory alkalosis.

It is also best to maintain a reasonably high operating room temperature and to reduce all air movement caused by extraction fans, open windows, etc. to a minimum.

d) Blood transfusion and fluid therapy

Many birds, particularly small ones, die during or very soon after surgery through blood loss. Every effort should be made whilst operating to reduce this to a minimum. However, the effects of a predicted haemorrhage can to some extent be counteracted by administering blood or blood volume expanders prior to actual surgery (after induction of anaesthesia) or just before a hazardous part of the surgical procedure. If the PCV is below 25 l/l then blood should be given before an incision is made. Interspecies transfusion can be given provided that the bird is not going to need a second transfusion after 24 hours when antibodies to the first transfusion have started to build up. In consequence of this, it is helpful to have 2 – 3 ml of heparinized blood collected from donor pigeons or chickens available for administration. 0.5 ml can safely be given intravenously to a budgerigar at one time whilst 10 ml can be given to a macaw or large cockatoo. This quantity can be repeated 2 or 3 times during the surgical procedure.

If the PCV is above 55–60 l/l, then the bird is dehydrated and requires fluid therapy prior to surgery. Lactated Ringer's or Hartman's solution should preferably be used, although 5% glucose saline will suffice. 10% of the bird's body weight is given as an intravenous bolus prior to surgery but after administration of the initial anaesthetic.

Fluid can also be given by mouth or subcutaneous injection. For subcutaneous injection, the skin on the dorsal surface at the base of the neck is ideal. Alternatively, the inguinal region can be used but care must be taken in this area not to puncture the body wall.

e) Positioning of the patient

When operating on a bird, it is preferable to place the patient in either lateral or sternal recumbancy. The natural tendency of the surgeon is to place the bird on its back for a ventral approach, since it is more stable in this position, but the operator should try and avoid this method as the pressure of the viscera greatly reduces the volume of the air sacs. Marley and Payne (1964) working with chickens showed that if a bird is placed in dorsal recumbancy during anaesthesia its minute volume could be reduced by anything between 10–60%.

f) Instrumentation and essential equipment

As most psittacine birds are so much smaller than cats and dogs, magnification and good lighting are essential. Some avian surgeons consider the operating microscope is the best form of magnification. However, these instruments are expensive and require considerable practice on the part of the surgeon to be used effectively. For most purposes the use of a binocular loupe or magnifying spectacles is adequate. An inexpensive and effective method of magnification with shadowless illumination is to use a lamp commonly in use by many persons carrying out delicate work in industry. This is the use of a combined 3-diopter 5 inch diameter lens housed together with a surrounding circular fluorescent tube. (Arnolds Veterinary Products Ltd.). It has also been suggested that the fibre optic laparoscope, commonly used for the surgical sexing of birds can be mounted on a flexible arm and become a combined source of magnification and pin-point lighting. This is an excellent idea since the instrument is in constant focus but the field of view is rather restricted.

A selection of small scale instruments such as is used for ophthalmic surgery is also essential. The following list will be found useful for this purpose:-

1. A pairs of 4 ½ inch enucleation or strabismus scissors.
2. A pair of Lister's conjunctival forceps with 1 x 2 teeth.
3. Several pairs of straight and curved Halstead mosquito artery forceps.
4. A pair of fine needle holders. A pair of the above Halstead mosquito forceps will act as a substitute but sometimes the needle tends to rotate in the jaws.
5. Eye-lid retractors can be used as avian wound retractors.
6. An iris hook and a soft silver bulbous ended probe are useful for manipulating tissues. However, sterile cotton wool buds on wooden sticks can also be used for this purpose and at the same time act as swabs.
7. A Spreull's needle attached to a sterile 5 ml syringe can be used for suction and irrigation.
8. A selection of suitable suture material from 3 − 0 to 10 − 0 size all swaged onto round bodied needles with taper-cut points.
9. Light-weight transparent drapes can be made from suitable polythene sheeting. The gauge used for household food bags is suitable. The edges of a preformed operating hole can be strengthened with zinc oxide, masking or other suitable adhesive tape and the whole gas sterilised using ethylene oxide.
10. An operating stool is essential since, if the surgeon is seated with the arms resting on the table, there is better control of the hands.
11. A diathermy or electro-surgical unit is useful for incision of all tissues and helps control haemorrhage.

SURGERY OF THE SKIN AND THE ASSOCIATED TISSUES

a) Primary considerations

When compared with that in mammals avian skin is thin and because it contains less elastic fibres is not very resilient. The density of collagen fibres and hence the strength of the skin is more concentrated in the area between the rows of feathers or pterylae, Stettenheim (1972). The integument is only loosely attached to the underlying tissues except in those areas such as the skull, the synsacrum, the carpo metacarpus and the digits where it is directly attached to the underlying bone. Because of these factors avian skin tears easily particularly where it is attached to bone. Apart from the capilliaries there are numerous larger blood vessels in the skin and haemorrhage from these can be a problem. Because of the foregoing considerations, the initial incision in the skin is best made using either a diathermy needle or picking up the skin with forceps to form a 'tent' and nicking this with scissors. After making a small puncture a haemostat can be used to undermine the skin. Before the incision is extended the skin should be crushed with the haemostat along the proposed line of incision to reduce the risk of haemorrhage.

When suturing skin, if practical, it is better to place sutures in the feather tracts or apteria where the skin is strongest . Also, if suture material is swaged onto round bodied needles with trocar points there is less tendency for the skin to tear. The author's preference is to use 3/0 to 5/10 polyglactin ('Vicryl' Ethicon) which is more pliant than monofilament nylon and has less tendency to cut through the skin. Also, a personal preference is to use mattress sutures rather than single interrupted sutures. Harrison (1986) prefers a continuous interlocking suture.

b) Lacerated wounds and extensive trauma to the skin

In most cases where there is trauma to the skin alone and there is not serious damage to underlying structures, the wound is best left open for a few days to drain. The area can be cleansed daily with Dermisol (Beecham Animal Health) or Povidon-Iodine (Pevidene, Berk Pharmaceuticals Ltd.) solution. In those cases where the skin has been lost and there is insufficient to cover the wound, this area is best covered with a flexible hydroactive gel (Granuflex, E. R. Squibb and Sons Ltd.) to encourage epithelialization. Alternatively, a flexible isobutyl dental acrylic can be used to anchor the skin edges together and cover the gap between the edges. Adhesion is best achieved when the wound is dry and the edges of the skin are rolled slightly inward as described by Harrison (1986).

c) Subcutaneous abscesses

These commonly occur around the head of parrots in the periorbital region and often involve the paranasal sinuses. They are usually a sequel to chronic respiratory infection. (See Plate 5:6)

Abscesses may also be seen as pendulant swellings in the submaxillary region and as multiocular swellings in the carpo metacarpal area. In both these latter cases, they may be confused with neoplasms. Furthermore, the multiocular carpometacarpal abscess could be confused with a Xanthoma which commonly occurs in the same region, is distinctly yellow and is often quite vascular. (See Plate 5:1).

In all cases, the swelling should first be explored using an 18 gauge hypodermic needle. If pus is present it is usually caseous in nature as the white blood cells of birds do not contain lysosomes. The abscess should be opened using a No. 11 Swan Morton blade, inserting the point first and directing the cutting edge away from the body. Haemorrhage is not usually a problem but it might be wiser to crush the skin first before making an incision as described above. Swabs should be obtained for bacteriology and sensitivity testing. The pus can then be scooped out using a small Volkmann's spoon, a cotton wool bud or a spatulate-type dental scaler. The cavity should be thoroughly cleansed and then sutured. It is not left open as would be the case in a mammal.

Where pendulant submaxillary swellings are concerned it may be possible to dissect the abscess free without opening the surrounding capsule. Blunt dissection by inserting a closed haemaostat and then opening this to carefully break down the subcutaneous tissue, should be used. In the case of a multicentric abscess covering the carpal region where the skin in this area is closely attached to the bone, after dissecting out the abscess there may be insufficient skin to cover the wound. In this case the use of a hydroactive gel or flexible dental acrylic is indicated.

d) Feather cysts

These are often seen in parrots and may be confused with abscesses or neoplasms (See plate 5:2). They are usually seen in the region of the carpometacarpus but can be seen anywhere in the body. The cyst can either be incised and the contents evacuated or the complete cyst can be dissected free. In either case it is a wise precaution to use a rubber band clipped together with artery forceps to act as a tourniquet. If the cyst is just opened and evacuated the cavity can be cauterised using a silver nitrate pencil or it can be fulgurated by electro surgery. If the whole cyst, including the germinal layer attached to the bone, is carefully dissected free, great care should be taken to remove as little skin as possible and not to damage the neighbouring follicles.

Whichever method of surgery is used to deal with the problem, an area of fibrosed skin is liable to remain leading to a recurrence of the cyst. Plastic surgery to remove the offending area is not practical.

e) Neoplasia

Undoubtedly the most common subcutaneous tumour seen in psittacine birds is the lipoma. This very often, but not always, occurs over the sternum. In the budgerigar they are often quite large and may invade the thoracic inlet and be adherent to the crop. These tumours are often associated with secondary hypothyroidism caused by a deficiency of iodine in the diet. They may also be due to excessive food intake and inadequate exercise. Liposarcomata are sometimes seen in the same regions as lipomata but they are usually firmer in consistency and have a more extensive blood supply. In the case of the lipoma a reduction in the size of the tumour and an improvement in the general health of the bird should be achieved by dietary means before surgery is attempted. However, the process is slow and may take 4 or 5 months.

Calorific intake can be lowered by reducing the intake of high oil bearing seeds such as sunflower seeds, peanuts, hemp, rape, niger and sesame. Instead, white millet, wholemeal bread, fresh vegetables and fruit can be given. Yogurt, preferably plain, although one containing fruit may be more acceptable, together with hard boiled egg, chicken or turkey breasts to provide some protein should also be fed. A vitamin supplement, such as S.A.37 (Intervet Ltd.) or Vionate (Ciba-Geigy Ltd) should be added. Lugols iodine should be added to the drinking water, diluted one part in 7500, together with thyroxine (50 — 70 mcg. thyroxine crushed in 100 ml drinking water).

In the case of budgerigars the seed should be rationed to a heaped teaspoonful of seed twice daily and not given *ad libitum* as is the usual practice. Only white millet and fruit together with soluble vitamins in the drinking water should be given. Exercise can be increased by allowing the bird free flight out of its cage or with the bird perched on the hand the owner alternatively raises and lowers the hand to encourage flapping of the wings. This exercise should be carried out on a regular basis: at least 15 minutes three times a day are needed.

To remove the lipoma an incision is made over the mid line, preferably using an electrosurgical knife. The tumour is then freed from surrounding tissue by blunt dissection best carried out by inserting a closed pair of mosquito haemostats and then carefully opening these to break down the connective tissue. Each bleeding point must be meticulously controlled with particular attention being given to the main blood supply coming from the pectoral arteries on the underside of the tumour. These latter vessels are best clamped with an insulated haemostat which is then touched with the tip of a diathermy electrode (Ward's technique). Insulated bipolar ophthalmic forceps can be used as an alternative. Post operative haemorrhage into the operation site can sometimes occur after suturing, possibly as a result of a clotting defect due to hepatopathy. For this reason a preoperative assessment of the health of the liver as earlier described is a sensible precaution. Also, any redundant skin left after the removal of a large tumour should be trimmed so that the skin fits firmly over the underlying tissues. After suturing there should be no resulting dead space.

Other neoplasms such as haemangiomata, fibromata, fibrosarcomata and mixed cell tumours are occasionally encountered. The surgical principles as described above when dealing with lipomata are equally applicable. Also from time to time encapsulated and organised haematomata are seen and can be similarly dealt with.

f)   The uropygial gland
Adenomata and adenocarcinomata originating from the glandular epithelium of the uropygial gland are quite commonly seen in budgerigars and occasionally in other species (Gandal 1982, Petrak and Gilmore 1982). These tumours must be differentiated from impaction and abscessation of the gland. (See Plate 5:3).

As mentioned earlier, the skin in this area is firmly attached to the underlying synsacrum. Adenomata tend to be locally invasive and so, during the dissection to free the tumour, the skin can easily become torn and it can be difficult to cleanly dissect out the neoplastic tissue.

Removal of an affected preen gland does not seem to be a problem in the budgerigar or for that matter in other species of birds. Amazon parrots, which live in tropical rain forest, do not possess the gland and in many other species such as cockatiels, cockatoos and lovebirds the gland is reduced. Waterproofing the plumage does not therefore entirely depend on the secretion of the gland, and is more dependent on the interlocking integrity of the feather barbules.

THE HEAD
Subcutaneous swellings in the periorbital and submandibular regions have already been referred to earlier in this chapter.

Abscesses are commonly seen in the oral cavity of psittacines and these may be situated on or under the tongue. They are also seen sometimes partially obstructing the glottis and the choanal space, in which site they may occlude the common opening of the nasolachrymal ducts. These abscesses often start in the glands of the oral mucous membranes which, due to hypovitaminosis A, undergo squamous metaplasia and subsequently become blocked with keratin. The gland may also become secondarily infected with candida, trichomonades or bacterial organisms.

The abscess must be opened and debrided. It is not usually possible to suture these lesions in the oral cavity. Swabs must be taken for bacteriological and fungal culture and the lesions must be differentiated from pox infection or papillomata by biopsy.

Occasionally, tumours such as adenomata and granulomata caused by long retained foreign bodies will be encountered. Sometimes it is possible to deal with these using a fine-tip cryosurgical probe. However, great care must be taken to restrict the extent of the ice ball; it is very easy to destroy too much tissue.

Accidental wounds to the head

A startled bird, or one which is carelessly caught, may sustain collision damage and trauma to the head. Also, an attack by an aggresssive cage mate commonly results in a wound to the head.

Every effort should be made to preserve the skin covering the scalp since it is adherent to the underlying bone and not very mobile. It may be possible to mobilise skin from the dorsal part of the neck and to draw this forward to help cover the wound. Similarly, a wound affecting the upper eyelid may be repaired by carrying out a lateral canthotomy and sliding the skin forward from an area posterior to the eye. As far as possible avoid tension on the lower eyelid because it is this structure, rather than the upper eyelid, which is mainly responsible for closing the eye.

Enucleation of the eye

Before attempting eye enucleation, the following anatomical differences from mammals should be noted. The eyes are larger and relatively occupy a greater proportion of the volume of the avian skull. The two eyes in a bird are separated by only a thin plate of bone. In attempting to remove one eye in its entirety, the optic nerve of the contra-lateral eye as well as the optic chiasma, which is close at hand, may be damaged. The extra occular muscles have been greatly reduced so that the avian eye is much less mobile in its socket (compensated by greater mobility of the neck) and the globe of the eye fits very closely in the orbit.

The sclera is not only cartilagenous but is ossified in a ring of bony plates in the region of the corneal scleral junction.

Considering all these factors the best method is first to incise and remove the cornea. Next carefully dissect out the lens and iris and any free vitreous so that the eye is partially eviscerated rather than enucleated. Care is taken not to dig too deeply into the posterior pole of the globe. The cavity created can be plugged with an absorbent fibrin or gelatin sponge after which the conjunctive is sutured across the opening. Lastly, the margins of the eyelids are carefully trimmed and sutured together. The loss of one eye does not seem to severely incapacitate the bird since there are a number of recorded instances of wild birds which have lost one eye and have managed to fend for themselves.

In small birds it has been suggested that cryosurgery may be an alternative to enucleation. However, very great care would be needed to control the size of the ice ball.

Cataract surgery

Cataracts are sometimes seen in old birds (See Plate 5:5); they also occur as a result of trauma. If the condition is bilateral and the bird is incapacitated, surgical intervention may be justified.

Topical treatment with an antibiotic/corticosteroid ointment is commenced the day before surgery. Since the muscles of both the iris and ciliary body in birds are striated, relaxation of these and dilation of the pupil is achieved by the injection of D-tubocurarine chloride (0.05 mg) into the anterior chamber.

A 180° incision through the dorsal cornea just anterior to the limbus is made using a cataract knife. In birds an extracapsular extraction of the lens is the preferred method of lens removal. An anterior capsulotomy is carried out to remove as much of the anterior capsule of the lens as possible. A cystitome or a 25 gauge hypodermic needle with the tip bent to form a small hook can be used. The lens substance which is softer in birds than mammals and the bulk of which is separated from periphery by a fluid filled vesicle (King & McLelland 1974), can then be broken up by discission using the same instruments as for the capsulotomy. Care is taken not to damage the posterior lens capsule. The lens material is then carefully removed by alternate irrigation and aspiration using normal saline. The corneal incision is closed using 7 − 0 collagen. A modified extra capsular lens extraction technique used on two raptors is described by Kern et al. (1984). These workers made two incisions with a von Graefe knife into the cornea at 10 o'clock and 3 o'clock. A 22 gauge needle was inserted through the first incision and was attached to a 500 ml bag of lactated Ringers with added sodium bicarbonate. Slow infusion of fluid was carried out to maintain the volume of the anterior chamber. Anterior capsulotomy was performed after which an untrasonic tip was inserted into the lens to emulsify the contents by ultra sonic fragmentation. The lens material was then sucked out. The results of this technique, used in these two cases, were very good.

Cannulation of the infra-orbital sinuses

As a result of the intricate anatomy of the infra-orbital sinuses owing to multiple diverticulae and also due to the connection with the air sac system of the head and neck, chronic infection, particularly pseudomonas infection of these structures, sometimes fails to respond to medical treatment. There is a chronic rhinorrhea which may be purulent with or without dilation of the unsupported parts of the sinuses. These cases require cannulation of the sinuses and flushing with an appropriate antibiotic preparation. Bacteriological swabs are first taken from the choanal space to ascertain which antibiotic to use. Cannulation is a simple procedure which can sometimes be carried out without anaesthetic although light anaesthesia is usually required.

A 20 gauge hypodermic needle is inserted just dorsal to the angle of the mouth in a notch formed by the junction of the premaxillary and maxillary bones. This can best be palpated just below the skin surface when the mouth is opened. The maxillary bone in the bird is small and rod-like and forms the anterior part of the zygomatic arch (maxillary, jugal arch). The needle is advanced at an angle of 45° but not so far as the rim of the orbit otherwise the globe of the eye will be penetrated. Sometimes this area is noticeably distended and the needle can then be inserted into the point of greatest distension. After injection of the appropriate antibiotic excess fluid will usually exit through the nares and choanal aperture. The bird is best held, head downwards so that the fluid flows into the glottis.

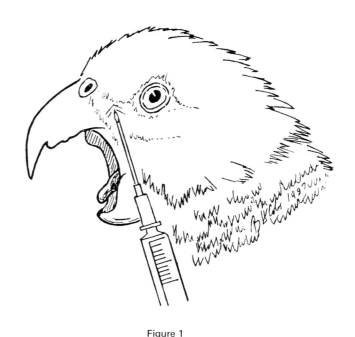

Figure 1

Cannulation of the infra-orbital sinuses

The needle is inserted just dorsal to the angle of the mouth, in a notch formed by the junction of the premaxillary and maxillary bones which can be palpated just below the skin surface when the mouth is opened and the skin stretched.

Hyperkeratinization of the cere and nares

Budgerigars will sometimes develop an excess keratinaceous horny growth of the cere, a condition known as brown hypertrophy. This is of no clinical significance unless the nares become blocked. The structure is bloodless and can be cut with scissors.

Larger psittacines may show rhinolyths or excessive dried exudate within the nares which can act as a ball valve (See Plate 18:4). This can be carefully extracted with a spatulate dental scaler, care being taken not to damage the small C-shaped opercula bone lying at the entrance to the nasal cavity. Swelling and distortion of the cere and external nares is also sometimes seen, particularly in the African Grey parrot (Psittacus erithracus), which is a response to a chronic rhinitis. Cryosurgery has been used to reduce the disfigurement but has only met with limited success and may result in further distortion of this area unless the ice ball is very carefully controlled.

The ear

Surgery is rarely required on this structure although Harrison (1986) reports the removal of a tumour from the wall of the ear canal.

The beak

Budgerigars are seen by most practitioners with overgrown or distorted beaks and occasionally the larger parrots are seen with similar problems. Usually, the upper beak is involved but sometimes the lower beak is affected. Disfiguration may be due to malnutrition such as that occurring in metabolic bone disease (See Plates 12:3) or due to localised diseases. Traumatic damage to the germinal cells at the base of the horn or, particularly in the case of the budgerigar, inflammatory reaction caused by the mite *Cnemidocoptes pilae* can be the cause of distortion. Tumours, particularly fibrosarcomata, should also be considered in the differential diagnosis. Often the beak is only distorted on the side below a suspected tumour mass. In the case of a suspected tumour, if size allows, a biopsy should be taken and cryosurgery, using a fine tip cryo-probe, can be used to destroy the neoplastic tissue. However, extreme care must be taken to control the size of the ice ball and it may be necessary to operate on more than one occasion. The rhamphotheca or heavily cornified covering of the underlying bone is a perpetually growing structure. During growth, the mineralized horny tissue gradually moves obliquely towards the tip and edges of the beak. All parrots use their beak, not only to crack nuts or seed, but to strip bark, dig in the soil for minerals and also to climb. Fruit eaters, of course, use the beak to extract fruit.

This constant daily use for a variety of tasks helps to maintain the beak in shape. Pet psittacines may not be offered the variety of activity necessary to keep the beak in trim and consequently their beaks may need regular attention. A beak which is once distorted, even if fashioned to normal shape, will eventually return to its deformed condition. Contrary to popular belief, cuttle bone and mineral blocks, neither of which are found in the normal environment of birds, do not help to keep the beak in shape. In all cases the beak can be trimmed with nail clippers and finished with fine sandpaper. If bleeding occurs this can be controlled with a silver nitrate pencil. With larger parrots a portable grinding tool is a valuable aid. These D.I.Y. tools are small, light in weight and can be held in one hand. They have a built-in rechargeable battery. A badly distorted beak can often be ground back to reasonable shape and the heat from the grinding tip helps to staunch any bleeding. Minor cases can be attended to without anaesthesia but in the case of a macaw with gross distortion of the beak, anaesthesia will be necessary. After reshaping, the application of a little vaseline helps to restore the gloss to the horn.

Beaks can be split or torn asunder through accident or aggression from other birds or even bites from the family dog. If the damage is a simple crack, repair can be achieved by using a household epoxy resin glue or better still a dental acrylic adhesive. Although epoxy resin glue is toxic if used internally, it does not have any adverse effect when used externally. A more extensive crack may need the use of stainless steel wire or P.D.S. (Ethicon Ltd.) sutures, which can then be reinforced by an overlayer of dental acrylic. The medical acrylic, because it exactly moulds to the shape of the underlying beak, gives good support. This moulded support is held in place by allowing liquid acrylic to fill one or two small holes drilled in the beak at converging angles. Alternatively, the holes can be undercut in the same way that a dental filling is held in a tooth cavity.

Cases will be encountered where part of the beak has been completely detached. If only the distal third beyond the level of the premaxillae has been lost, the injured part can be smoothed and any exposed holes plugged and there will be a reasonable chance of regrowth. If the damage is more extensive and particularly if the germinal layer has been damaged, regeneration rarely, if ever, occurs. In these cases the fitting of a prosthetic beak can be considered. There are few papers in the scientific literature on this subject although newspaper reports are seen from time to time. Budden (1987) Fry (1986) and Sleamaker (1983) report such cases. Materials such as fibreglass, 'Technovit 609' (Kulzer and Co.) and dental acrylic have been used to make the prosthesis. The author has on two occasions used high density polyethylene, a material employed in making human artificial hip joints. The problem with these methods is the permanent and satisfactory long term fixation of the prosthesis to the remainder of the premaxillae or prefrontal bone. The methods used have included the use of Kirschner wires placed in a cruciate pattern and further reinforced with a figure of eight stainless steel wire placed around the pins. A layer of dental acrylic with penetrating holes as described above, has been used. Sleamaker (1983), operating on a Salmon-crested cockatoo, used a combination of orthodontic wire with acrylic and reports the prosthesis stayed in place for over two years.

However, in the vast majority of cases, due to rough usage by the bird when climbing, the attachment works loose in a month or two. This is due to pressure erosion of the delicate trabeculae forming the bone of the avian skull.

Most birds soon learn to adapt to feeding on an entirely soft food diet. Also, they learn to climb gripping with the tongue and lower beak so that, apart from the obvious cosmetic improvement, it is questionable whether the fitting of a prosthesis is justifiable. The author has not been able to find out if the loss of the upper beak has stopped a breeding bird from effectively feeding its young or has affected courtship behaviour.

The neck and thoracic inlet

Foreign bodies can lodge in both the oesophagus and trachea and may require surgical removal. In small birds it may be possible to locate the foreign body by transillumination of the trachea using a powerful point source of light such as that emitted from the end of a fibre optic light guide. In the first instance removal should be attempted via the oropharynx using either biopsy forceps or crocodile forceps in the larger birds. Very often the foreign body lodged in the trachea is seed. In this case, to maintain the patient's airway and, if necessary gaseous anaesthesia, a cannula is placed in the abdominal airsac as described on page 26. If a tracheotomy has to be carried out, a transverse incision rather than a longitudinal incision is advisable because access to the lumen of the trachea and subsequent suturing is easier. It is not practical to approach the syrinx directly because the syrinx lies just posterior to the level of the coracoid bones beyond the thoracic inlet. The lumen of the syrinx can only be approached via an incision in the posterior third of the trachea.

When operating on a tumour or an encapsulated haematoma in the neck, the surgeon should take into account that the right jugular vein is better developed than the left and that the external carotid arteries do not form from the internal carotids until near to the base of the skull. The right internal carotid artery is positioned well under the cervical vertibrae but the left internal carotid artery is situated close to the left jugular vein as is the vagus nerve.

Surgery of the crop

Impaction of the crop is not often seen in adult parrots although crop stasis and a pendulous crop are sometimes seen in hand reared neonates. Crop stasis in recently hatched birds is discussed in Chapter 21 'Breeding'. This usually results from feeding an unsuitable diet or food which is too cold (less than 100°F or 37°C). Food which is too hot (105°F or 40.6°C) can cause necrosis and subsequent fistula formation (Giddings 1986). Also laceration of the crop may be caused by the careless use of a crop tube during medication or feeding.

As the temptations on parrot breeders increases to produce more youngsters, these problems are likely to be seen more often by clinicians. Non-surgical treatment of crop stasis is discussed in Chapters 7 and 21. If surgery is required, incision into the crop should be made into the area of greatest distension. In neonates this can be carried out without anaesthesia and in the adult only light anaesthesia is required as pain sensation in this area is minimal. After emptying the contents, the crop wall should be sutured with an inverting Lembert suture and the skin should be sutured separately.

In the case of fistulae, food may have leaked into the subcutaneous tissue and started to decompose. These birds may have been left sometime before being presented to the veterinarian and may be very ill. Great care in the use of anaesthesia is required. Both trachea and oesophagus are best intubated. In the case of the latter this is to assist the surgeon to locate the oesophagus and crop. All diseased tissue must be thoroughly debrided so that only healthy tissue is sutured. Polyglactin (Vicryl, Ethicon Ltd.) is better for suturing the crop than cat gut which may be too readily absorbed. A drain of soft plastic tube leading from the subcutaneous tissues and sutured to the skin is helpful where space allows for insertion. This drain can be flushed with sterile saline and antibiotic daily.

Subcutaneous emphysema

This condition occurring around the thoracic inlet and possibly extending over the thorax may be due to rupture of the cervical or interclavicular air sacs. The condition will often resolve spontaneously or can be deflated with a hypodermic needle.

INTRA ABDOMINAL SURGERY
Pre-operative considerations

Entrance to the abdomen will most likely be required for the following reasons:-

1. Exploratory laparotomy.
2. Proventriculotomy.
3. Ventriculotomy.
4. Removal of a neoplasm.
5. Relief of an impacted oviduct.
6. Hysterectomy.

The customary approach has been ventrically through a mid-line incision but a flank approach often gives better access to many organs including the gonads, kidneys, adrenals, lungs and proventriculus. Also, as mentioned in the chapter on anaesthesia, there is less tendency for a reduction in size of the air sacs if the bird is positioned on its side rather than on its back, should a large space occupying lesion be present.

Exploratory laparotomy using a ventral approach

This has, to some extent, been replaced by laparoscopy. The simplest approach is through the linea alba but, depending on which organs the surgeon wishes to operate on, an incision can be made to either side of the mid-line. The linea alba is picked up with rat-toothed forceps to hold it away from the underlying viscera and a small stab incision is made with either a scalpel or preferably with a pair of fine pointed scissors. From the initial stab incision the opening is extended, using blunt pointed scissors, from the edge of the sternum to just cranial to the pubic bones. If the incision is carried too far towards the cloaca, the intestinal peritoneal cavity and both right and left abdominal air sacs may be entered and this may not be necessary. The primary incision can be extended by one or more incisions at right angles, so as to form flaps. Depending on whether the surgeon has made his entry into the right or left side, the first cavity entered is the right or left vertical hepatic cavity lateral to which lie the posterior walls of the left and right posterior thoracic air sacs. On the floor of the compartment (anatomically the dorsal area of the recess) is a membrane, the post hepatic septum, underneath which lie the viscera closely interwoven with the two abdominal air sacs. Since the post hepatic septum acts as a fat depot, this may first be seen as a pad of fat which obscures the organs beneath. Alternatively, in a thin bird with no sign of airsacculitis or peritonitis, the viscera can clearly be identified beneath the post hepatic septum. If the septum is clear try to incise this without damaging the underlying air sacs. If fat is present this must carefully be dissected away. If the air sacs remain intact they can be seen to inflate and collapse with each respiratory movement. If possible the air sac should be carefully detached from the body wall by blunt dissection and only incised if necessary to gain access to a particular organ. In this way the rest of the air sac system remains intact and functional.

In parrots, the gizzard lies more or less centrally with its cranial part under the edge of the sternal plate and its ventral end emerging through the post hepatic membrane. There is a vertical membrane, the ventrical mesentery, attached to the ventral border of the gizzard and running towards the linea alba. The proventriculus lies anterior to the gizzard and is more accessible via a lateral approach.

On the surgeon's right side (anatomically the left side of the bird) lies most of the intestine beneath which is the uterus and oviduct.

Gastrotomy or ventriculotomy

The gizzard is held rather firmly in position by the membranes mentioned above and is also attached to the liver by the falciform ligament. The muscular wall is thick and haemorrhage from the muscle can be a problem if diathermy is not used. It is best to make the incision through the tendonous area on the anterior lateral border but care should be taken at the anterior end at the junction with the proventriculus. This region is not always very accessible from a ventral incision and there is here a large branch of the coeliac artery. Suturing the organ can be difficult and it is impossible to achieve an inverted Lembert type suture.

For the relief of impaction or the removal of a foreign body, it is probably safer and easier to approach the lumen via an incision in the proventriculus as described below.

Surgery for removal of an impacted egg

The diagnosis must firstly be confirmed by radiography although usually there is a history of the bird having layed a number of eggs then stopped and later becoming unwell.

The surgical approach is through the mid line. Access to the operating area can be increased by making a second incision at right angles to the first and just anterior to the left pubic bone. The pubic artery lies close to this bone. The distended oviduct containing the egg is situated on the left and displaces the abdominal viscera to the right. Often the egg will be felt rather than seen, lying below a pad of fat (in the left post hepatic septum). The uterus is exposed by careful blunt dissection of the fat sufficiently to permit extraction of the egg. As the wall of the oviduct can be very difficult to suture once it has collapsed after removal of the egg, it is a wise precaution to preplace two sutures. Removing the thin shelled parrot's egg intact without fracturing it can be tedious. A sterile coffee spoon will be found helpful for this purpose and an adequate incision must be made. Care must be taken to avoid rupturing the blood vessels which run over the surface of the oviduct. If the egg should break, the contents should not be spilt into the abdomen and care must be taken to avoid lacerating the oviduct wall with sharp, pieces of shell.

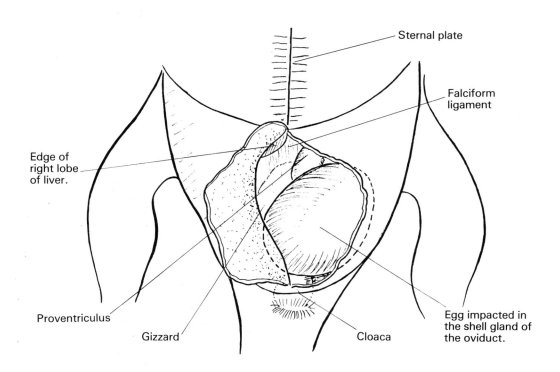

Figure 2

Diagrammatic representation of the ventral aspect of the abdomen after incision of the abdominal muscle. The egg impacted in the shell gland part of the oviduct has displaced the intestine to the right side of the abdomen and is hard against the pubic bone on the left.

Another method of dealing with an impacted egg described by Rosskopf and Woerpol (1982) is to aspirate the contents of the egg via a hypodermic needle (18 gauge is suitable) inserted through the unopened abdominal wall. When doing this, the egg needs to be held quite firmly through the abdominal wall and the needle needs to be thrust quite forcibly. If one is not careful the needle can glide off the egg shell. After evacuation of the egg contents the shell collapses. The bird is then given an injection of oxytocin 3 — 5 i.u./Kg and calcium boroglutinate (100 — 500 mg/Kg) and expulsion of the egg will often take place within 2 days. In the author's experience this technique is hazardous. The shell does not always collapse. Also the shell may fracture into large pieces and lacerate the oviduct.

Surgery of the Cloaca

An egg impacted in the lower reproductive tract (vagina) where it joins the cloaca sometimes causes tenesmus and leads to prolapse of the cloaca. Within a few hours the cloacal tissues become congested; it then dries and becomes necrotic. This condition must be distinguished from a cloaca impacted with dried urate and faecal matter.

The prolapsed cloaca should be first moistened with normal saline. After lubrication with a suitable lubricant such as petroleum jelly, liquid paraffin or K.Y. jelly, the egg can sometimes be gradually eased out by using a blunt ended instrument such as the bulb of a thermometer. This should carefully be rotated around the periphery between the egg and the exposed constricting tissues. After removal of the egg, the oviduct and the cloaca may remain prolapsed. The intestine, rectum or ureter may be contained within the prolapsed tissue. After the tissues have been carefully replaced, an injection of oxytocin and calcium as debrided above may encourage the oviduct to contract. Rosskopf, Woerpol and Pitts (1983) have used No. 0 stainless steel wire sutures around the vent to restrict further prolapse. These same workers have also used cloacopexy, that is suturing the cloaca to the abdominal wall. To make this easier, an assistant wearing a finger cot, or a suitably sized blunt instrument, pushed the cloaca back into the operation area.

Harrison (1986) prefers to carry out a cloacotomy to reduce the size of the cloacal orifice. The superficial epithelium lining the opening of the cloaca is debrided and several simple interrupted sutures are placed in position to reduce the size of this orifice.

Access to the cloaca may be required not only for cloacopexy but also to remove an enterolyth impacted in the cloaca. This is easily achieved using a mid line incision between the two pubic bones.

Papillomata are sometimes seen protruding from the cloaca and may require removal. This can usually be achieved through the cloacal orifice. However, these structures may be found to be quite vascular so that removal is best achieved using cryosurgery. They are probably viral in origin and may recur. They may also be concurrently found in the oropharynx.

Cloacal prolapse as a result of straining is discussed on page 79.

Hysterectomy

This has been used by a number of workers as a method of controlling persistent egg laying which is unresponsive to injections of medroxyprogesterone. Smith (1985) describes the method used in the cockatiel. Exactly how removal of the oviduct inhibits persistent egg laying is not well understood. The oviduct alone is removed and the ovary is left in situ. The lateral approach as described for proventriculotomy below is the simplest method when dealing with the non-gravid uterus. After opening the operating site, the dorsal suspensory ligament of the proventriculus is found in the depth of the cavity. From the ovary and running posteriorly is the fan-like infundibulum continuing into the oviduct which can be traced to its junction with the vagina and cloaca. The whole of this area is served by a number of delicate blood vessels.

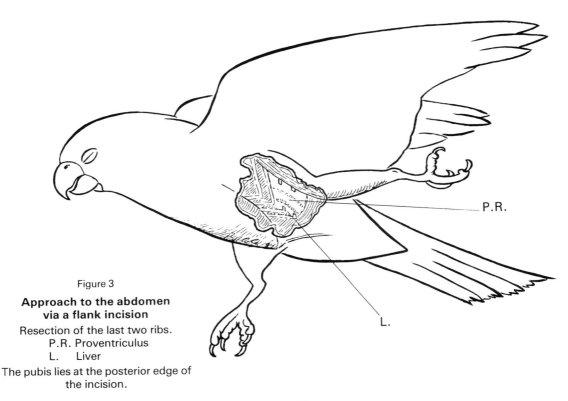

Figure 3

**Approach to the abdomen
via a flank incision**

Resection of the last two ribs.
P.R. Proventriculus
L.   Liver
The pubis lies at the posterior edge of
the incision.

Approach to the abdomen via a flank incision

The parrot is placed in right lateral recumbancy and the whole of the left side including the medial side of the left leg is prepared for surgery. The left leg needs to be held aloft away from the surgical field.

An incision is made extending from just above the dorsal end of the seventh or eighth rib to end a little anterior to half way along the pubic bone. The line of the incision is at a slight angle to the vertebral column and almost parallel to the pubic bone. The incision through the skin is followed through the muscle to reach the ribs and the pubic bone. The surgeon should be aware of the pubic artery lying just anterior to the pubic bone. The muscle over the last two ribs is cleared and the latter are carefully elevated from the underlying tissue. These ribs can then be resected near their junction with the vertibrae and also at their junction with the sternal ribs. This whole section of the body wall can then be removed. During this process care should be taken not to damage the lung lying under the dorsal area of the ribs or the liver under the ventral part of the incision. Haemorrhage from the intercostal arteries running along the posterior surface of ribs can be a problem and must be meticulously controlled by clamping or by diathermy.

In the recess which has been thus exposed in the dorsal part lies the fluctuating wall of the abdominal air sac. In the ventral part lies the proventriculus and left lobe of the liver.

Proventriculotomy

The viscus should carefully be freed from the surrounding tissues and gradually elevated into the operation site. Great care must be taken not to rupture any of the several branches of the coeliac artery supplying this area. Stay sutures can be used to anchor the organ in position and before proventriculotomy is performed the surrounding area should be packed with sterile swabs. Once opened, the impacted or dilated proventriculus can be gently flushed of its contents using warm saline. A number of sterile 10 ml hypodermic syringes and a Spreull's needle are useful for irrigation and aspiration.

Abdominal neoplasms

Tumours in the abdominal cavity nearly always involve the gonads but occasionally the kidneys and other viscera are involved in neoplastic change. Except where the liver is involved, a lateral approach with resection of the last two or three ribs to give adequate exposure provides the best access. The main problem is that by the time the condition has been accurately diagnosed, the tumour is often large in relation to the size of the bird. Also the blood vessels supplying the gonads are short. The arteries to the testes come from the anterior renal arteries whilst the ovarian artery arises directly from the aorta. In both cases the veins drain directly into the posterior vena cava. Good magnification and pinpoint lighting are essential. Clamping the blood vessels with mosquito forceps or even using electrosurgery is hazardous.

The key to success is to be able to see what one is doing and carry out the operation quickly.

Egg peritonitis and ascites.

Fluid in the abdomen diagnosed by palpation, radiography and paracentesis using an 18 − 24 gauge needle inserted into the mid line, can be drained using a Penrose drain. The needle should be directed almost horizontally and directed towards the bird's right side to avoid puncture of the gizzard. When in position, the drain can be held in situ by anchoring it to the skin and abdominal musculature. The abdomen can be flushed with antibiotics for 2 − 3 days prior to surgery if this is required.

ORTHOPAEDIC SURGERY

General considerations

Most psittacines presented to the veterinarian with fractures will not have to carry out sustained flight. At best they will be kept in an aviary and may well spend the whole of their life in a cage. Because of this, restoration of full wing function is often not essential. However, a parrot which cannot use its feet to perch and at the same time present food items to the beak will be disabled. However, parrots do adapt to their disabilities quickly; they can manipulate nuts in the mouth using only the tongue and beak and they soon learn to feed on soft foods.

Avian long bones are essentially a thin hollow cylinder of hard porcelain-like bone. Within the lumen of this tube is a reinforcing network of struts or trabeculae each positioned to counteract the twisting and torsional stress imposed on the bone during flight. Avian bones are consequently brittle and shatter easily, particularly in the smaller birds. They do not give good anchorages for orthopaedic implants.

Because of all the foregoing considerations perfect restoration of injured long bones in parrots is not always possible and may not be necessary. It is often safer for the bird's survival and wiser to be satisfied with an end result where the healed bone is somewhat distorted but still maintains reasonable function.

Parrots sustain fractures from a variety of causes; they may be attacked by a cage mate or by the family dog, or they may be suffering from metabolic bone disease. Also, objects around the home or pet store may fall on them or they will pull objects on top of themselves when climbing. Doors may slam on them or the smaller species may inadvertently be trodden on by their owners.

In all cases the bird must be allowed to recover from the initial shock for up to 48 hours. Considerable haemorrhage can occur around fracture sites. After recovery an accurate diagnosis using radiography must be made. Usually, a dorso-ventral projection is all that is necessary for the diagnosis of orthopaedic cases. In this way a course of action can be planned and an accurate prognosis can be given to the client.

In many cases external splinting which does not involve extensive surgery will suffice. Fractures of birds' bones heal in a similar way to those in mammals. Bush, Montali, Novak and James (1976) showed that both the fibrous union and subsequent cartilagenous callus were derived from both the periosteum and endosteum. Healing was probably a little faster in birds than in mammals and probably took place most rapidly in the smallest birds. Under optimal conditions, when infection is absent and there is no movement at the fracture site, cancellous bone formation can be seen on X-ray in as little as eight days. The very rapid healing which appears to occur in small birds such as budgerigars in a matter of 7 — 10 days is due to fibrous tissue; true boney union takes at least 3 weeks and complete healing with remodelling at least 6 weeks.

The use of pre-operative and post operative antibiotics is essential for all cases where internal fixation methods are used.

THE PECTORAL LIMB

The clavicle
This bone in the parrot is thin and if fractured by itself is unlikely to be diagnosed unless a sharp end of bone penetrates a vital structure at the thoracic inlet. There is no form of splinting which is practical and these cases are best left to heal with cage rest alone.

The coracoid
This stout bone is the main supporting structure of the wing which helps to counteract the force of compression exerted by the main flight muscles, the pectorals. The fracture cannot be splinted effectively using an external support and if left alone in a large bird is likely to produce a gross distortion of the carriage of the wing. The fracture is best dealt with using an intramedullary Steinmann pin. The bone is approached by carefully dissecting the supra-coroideus (superficial pectoral) muscle away from the clavicle which can be palpated subcutaneously. Care must be taken when manipulating the fractured halves of the coracoid since the great blood vessels from the heart are situated directly beneath this area. In small birds the fracture is best left to heal by cage rest but this may take several months.

Luxation of the shoulder joint
Although seen on a number of occasions in other species, the author has not seen this condition in parrots. In other types of birds it is almost always due to the tendon of the supracoroideus being stripped from the muscle belly and it is very difficult to deal with surgically.

The humerus
This bone is most often fractured in its middle or lower third where it is least protected by encircling muscle. Usually, the fractured segments are well displaced because of traction and axial rotation on the proximal segment caused by the pectoralis muscle. The distal segment is often displaced towards the radius and ulna by contraction of the extensor muscles of manus. The bone will eventually heal if the wing is strapped

in a folded position to the side of the bird's body. This is the preferred routine together with cage rest where the fracture is simple, not grossly distracted and uncomplicated by infection. However, healing is slow and may take 6 − 8 weeks. Also the parrot may not tolerate prolonged bandaging and may have to be restricted with an Elizabethan collar. However, this is often not necessary if the bandage is comfortable. In all cases where the fracture is compound and where the bird is over 100 grams in body weight it is best to resort to intramedullary pinning. However, any superimposed infection must first be treated and the area must be debrided with the removal of all necrotic pieces of bone. It is probably better to exit the pin through the proximal end of the bone because the shoulder joint is less liable to injury than the elbow joint. Even in those cases where intramedullary pinning has been used, strapping to the body will be required for the first few days post operatively to prevent axial rotation of the bone. However the strapping should not be left in position for more than a week. Other methods of internal fixation for reducing fractures of the humerus have been used in other families of birds. These include Kirschner splints and shuttle pins. They are described by the author in another publication (Coles 1985).

In those cases where the distal segment is very short, good reduction of the fracture is very difficult and whatever method is used, the prognosis is poor. In most other cases, providing superimposed infection has been overcome, healing will eventually take place and the prognosis is reasonable.

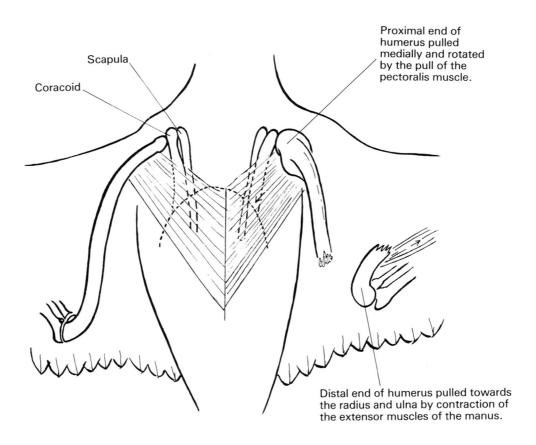

Figure 4
The use of this diagram is by permission of the Publishers, the Editor and the Author of Avian Medicine and Surgery.

Dislocation of the elbow joint
Although this has been seen by the author in numerous other species of birds, it has not been seen in parrots. No satisfactory method has yet been devised for dealing with this problem in other species.

Fractures of the radius and ulna

In about half of these cases only one or other of these two bones is fractured. In these cases it is best to leave the wing alone and only to carry out cage rest for 3 – 4 weeks. The unfractured partner of the two bones will act as a splint for the injured bone.

If both bones are fractured then some form of external splint will be required. The simplest method in parrots is to bandage the wing in the folded position first using a figure-of-eight bandage around the manus and the radius and ulna and finally bandaging the wing to the body. If the fracture is compound, a medicated dressing over the wound can be incorporated into the above bandage. In the larger parrots a more robust form of external splint may be required. One method is to suture over the fracture a slab of Hexcellite (Hexcel Medical Products), Zimflex (Zimmer) or Vetacast (Animal Care Products) casting tape padded beneath with polyurethane foam. The sutures are taken through the mesh of the splinting material through the skin and around the shafts of the secondary feathers near to where these are anchored to the bone. If most of the covert feathers are plucked and the skin is first moistened with alcohol, then the individual parts of the anatomy can be more readily discerned. The sutures should be placed in front of the interemigial ligament and care should be taken to avoid the ulna artery and vein. All sutures should be replaced before tying. The whole splint can then be incorporated in a figure-of-eight bandage.

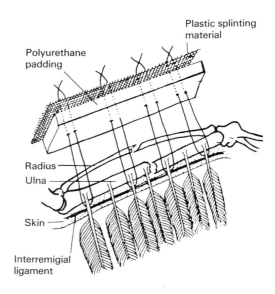

Figure 5
Method of external splinting of the fractured ulna using a mesh of plastic splinting material.

The use of this diagram is by permission of the Publishers, the Editor and Author of Avian Medicine and Surgery.

If internal fixation has to be adopted this is best carried out using a Kirschner splint rather than an intramedullary pin because, wherever the pin emerges from the bone, it is liable to damage the neighbouring joint.

Fractures of the carpometacarpus and digits

In all cases of fractures effecting this region in psittacines the method of choice is external splinting. The bones in this area are too small in parrots to consider using any type of internal fixation although this has sometimes been used in some very large birds of other species.

A method of external splinting used by the author for many types of birds of all sizes from 50g to 1500g in body weight, is to use a piece of disused X-ray film. This is bent over the leading edge of the wing so that the fracture is sandwiched between the two halves. The whole is then held in position by sutures passed through the film and into the skin and between the shafts of the primary feathers. Just posterior to the carpometacarpus is the ulnocarporemagial aponeurotic sheet which helps to give firm support to these sutures. This splint is light in weight and will hold the bones sufficiently rigidly for healing to take place. If the fracture is compound and damage to the soft tissues has occurred, a slab of Hexcelite or Vetcast cast tape can be sutured to this area, as described above for fracture of the radius and ulna. This type of splint can be positioned either dorsally or ventrally away from the wound which can then be dressed daily with medicaments.

Feather cutting to restrict free flight

Practitioners are often asked to carry this out either to stop the parrot flying forcibly around the house or to inhibit the bird if taken into the garden. Amputation of the wing tip for this purpose is not usually necessary or desirable in parrots. Simply cutting most of the flight feathers will suffice. Providing the feather is not cut whilst in the growing stage (i.e. 'in the blood') it will not bleed. It is best to cut all but the outer two or three primary feathers and all the secondaries down to a level just beyond the edge of the covert feathers. The outer primaries which are left then act to cover the defect in the wing when it is folded in the resting position. Cutting the feathers should be done carefully because carelessly carrying out this task with blunt scissors can cause irritation to the parrot and be the start of feather plucking. It is important to cut the feathers on one wing only since many birds are able to fly short distances if both wings are cut at the same time.

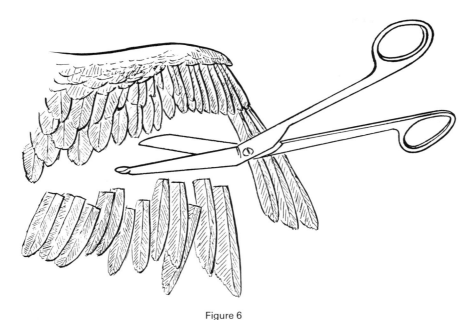

Figure 6
Feather cutting to restrict free flight
Most of the flight feathers are cut leaving only the outermost two or three primary feathers.

Amputation of the wing tip

Whilst pinioning or amputation of the wing tip in parrots to stop flying is not usually necessary, this may be needed to alleviate persistent self trauma and bleeding of this area. This sometimes starts with, or results in, more generalised feather plucking. Also, amputation may be required to relieve the condition known as 'Angel wing' or slipped wing. This condition is not uncommonly seen in waterfowl and also occasionally occurs in budgerigars, conures and macaws. There is an outward rotation of the carpal joint. This may be genetic in origin or possibly due to malnutrition during the time when the skeleton is being mineralised.

At the start of the operation all the covert feathers are plucked from the area and the skin is moistened with alcohol. In this way the underlying structures can easily be seen. A tourniquet is placed around the carpal area just proximal to the alula digit. The ligature must also pass through the interosseous space, in a figure-of-eight fashion, so that the interosseous artery is trapped. An incision is made around the entire wing tip at the level of the distal end of the third and fourth metacarpal bones. Skin and muscle are then carefully teased back to expose the proximal ends of these bones. At this point amputation is then carried out using bone forceps or strong scissors. Finally, the skin and muscle are sutured back across the ends of the bone to form a protective pad of tissue. Failure to provide this pad often results in wound breakdown. Post operatively, the whole wing must be bandaged to the body and an Elizabethan collar may be necessary. Success depends on cleanly cut tissues using sharp instruments, minimal haemorrhage and sutures which are not too tight. In this way the tissues heal rapidly without any further tendency to self trauma.

THE PELVIC LIMB

The femur

The proximal part of the leg in birds is well covered by muscle and a fold of skin extends from the lateral surface of the leg to the side of the body wall over the ribs. Because of this, an external splint is difficult to apply effectively. Rousch (1980) describes the use of a Hexcelite cast enclosing the whole leg except for the foot. This cast is then extended as a tongue wrapping dorsally over the body to the contralateral side. This part of the splint is bound in position with an elastic adhesive bandage. Care needs to be taken to pad the whole splint with polyurethane foam and not to restrict respiration or defaecation.

The use of an intramedullary pin with the pin exiting through the stifle is a simple procedure and is the method preferred by the author. The femur is easily approached from the anterio-dorsal aspect and the overlying muscle can be split in the direction of its fibres. Rotation is unlikely to occur but can be prevented in large parrots by using a stack of two or three small diameter pins.

The tibiotarsus

A number of techniques have been devised for dealing with fractures of this area. Because of the conical shape of the muscles surrounding this part of the leg, external splinting is difficult. Redig (1986) describes a method of using a modified Schroeder-Thomas splint combined with intramedullary pinning which gives very good stability. However, the surgeon must make sure the device does not become too bulky and cumbersome.

For making these splints Redig used coat hanger wire for birds the size of, and above the weight of, Amazons and cockatoos. The author has used aluminium rod of approximately the same diameter (2mm). Another method of external splinting used in conjunction with intramedullary pinning, is to encase the whole leg from stifle to hock in ½" thick polyurethane padding. A ½" aluminium finger splint is then bent over the stifle in the form of an inverted 'U' and again round the back. Both joints are slightly flexed and in the normal standing position. The whole is then bound tightly with a thin self-adhering co-elastic conforming bandage. This makes a comfortable and effective splint and enables the bird to place the leg lightly on the ground. Admittedly the splint does not apply any longitudinal traction to the leg as does Redig's modified Schroeder-Thomas splint but this is not necessary when intramedullary pinning is used. In cases where the tibiotarsal fracture is badly comminuted the Redig method without any attempt at open reduction gives the best chance of resolution.

In some cases the author has successfully used a method of Kirschner splinting and this is described elsewhere (Coles 1986).

Fractures of the tarsometatarsal bones

Whether these fractures are simple or compound they are best tackled using an external splint as the bones are too small for internal fixation. The whole area should be well padded with polyurethane foam and encolsed in a splint made of Hexcelite or Vetcast casting tape. This is then bound firmly to the affected parts with a self-adhering co-elastic confriming bandage before the plastic splinting material has begun to set. This method provides a comfortable, firm splint.

The Altman type tape splint

Fractures of the tibiotarsus and tarsometatarsus in small birds up to the size of cockatiels can be supported by a splint made from any adhesive tape. Zinc oxide plaster is the material most commonly used. Two pieces of adhesive tape are placed on either side of the limb so that the sticky surfaces face each other. The protruding flanges of tape are then crimped together with artery forceps so that the tape grips the leg firmly. Several thicknesses of tape can be used to increase the strength of the cast. Also match sticks, cocktail sticks or swab sticks can be incorporated between the layers of tape to add strength. The splint can be removed by dissolving the adhesive in ether or other solvent.

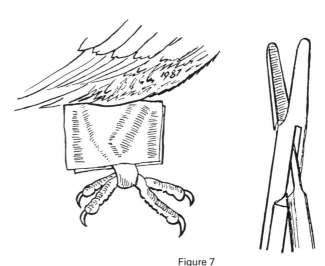

Figure 7
The Altman type tape splint
Two pieces of adhesive tape are placed on either side of the fractured limb with the sticky surfaces facing each other.

Fracture of the digits.
The most effective method of dealing with these is to firmly bandage the whole foot over a ball of gauze or preferably over a small shaped block of polyurethane foam. A self-adhesive co-elastic conforming bandage is most useful for this purpose. The bandage should include the metatarso-phalangeal joint.

Fractures of the skull
These are not often seen because the trauma necessary to produce the fracture is usually fatal. However, Harrison (1986) reports successfully repairing a fractured skull with dental acrylic.

REFERENCES

ALTMAN, R. B. (1987) in: Diseases of Cage and Aviary Birds, (Ed. M. L. Petrak) p. 260, Lea and Febiger, Philadelphia.

BUDDEN, P. G., OTTY, S and WOOLOCK, D. (1987) personal communication.

BUSH, M., MONTALI, R. I., NOVAK, R. G. and JAMES, F. A. (1976). The Healing of Avian Fractures. A histological xerodiographic study. Amer. Animal Hospital Association Journal 12 (6) p. 768-773.

COLES, B. H. (1985) Avian Medicine and Surgery, p. 153, Blackwell Scientific, Oxford.

FRYE, F. L. (1984) Prosthesies enhance quality of life, p. 931-935, Vet. Medicine.

GANDAL, C. P. (1982) Anaesthetic and Surgical techniques, p. 319 in Petrak, M. L. (Ed.) Diseases of Cage and Aviary Birds, Lea and Febiger, Philadelphia.

HARRISON, G. J. and HARRISON L. R. (1986) Clinical Avian Medicine and Surgery, pp 564, 566, 578, 580, 593 and 658. W. B. Saunders, Philadelphia.

KALLIAS, G. V., WEHRMANN, S. and STETTER, E. R. (1984) Enterolithiasis in an Umbrella cockatoo, p 1407, J.A.V.M.A. Vol. 185.

KERN, T. J., MURPHY, C. J. and RIIS, A. C. (1984) Lens extraction by phamaco-emulsification in two raptors, p. 1403, J.A.V.M.A. Vol 185.

KING, A. S. and McLELLAND, J. (1984) Birds: their structure and function, p. 290. Baillière Tindall, London.

KING, A. S. and PAYNE, D. C. (1964) Normal breathing and the effects of posture in Gallus domesticus. Journal of Physiology, 174, 340-347.

PETRAK, M. L. and GILMORE, C. E. (1982) Neoplasms in: Petrak, M. L. (Ed.): Diseases of cage and Aviary Birds, p. 319, Lea and Febiger, Philadelphia.

REDIG, P. T. (1986) Modification of the Schroeder-Thomas splint for birds, in: Harrison: Clinical Avian Medicine and Surgery, p. 391. W. B. SAUNDERS, Philadelphia.

ROSSKOPF, W. J. and WOERPEL, R. W. (1982). Abdominal Surgery in Pet Birds, Modern Veterinary Practice, 63 (2), 889-890.

ROSSKOPF, W. J., WOERPEL, R. W. and PITTS, B. J. (1983) Surgical repair of a chronic cloacal prolapse in a Greater Sulphur Crested cockatoo (Cacatua galenta galenta), veterinary medicine/Small Animal Clinician 78 (5), 719-724.

ROUSCH, J. C. (1980) Avian Orthopaedics, in Kirk, R. W. (ed.), Current Veterinary Therapy VII, pp. 662-673, W. B. Saunders, Philadelphia.

SLEAMAKER, T. F. and FOSTER, W. R. (1983) Prosthetic beak for a Salmon-Crested cockatoo, J. A. V. M. A., Vol, 183 No. 11 p 1300.

SMITH, R. F. (1985) Hysterectomy to relieve reproductive disorders in birds, Avian/Exoic Practice, Vo. 2 (1) pp. 40-43.

STETTENHEIM. P. (1972) The Integument of Birds, in: Avian Biology, Vol. 11 (Eds. Farner, King and Parks), 7 Academic Press, New York/London.

Chapter 6

SURGICAL SEXING AND DIAGNOSTIC LAPAROSCOPY

T. M. Eaton B.Vet.Med., M.R.C.V.S.

INTRODUCTION

In many species of psittacine birds, there are no external differences between the male and female (i.e., they are monomorphic) and in some sexually dimorphic species the differences are not apparent until the birds are several years old. Accurate determination of the sex of a bird is therefore fundamental to a successful breeding programme in such species.

Many sexing techniques used in the past have been inaccurate, leading to improperly paired birds with the resultant economic loss and frustration of the breeder. Relying on differences in the weight or size of birds is hazardous in the extreme. Radiography is unreliable. Faecal steroid analysis is reliable but expensive and takes a long time. Cystological examination of chromosomes is also expensive and needs very sophisticated equipment.

Internal examination of the abdomen provides a reliable method of sex differentiation. It has the added advantage of allowing examination of other organs and tissues for diagnostic purposes.

The presence of air sacs in the bird facilitates laparoscopic examination by allowing a large number of organs to be examined through one incision. As birds have no diaphragm, the lungs, major blood vessels and heart can be examined as well as the abdominal organs and biopsy samples can be collected if required.

EQUIPMENT

Various pieces of equipment may be used for the internal examination of birds.

(i) Auroscope

The auroscope is simple and cheap and, where only the occasional bird is examined, this instrument would be acceptable. The disadvantages are (a) that there is a direct pathway of contamination down the instrument (b) that quite a large incision is required (c) that the magnification and intensity of the light are very poor. While these factors may not be so important in the larger bird they preclude the use of this instrument in the smaller species.

(ii) Focuscope

This is essentially an endoscope fitted to an auroscope handle. The light source is powered by batteries but is carried by a fibreoptic system. The detachable endoscope fitting can be sterilised and requires a smaller incision than an auroscope. The eye piece has a focusing system so that external adjustment can give different internal views. The advantages of the focuscope over the auroscope are better illumination and a far wider field of view. Also, sterilisation is easier and the chances of introducing infection are far less. The cost of the focuscope is relatively moderate and the system is a great improvement on the auroscope.

(iii) Endoscope

This is the preferred instrument for those performing the procedure regularly. It provides excellent illumination and magnification and requires a very small incision. The only disadvantage is that it is expensive.

Endoscopes vary between 2.2mm and 10.0mm in diameter. In choosing the size of endoscope, one has to balance the fact that the smaller endoscope causes less damage on insertion, against the fact that the smaller endoscopes are rather fragile. The lens system of the endoscope varies in the angle of viewing from straight ahead, to 90° to the line of the endoscope. The author prefers a human arthroscope which is a 4.0 mm endoscope with a viewing angle of 25°.

The halogen light source is powered from the main electricity supply, which might restrict the places where the instrument could be used. The light is carried through a flexible fibreoptic cable to the endoscope. The light passes down the endoscope parallel to a lens system. The lens system cannot be focused; focusing is achieved by altering the distance of the end of the endoscope from the object to be viewed.

The various accessories supplied include a trochar and cannula, biopsy forceps, suction tubes and cameras.

STERILIZATION OF EQUIPMENT
The endoscope is a system of light conducting fibres and lenses sealed in a metal tube. However carefully chemical or heat treatment is used, there is a danger that the seals will break down in time.

Alcohol can be used, but is not very effective unless a long period of immersion is used.

Heat treatment (including autoclaving) causes damage quite easily.

There are various chemicals on the market for use for cold sterilisation. The one favoured by the author is Cidex (activated glutaraldehyde solution). The advantage of this solution is its effective action; the main disadvantage is that it is corrosive to tissue. Rinsing the instrument under tap water removes the chemical and has not caused a practical loss of sterility. To use sterile water would add to the cost, as large volumes would be required.

ANAESTHESIA (See Chapter 2)
Halothane, Methoxyfluorane or Alphaxelane/alphadone ('Saffan', Glaxo) can be used but a combination of Ketamine and Xylaxine is preferred.

PREPARATION OF THE BIRD AND POSITIONING
The bird is placed on its right side and restrained with the left hand, in the case of a right handed operator. The bird can be restrained using strips of adhesive plaster but, as the bird may need to be moved during the examination, holding the bird with the hand gives greater flexibility.

The upper hind leg is drawn forward. The posterior point of the sternum is followed dorso-laterally until a notch is felt. This lies between the sternum and the rib. The shape of the notch and its relative position vary greatly with the species of bird.

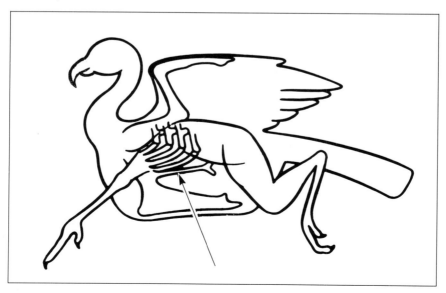

Figure 1

As few feathers as possible are plucked from the area of the notch exposing an area approximately 1cm in diameter. The skin is then swabbed with disinfectant and the surrounding feathers are smoothed away from the prepared site.

Using pointed 6 inch straight scissors, a puncture incision is made in the centre of the notch. The points of the scissors are pushed cranially and dorsally almost parallel with the body surface. If the wrong angle is followed, the heart may be punctured. A distinct 'pop' is felt as the points enter the air sac (similar to that felt when an intravenous needle enters a vein). The blades are opened slightly, to enlarge the hole.

The scissors are withdrawn and the endoscope is inserted very quickly. Delay and movement cause an overlap of the layers of tissues, which makes insertion difficult. The tip of the endoscope should now be in the abdominal air sac.

A trochar and cannula may be used for this procedure to reduce the likelihood of the tip of the endoscope being obscured by blood but the incision this makes is larger than if scissors are used. The operator should be seated at a table, with his elbows resting on the surface to ensure that movements of the endoscope are very finely controlled.

The endoscope gives a wide field of view and the magnification is considerable. It is manoeuvered towards the gonads. During this manoeuvring various tissues such as lung, liver, kidney and spleen can be examined. The lens system is fixed, so focusing is achieved by moving the endoscope backwards and forwards (Plate 6:1).

Care must be taken not to touch any tissue in the abdomen, except muscle, to minimise haemorrhage.

The tip of the endoscope is moved close to the caudal border of the left lung. Occasionally the air sac is thin enough to see through, but normally it must be punctured by gentle pressure from the end of the endoscope, avoiding any of the blood vessels which cross the air sac wall. Puncture of the air sac appears to give rise to no ill effects. Having passed through the air sac wall, the left kidney should be seen dorsally and the spleen and the left adrenal gland ventrally. The kidney is a multiple, lobulated organ and is recognised by its crinkled, fissured surface.

The spleen is usually rounded and is often speckled. The adrenal gland is variable in shape and colour and could be confused with a gonad. Ventral to the spleen and the left adrenal gland lie the gonads. Below this level lie the intestines.

If the incision in the abdominal wall is too caudal, the air sac will be missed and direct entry into the abdomen is made. Approach from this angle is almost impossible because of the coiled intestines which are continually moving. Should this occur, a fresh start must be made.

The testes are paired but from the approach described, usually the left testis only is seen. The colour of the testis varies, but is usually pale yellow and may have blood vessels over the surface. The smooth surface of the testis is characteristic (Plate 6:2).

The ovary is a single gonad and lies on the left of the bird. In the mature bird it is unmistakeable as it is covered with maturing follicles and resembles a bunch of grapes (Plate 6:3).

The immature ovary is far more difficult to recognise (Plate 6:4). It is very variable in shape, and in some cases resembles a testis in texture. However, even the most immature ovary is fairly granular in texture and is usually irregular in outline. In very young birds differentiation may be impossible, in which case the procedure should be repeated when the bird is older.

When the endoscope is removed, the various layers through which the stab incision has been made slide over each other and close the wound.

The area should be cleaned and disinfected. If a correct antiseptic technique has been carried out, no routine antibiotic therapy is necessary. In the case of the aseptic technique failing, antibiotics should be given. Should there be any bleeding from the wound at the end of the operation, a single suture can be used.

Identification is usually necessary where several birds are examined. A colour spray may be used or a dab of nail varnish. Leg rings are difficult in the parrot family, as most are quickly removed by the bird. The best method is to tatoo the bird under one wing. There is an area relatively free of feathers, close to the body on the underside.

PROBLEMS LIKELY TO BE ENCOUNTERED

The risks of this procedure must be clearly explained to the owner.

Using the Ketamine/Xyalzine mixture, the anaesthetic risks are minimal.

Should the endoscope become filmed in blood or should blood enter the fluid in the abdomen, the whole field becomes fogged and further examination is impossible. Although the blood quickly clots, prolonged anaesthesia is necessary to allow the field to clear so that it is advisable to discontinue and repeat the procedure after approximately one month.

Chronic infection causes adhesions within the abdomen and infection of the air sacs causes thickening and opacity of the walls. In either case it is unlikely that the procedure can be carried out successfully.

Every effort should be made to ascertain from the owner the state of the bird's health before endoscopy is performed in order to minimise the risk of operating on an ill bird which is showing minimal or no clinical signs.

RECOVERY (See also Chapter 2)

The bird is examined for any external faults or damage to feathers. The bird should be cleaned, and the feathers smoothed. It is then laid on clean paper on the floor of the cage or container. Four hours should be allowed for full recovery before the bird is returned to the owner.

Chapter 7 # THE GASTRO-INTESTINAL TRACT

K. Lawrence B.V.Sc., F.R.C.V.S.

The digestive tract of birds differs from that of mammals in a number of ways:-

1. Birds have no teeth and seeds are dehusked and then swallowed whole without being chewed.

2. The saliva of birds contains no enzymes.

3. Food is stored in the crop, a distensible diverticulum of the oesophagus, to allow softening. The crop is well developed in most groups of parrots except the lories which eat a liquid diet.

4. Softened food from the crop enters the proventriculus (true or glanular stomach) before passing into the thick walled, keratin lined ventriculus (gizzard) for grinding. Again, in those species of parrot with a liquid diet, the ventriculus has thinner, less muscular walls which do not have a keratinoid lining.

5. The relatively short intestine terminates at the cloaca, a three chambered organ. Faeces are stored in the coprodeum, the ureters enter the urodeum and both communicate to the exterior via the proctodeum. A pouch-like diverticulum of the proctodeum is called the Bursa of Fabricius, the source of the B-lymphocytes.

6. Many groups of birds such as the galliformes (quail, pheasants and fowl) and raptors (birds of prey and owls) have well developed paired caecae. The caecae are, however, completely absent in all species of psittacines.

The clinical anatomy of the Amazon parrot *(Amazona sp)*, including the gastro-intestinal tract, has been described by McKibben and Harrison (1986). Avian digestive physiology has been reviewed by King and McLelland (1979), Sturkie (1976) and Ringer (1986). Little of the information, however, relates directly to psittacines and is based on detailed studies in the fowl *(Gallus domesticus).* Much of what has been learned in the study of poultry has been extrapolated to other species. Even though this is often the only option, this has obvious risks which should be appreciated.

CLINICAL SIGNS OF INTESTINAL DISEASE
In order to present information about the diseases of the intestine that have been diagnosed in parrots, the clinical signs have been listed in Table 1 with some of the principal causes. The conditions will be described in the order set out in the table.

Table 1:

**Clinical Signs of Intestinal Disease in Psittacines and
the Major Causes**

Vomiting — regurgitation
  a) Courtship behaviour
  b) Crop impaction
  c) Sour crop
  d) Candidiasis and Trichomoniasis
	Passing undigested whole seeds
	  a) Lack of grit
	  b) Enteritis
	  c) Gizzard (ventriculus) atrophy

Swollen neck
  a) Crop impaction
  b) Sour crop
  c) Thyroid hyperplasia
	Straining, cloacal prolapse & constipation
	  a) Persistent diarrhoea
	  b) Egg laying
	  c) Cloacal papillomas
	  d) Dehydration
	  e) Excess grit or dietary fibre
	  f) Abdominal tumour

Diarrhoea
  a) Systemic disease
      1. Viral infections
      2. Bacterial infections
      3. Chlamydial infection
  b) Enteritis
      1. Bacterial enteritis
      2. Fungal enteritis
      3. Protozan enteritis
      4. Parasitic nematodes
      5. Parasitic cestodes
	Weight loss/wasting
	  a) Systemic disease
	  b) Malabsorption
	  c) Parasitic nematodes and cestodes
	  d) Malocclusion

Vomiting — regurgitation

a. Courtship behaviour

Neurotic imitation courtship feeding is very common in bored male parakeets. Individuals will attempt to feed cage toys, their image in a mirror or even the owner. The boredom can be relieved by frequent changes in the cage furnishings or the provision of a mate. The objects of the bird's affection should also be removed. Some birds will have lost weight by the time they are presented for examination; under these circumstances, an intramuscular injection of medroxyprogesterone acetate (Perlutex for injection, Leo Laboratories) at a dose rate of 50 mg/kg bodyweight may prove useful.

b. Crop impaction

Crop impaction causes the development, over the course of several days, of a large pendulous swelling at the base of the neck. The mass is usually hard but deformable.

This is not a specific entity but the sign of one of a number of conditions affecting the crop. The condition in recently hatched birds is discussed in Chapter 21 ('Breeding'). In mature birds the most common cause is the eating of excessive fibrous food or grit but stricture of the opening of the crop into the oesophagus does occur particularly in association with enlargement of the thyroid glands.

History taking and a detailed clinical examination will establish the underlying cause, which may have to be treated to prevent recurrence. If the contents of the crop are dry and difficult to break up, vegetable oil can be administered orally to soften the obstruction before it is manually milked from the crop. A more fluid content can literally be poured out of the crop, by carefully tipping the bird upside down. In a few cases the obstruction can only be removed surgically.

c. Sour crop

In this condition the lining of the crop becomes inflamed and ulcerated. The first signs of the condition seen by the owner are usually regurgitation and soiling of the beak and neck feathers with regurgitated material. Fluid removed from the crop may smell strongly, or be blood tinged or of a mucoid texture.

The causes of sour crop are very varied but the most common are the provision of spoiled food, irregular feeding and stress. These factors predispose the crop to secondary infection.

Treatment consists of milking the contents from the crop three times daily and administering an antibiotic, kaolin and pectate mixture (Kaobiotic suspension, Upjohn Ltd) by crop tube. The addition of a small amount of sodium bicarbonate has been suggested to counter acidity. Some birds are in poor condition when examined and supportive therapy may prove invaluable.

d.   Candidiasis and Trichomoniasis

Candidiasis is caused by an infection with the fungus *Candida albicans*. The condition usually affects the upper alimentary tract including the oesophagus and crop. Young hand-reared psittacines have proved to be very susceptible to infection, which may spread systematically. In older birds, a predisposing factor should be looked for as *Candida* is a normal inhabitant of the gastro-intestinal tract of healthy individuals (Keymer 1982). The clinical signs of Candidiasis are very variable depending on the severity of the lesions, but one of the most common is regurgitation. A thickened crop may be palpable and if it is examined in the anaesthetised bird either, using an auroscope or a rigid endoscope, characteristic lesions will be evident. Insufflation may be necessary to facilitate examination of the crop mucosa. The lesions of *Candida albicans* may vary from small areas of white streaking to a severe diphtheresis described by Steiner and Davis (1981) as resembling a turkish towel covered in cottage cheese.

Microscopic examination of material from the crop wall or crop content, stained with lactophenol cotton blue, can provide evidence of an infection. *Candida* normally exists as a yeast-like cell in healthy birds but if there is an active infection of the tissues of the crop blastospores or hyphae are identifiable. Treatment is usually successful using nystatin (Nystan oral suspension, E. R. Squibb and Sons Ltd), applied directly to the lesions. In debilitated individuals supportive therapy will be essential to ensure recovery.

Trichomoniasis is considered also with Candidiasis because the lesions in the crop are often indistinguishable. However, microscopic examination of the crop content will differentiate the two conditions. Trichomonads are rapidly moving rounded protozoa bearing flagellae. They have been likened to mobile light bulbs travelling in straight lines, but capable of sudden changes in direction. In thicker exudates they will often be seen as specks of spinning light. Trichomoniasis is usually only seen in budgerigars *(Melopsittacus undulatus)*. Treatment is by oral administration of metronidazole (Flagyl, May and Baker).

Control of both Candidiasis and Trichomoniasis in a flock can be accomplished by regular use of chlorhexidene (Hibitane Concentrate, Coopers Animal Health) as a 2 per cent solution in the drinking water.

SWOLLEN NECK

    a.   Crop impaction — see vomiting.

    b.   Sour crop — see vomiting

    c.   Thyroid hyperplasia — see page 159

DIARRHOEA

Ensley (1979) has described the normal appearance of bird's faeces and has cautioned that the nature of the droppings is dependent on diet and the amounts of water consumed by the bird.

a.   Systemic diseases

Diarrhoea is a clinical sign associated with many systemic infections.

    1. Viral infections

        Coronavirus in Cape Parrots *(Poicephalus robustus)* — Harrison (1986).

        Herpesvirus in Double Yellow-headed Amazons *(Amazona ochrocephala)* — Lowenstine (1982).

        Inclusion body pancreatitis *(Agapornis roseicollis* and *A. lilianae)* — Wallner-Pendleton *et al.* (1983).

        Pacheco's Disease in African Greys *(Psittacus erithacus)*, Amazon Parrots *(Amazona* sp and *Pionus* sp), Budgerigars *(Melopsittacus undulatus)*, Cockatiels *(Nymphicus hollandicus)* , Cockatoos *(Cacatua* sp), Conures *(Aratinga* sp and *Cyanoliseus* sp), King Parrots *(Alisterus* sp), Lovebirds *(Agapornis* sp), Lories *(Eos* sp) and Macaws *(Ara* sp — Kitzing (1981).

Paramyxovirus Group 3 in Budgerigars *(Melopsittacus undulatus)* — Hirai *et al.* (1979).

Paramyxovirus Unclassified in Budgerigars *(Melopsittacus undulatus)* and Rainbow Lories *(Trichoglossus haematodus* — Mustaffa-Baylee *et al.* (1974).

Reovirus in Grey-cheeked Parakeets *(Brotogeris pyrrhopterus* — Mohan (1984).

2. Bacterial infections

Campylobacter jejuni infection produces a characteristic hepatitis which is often accompanied by diarrhoea. There are few descriptions of this condition in psittacines and in most an intercurrent bacterial infection or parasitic infestation was described. The treatment of choice is the macrolide group of antibiotics such as tylosin or erythromycin.

Escherichia coli. The enteric signs of *E. coli* infection may be associated with a septicaemia or a localised infection in the intestine (see Chapter 17).

Mycobacterium avium (Avian tuberculosis) causes a chronic wasting disease in which diarrhoea, polydipsia and polyuria are also described. (see Chapter 16).

Pseudomonas and *Aeromonas.* Dolphin and Olsen (1978) considered that *Pseudomonas* produce the most severe enteric infections in companion birds. The degree of severity is variable but a haemorrhagic enteritis with an associated sloughing of the intestinal mucosa is not uncommon. These enteric signs are usually accompanied by evidence of septicaemia. An *Aeromonas hydrophila* infection in Cockatiels *(Nymphicus hollandicus)* was described by Panigrahy *et al.* (1981) in which the clinical signs were diarrhoea and emaciation. The causative organisms must be identified on culture and an antibiotic sensitivity test performed. Treatment may prove difficult with gentamicin (Genticin paediatric injection, Nicholas Laboratories Ltd) and carbenicillin (Pyopen, Beecham Research Laboratories) often being the only effective agents.

Salmonellosis (see Chapter 17) is a common condition, especially during the quarantine period after importation. Many psittacine species are very susceptible, especially African Grey Parrots *(Psittacus erythacus)* and some species of lories *(Eos* sp). The clinical signs are very variable with both acute and chronic manifestations including anorexia, diarrhoea, polydipsia and polyuria. The post-mortem features (see page 155) may be indicative of a *Salmonella* infection and culture will confirm the diagnosis. Treatment of affected birds is often unrewarding so sensitivity and likely antibiotic tissue levels should be considered carefully before the administration route and antibiotic are chosen.

Pseudotuberculosis (see Chapter 16) is caused by *Yersinia pseudotuberculosis.* The more acute form of the disease is typified by weight loss, dehydration, diarrhoea and respiratory difficulties. In the chronic form tubercle-like granulomata are found on post-mortem examination. If the condition is confirmed bacteriologically, euthanasia of affected birds and antibiotic treatment of healthy contacts must be considered.

3. Chlamydial infection (see Chapter 13)

Psittacosis must be considered in the differential diagnosis of diarrhoea in psittacines, especially if there is evidence of respiratory involvement.

In all these conditions the birds appear very similar on clinical examination. They show the clinical signs of the 'sick bird syndrome': ruffled feathers, inappetance, polydipsia, lethargy and abnormal behaviour. The bacterial infections can only be distinguished by bacteriological examination of faeces or post-mortem material. Regardless of cause, careful nursing and supportive therapy are essential, as well as the use of an appropriate antibiotic. In cases of avian tuberculosis and pseudo-tuberculosis, therapy is ineffective and euthanasia is necessary. The importance of stress in the genesis of the disease and of improved hygiene in the control and prevention, should be emphasised.

b.   Enteritis

1. Bacterial enteritis

Bacterial enteritis as a discrete entity is very rare. It is usually associated with a systemic disease which has enteric manifestations. However, the recovery of coliforms alone from faecal samples, especially in birds with diarrhoea, is a definite indication of their involvement. Oral antibiotics and fluid replacement therapy both have important roles to play in successful treatment. Coliform enteritis is often complicated by toxaemia and the use of kaolin or pectate-based antibiotic mixtures is advised.

2. Fungal enteritis

Mycotic enteritis can occur as an extension of a candida infection from the crop, but this is rare. More usually it is the consequence of the long term use of oral tetracyclines. This is especially common in quarantine when prophylactic treatment of psittacosis *(Chlamydia psittaci)* has been authorised. Treatment with nystatin by gavage has proved effective. Prevention may be accomplished by adding chlorhexidene (Hibitane Concentrate, Coopers Animal Health) to the drinking water to provide a 2 per cent solution. Medicated drinking water should be provided for five days, every two weeks.

3. Protozan enteritis

Two protozan parasites have been described in psittacines. They are *Giardia lamblia* and coccidia *(Eimeria* and *Isopora* sp).

Giardia is a very common parasite of psittacines; it is a flagellate from the family Hexamita. Scholtens *et al.* (1982) recovered cysts and trophozoites from two-thirds of the healthy parakeets they examined. Barnes (1986) reported that Californian veterinary practitioners consider *Giardia* one of the most common of the gastrointestinal parasites of pet birds. The highest rate of recovery is usually in young birds, the infection being thrown off as they become older. Clinical problems associated with *Giardia* can be varied; weight loss ('going light' in budgerigars and other parakeets) intermittent diarrhoea, steatorrhoea, dry, flaky skin and feather plucking have all been reported.

Jones and Carroll (1977) and Panigrahy *et al.* (1981) have described a debilitating syndrome in budgerigars *(Melopsittacus undulatus)* nestlings associated with Giardiasis. If left untreated up to 100 per cent of the affected nestlings died. Treatment with dimetridazole ('Emtryl', May and Baker) controlled the condition.

The most common manifestation of Giardiasis is a more acute disease typified by ruffled feathers, lethargy, depression, debility and diarrhoea. The faeces are quite distinctive with a greasy, mucoid appearance and a foul smell. The characteristic faeces are caused at a steatorrhoea associated with malabsorption caused by the *Giardia.* If left untreated up to 50 per cent of affected birds will die.

A further manifestation of *Giardia* infection of the intestine has been reported (Barnes, 1986, attributed to Fudge). Dry, flaking skin and episodes of feather pulling and pruritis were caused by malabsorption and an allergic reaction. Successful treatment of the *Giardia* led to a cessation of the clinical signs.

Diagnosis of Giardiasis can pose problems. Scholtens *et al.* (1982) have recommended the following schedule for faecal examination for cysts and trophozites:-

(i)   Faeces must be examined within 30 minutes of being passed by the bird.

(ii) Faeces should be mixed well with 2-3 drops of normal saline on a glass slide and covered with a coverslip.

(iii) The preparation should be examined under at least x100 magnification with the condenser diaphragm nearly closed.

Examination of intestinal scrapings for trophozoites can be undertaken on post-mortem material, but recovery rates may be low, as the trophozoites only live for a short period after the death of the bird. There are rarely any specific lesions found during a post-mortem examination, although occasionally the distal portion of the small intestine may be distended with an off-white to yellow creamy material.

Giardia can cause enteritis in man and the zoonotic potential of this protozoan should be considered when treatment and control are discussed.

Coccidiosis was not regarded as a serious disease of psittacines until Panigrahy *et al* (1981 reported on the condition in budgerigars *(Melopsittacus undulatus).* In aviary birds coccidiosis was shown to cause significant mortality. The clinical signs were bloody diarrhoea and those associated with the 'sick bird syndrome'. Microscopic examination of wet mounted faecal smears revealed typical oocysts, which were not speciated.

Treatment with a sulpha drug ('Sulphamezathine', Coopers Animal Health — 0.2% solution in drinking water for 5 days) or a potentiated sulphonamide ('Septrin' paediatric suspension, Wellcome — 2 ml/kg feed) will effectively control mortalities, but for long term control reduced stocking rates and improved hygiene are essential.

4. Parasitic nematodes

While only *Capillaria* infestation is usually accompanied by a diarrhoea, all the species will be considered in this section. Four main genera of nematodes are implicated in parasitic conditions of the psittacine intestine, *Capillaria, Ascaridia, Spiroptera* and *Tetrameres.*

Spiroptera and *Tetrameres* have indirect life-cycles involving intermediate hosts, and are therefore rarely involved in long-term captive cage and aviary birds. Both cause acute death and wasting with nodule formation in the wall of the proventriculus and ventriculus. The eggs found in the faeces are thin shelled and embyonated.

The two common nematodes implicated in intestinal parasitism are *Capillaria* and *Ascaridia.* In a survey of 153 psittacines, Lawrence (1983) reported that 104 (68%) were infected with *Ascaridia* and 38 (25%) with *Capillaria* while 11 (7%) had a mixed infestation. In general no clinical disease was associated with *Ascaridia,* although damage to the gut wall by migrating larvae, obstruction of the gut lumen by adults, competition for nutrients and perforation of the intestinal wall have all been described.

The adults inhabit the distal duodenum and proximal intestine. Large numbers of eggs are passed in the bird's droppings and develop in moist, warm conditions to the infective laval stage. The life cycle is direct.

Diagnosis of an infestation depends on finding characteristic eggs in the faeces. However, this may prove unreliable if the problem is caused by migrating larvae, which are sexually immature i.e. not laying eggs.

At post-mortem, ascarids are readily seen and recognised from their large size and pinkish-brown colour. Capillarids are easily missed as they are small, transparent and often obscured by intestinal mucus.

In view of the great potential of parasitic infestations for causing disease or contributing to a weakening of the bird which predisposes to concurrent infections, regular anthelmintic treatment of aviary birds has been recommended (Smith 1980). As explained in Chapter 20, medication of drinking water is a poor second best to individual treatment. Nevertheless, levamisole (often sweetened with sucrose) is regularly used for water medication. The empirical dosage used is a 1 in 40 dilution of 7.5% W/V solution ('Nemecide', Coopers Animal Health).

Preferably, birds should be medicated individually using fenbendazole (Panacur, Hoechst UK Ltd) administered by crop tube. Alternatively, ivermectin (Ivomec, MSD Aqvet) may be injected intramuscularly (for dosages see Chapter 20). Mebendazole is contraindicated in parrots.

As both *Capillaria* and *Ascaridia* have direct life-cycles improved hygiene is essential for long-term control.

5. Parasitic cestodes

Tapeworms can cause a variety of clinical conditions from wasting to bloody diarrhoea, dependent on numbers present. They are rarely a problem of long-term captives as the life-cycle is complex, requiring at least one intermediate host. Smith (1980) has suggested that recently imported nectar-feeding parrots are likely to carry very high burdens. The tapeworms are readily seen in the small intestine on post-mortem examination or proglottids, egg packets or eggs may be found in the faeces. Treatment either parenterally or orally using praziquantel ('Droncit', Bayer) has proved very effective.

Passing undigested whole seeds

a)   Lack of grit

Grit is essential for the grinding of the softened and partially digested seeds entering the gizzard (ventriculus). Provision of insufficient grit will lead to whole seeds entering the intestine. They will pass through in a relatively unchanged form producing characteristic faeces. Grit should be reintroduced gradually, to avoid crop impaction. In laying hens, the grit of choice should contain ground oyster shells as a source of calcium.

b)   Enteritis. See Giardia.

c)   Gizzard (Ventriculus) atrophy
Steiner and Davis (1981) suggest that atrophy of the muscle of the gizzard is related to a vitamin E/Selenium deficiency.

Straining, cloacal prolapse and constipation. (See also Chapter 9).

a)   **Straining** may be associated with persistent diarrhoea or attempts by a hen bird to lay an egg. Constipation can also cause straining, but this is a rare condition in cage and aviary birds. A more commonly described condition associated with tenesmus is the presence of papillomas in the cloaca. Sundberg *et al* (1986) have reported the condition in a variety of psittacines including Amazon parrots (*Amazona* sp), macaws (*Ara* sp), conures and parakeets. They resemble, and are often confused with, cloacal prolapses. Treatment, except for cryosurgery, is usually to no avail.

b)   **Cloacal** prolapse is not a uncommon sequel to straining. The cloaca becomes swollen, oedematous, inflamed and caked with faecal material. The successful return of the prolapse requires a reduction in size of the prolapse and lubrication. After cleaning the prolapse to remove as much faecal material as possible a very fine sugar, such as icing sugar, is applied to reduce the swelling. A lubricant such as a vegetable or mineral oil is then liberally applied before the prolapse is gently returned using the bulb of a thermometer to reposition it and act as a marker while a purse string suture is inserted. The most successful suture material to use is chromic catgut with an attached round bodied needle. This minimises trauma and removes the need to catch the bird again for removal. The prolapse will recur if the underlying cause for the straining is not treated. (See also page 60.)

c)   **Constipation** is rare in cage and aviary birds. It is seen in dehydrated and obese individuals, and can be caused by excessive ingestion of grit or fibrous foods. Initially, treatment must alleviate the underlying cause and then lubrication can be achieved by administering vegetable or mineral oils by crop tube or by enema. The addition of fruit to the diet will make the faeces looser, as will the addition of a small amount of salt to the drinking water. One cause of constipation that must not be ignored is the pressure of an abdominal tumour on the rectum. In such cases however, there is usually evidence of abdominal enlargement.

Weight loss/wasting

a)   Systemic disease — see Enteritis

b)   Malabsorption — see Enteritis, Giardia

c)   Parasitic nematodes and cestodes — see Enteritis

d)   Malocclusion of the beak can lead to difficulties in prehension of food leading to poor growth, weight loss and wasting. The malocclusion may be caused by poor incubation technique, malnutrition, trauma or infections. (See Pages 56 to 57.)

REFERENCES

BARNES, H. J. (1986). Parasites. In: Clinical Avian Medicine and Surgery. Editors G. J. Harrison and L. R. Harrison. Saunders Philadelphia USA. pp 472-485.

DOLPHIN, R. E. and OLSEN, D. E. (1978). Bacteriology of companion birds. Veterinary Medicine/Small Animal Clinician. **73**; 359-361.

ENSLEY, P. (1979). Caged bird medicine and husbandry. Veterinary Clinics of North America: Small Animal Practice. **9**; 499-525.

GERLACH, H. (1986). Viral diseases. In: Clinical Avian Medicine and Surgery. Editors G. J. Harrison and L. R. Harrison. Saunders Philadelphia USA. pp 408-433.

HARRISON, G. J. (1986). Editor's note Viral Diseases. In: Clinical Avian Medicine and Surgeryy. Editors G. J. Harrison and L. R. Harrison. Saunders Philadelphia USA. p 432.

HIRAI, K., HITCHNER, S. B. and CALNEK, B. W. (1979). Characterisation of paramyxo-. herpes-, and orbiviruses isolated from psittacine birds. Avian Diseases. **23**; 148-163.

JONES, D. M. and CARROLL, M. M. (1977). Debilitating syndrome in budgerigars *(Melopsittacus undulatus)*. Veterinary Record. **101**; 188-190.

KEYMER, I. F. (1982). Mycoses. In: Diseases of Cage and Aviary Birds. Editor M. L. Petrak. Lea and Febiger Philadelphia USA. pp 599-605.

KING, A. S. and McLELLAND, J. (1979). Form and Function in Birds. Vol 1. Academic Press, New York.

KITZING, D. (1981). Zur Charakterisierung eines mit dem ILT-Virus seologisch verwandten Herpesvirus aus Amazonen. Dissertation Medical Veterinar, Munchen.

LAWRENCE, K. (1983). Efficacy of fenbendazole against nematodes of captive birds. Veterinary Record. **112**; 433-434.

LOWENSTEIN, L. J. (1982). Diseases of psittacines differing morphologically from Pacheco's disease, but associated with herpesvirus-like particles. Proceedings of the Thirty first Western Poultry Conferences, Davis Californian USA. pp 141-142.

McKIBBEN, J. S. and HARRISON, G. J. (1986). Clinical anatomy with emphasis on the Amazon parrot. In: Clinical Avian Medicine and Surgery. Editors G. J. Harrison and L. R. Harrison. Saunders Philadelphia USA. pp 31-66.

MOHAN, R. (1984). Clinical and laboratory observations of reovirus infection in a Grey-cheeked Parrot. Proceedings of the International Conference on Avian Medicine, Toronto Canada. pp 29-34.

MUSTAFFA-BABJEE, A., SPRADBORROW, P. B. and SAMUEL, J. L. (1974). A pathogenic paramyxovirus from a budgerigar. Avian Diseases. **18**; 226-230.

PANIGRAHY, B., MATHEWSON, J. J., HALL, C. F. and GRUMBLES, L. C. (1981). Unusual disease conditions in pet and aviary birds. Journal of the American Veterinary Medical Association. **178**; 394-395.

RINGER, R. K. (1986). Selected physiology for the avian practitioner. In: Clinical Avian Medicine and Surgery. Editors G. J. Harrison and L. R. Harrison. Saunders Philadelphia USA. pp 67-81.

SCHOLTENS, R. G., NEW, J. C. and JOHNSON, S. (1982). The nature and treatment of giardiasis in parakeets. Journal of the American Veterinary Medical Association. 180; 170-173.

SMITH, G. A. (1980). Sick birds, causes and care. In: Parrots, their Care and Breeding. Rosemary Low. Blandford Press Poole UK. pp 99-110.

STEINER, C. V. and DAVIS, R. B. (1981). Caged Bird Medicine — Selected Topics. Iowa State University Press Iowa USA.

STURKIE, P. D. (1976). Avian Physiology. Springer-Verlag New York USA.

SUNDBERG, J. P., RANDALL, E. J., O'BANION, M. K., BASGALL, E. J., HARRISON, G. J., HERRON, A. J. and SHIVAPRASAD, H. L. (1986), Cloacal papillomas in psittacines. American Journal of Veterinary Research. **47**; 928-932.

WALLNER-PENDLETON, E., HELFER, D. H., SCHMITZ, J. A. and LOWENSTEIN, L. (1983). An inclusion-body pancreatitis in Agapornis. Proceedings of the Thirty second Western Poultry Conference. Davis California USA. p 99.

Chapter 8 # THE RESPIRATORY SYSTEM

M. P. C. Lawton B.Vet.Med.,Cert.V.Ophthal., M.R.C.V.S.

J. E. Cooper B.V.Sc., D.T.V.M., F.I.Biol., Cert.L.A.S., F.R.C.V.S.

The respiratory system of birds is complex and liable to many disorders, which makes respiratory disease one of the most commonly encountered disorders in psittacine birds (McDonald 1980). The basic anatomy is similar to that of mammals but in addition to the upper respiratory tract and lungs there is an extensive system of air sacs which play a part in respiration as well as having other functions. Birds have no larynx but a syrinx at the distal end of the trachea prior to its bifurcation into the two bronchi.

The physiology of the respiratory system of birds is discussed in Chapter 2. The important point for the practitioner to remember is that when air is inhaled it goes via the trachea through the lungs via the tertiary bronchi into the air sacs. Only on exhalation does the air pass from the air sacs into the lungs for gaseous exchange. This mechanism, which is unique to birds, is important in terms of disease and diagnosis and also relevant to the use of inhalation anaesthesia (see Chapter 2).

Another important difference from mammals is that birds have no diaphragm; there is one body cavity, known as the coelomic cavity. The bird's lungs are semirigid and are positioned against the thoracic vertebrae and the dorsal parts of the thoracic ribs (McDonald 1980), thus preventing collapse. This clearly has advantages in flight since the heavier viscera lie ventrally. Respiration depends largely upon muscle movements, particularly of the intercostal muscles, moving the ribs while the abdominal muscles help to move the sternum. The air sacs also act as bellows; increased intracoelomic pressure due to muscular contraction helps force the air out of the air sacs and through the lungs. The air sacs hold 80% of the volumetric capacity (Coles 1985). This, however, is dead space, as there is no gaseous exchange in the avascular air sacs.

The relative positioning of the viscera and respiratory tract means that birds are particularly susceptible to respiratory embarrassment if, for example, there is an intra-abdominal mass/fluid or other pressure within the body cavity or if the bird is turned on its back.

The glottis of the bird is readily visible. It lies at the base of the tongue, thus facilitating endotracheal intubation or intratracheal medication. However, if a bird is clumsily positioned on its back, for example, during sedation or anaesthesia, the large fleshy tongue may fall back and occlude the glottis thus exacerbating any respiratory embarrassment.

RESPIRATORY DISEASES

The clinical signs seen in a bird with respiratory disease are very similar, irrespective of the aetology. It is usually only the severity that varies.

Clinical signs may include any or all of the following:-

Nasal Discharges — serous, mucoid, purulent or a combination of the three. The discharge may be caked around the feathers and beak or be seen coming from the nares.

Blocked Nares — often associated with chronic infections. Rhinoliths are the most common cause of the blockage although dried nasal discharges and inhaled foreign bodies may also be responsible.

Sneezing — May be mild or explosive, frequent or infrequent.

Coughing — may be intermittent and chronic, but rarely productive.

Conjunctivitis, blepharitis, proptosis, swelling around the eye or ocular discharges may often be part of a respiratory disease.

Tail Bobbing — how obvious this is will depend on the degree of the respiratory distress. The increased effort in breathing leads to an upward wagging of the tail feathers. This feature may be hidden if the bird is on the floor of a cage.

Loss of Voice — or change of pitch is generally a sign of pressure on the trachea or syrinx. Degrees of dyspnoea may be associated with a clicking sound on respiration. Often the head is held pointing upwards.

Ruffled Appearance — the general signs of a 'sick' bird. In severe pneumonic conditions the main presenting signs may be a ruffled appearance and partially closed eyes (Plate 8:1). The bird often keeps nodding off to sleep (Arnall and Petrak 1982).

Inability to Perch or climb — usually only seen in severe or chronic respiratory disease, when the bird does not have sufficient energy to perch or move. If it does perch then the rocking associated with the respiratory movements may cause it to fall.

Cyanosis — usually of the feet and cere and is a very grave sign, usually only seen in birds near death (McDonald 1980).

The above clinical signs may be disguised by the bird, especially when it is first presented in the surgery. One should always allow the bird some time to settle down (for example, while taking the case history); examination may then reveal the more subtle signs. Observing the bird without being seen — for example, through a keyhole in the door or a hole in a cardboard box may prove helpful (Cooper 1987).

RESPIRATORY DISEASE AETIOLOGY

Arnall and Petrak (1982) reviewed the causes of respiratory diseases and other systemic diseases which may cause respiratory signs.

The aetiology of respiratory disease can be simple or multiple, but can be conveniently divided into:-

> Bacterial
> Viral
> Fungal
> Parasitic
> Neoplastic (very rare)
> Nutritional
> Mechanical obstruction
> Allergic

BACTERIAL RESPIRATORY DISEASE

The clinical signs are usually associated with blepharitis, conjunctivitis and sometimes swelling of the sinuses. Diagnosis is based on culture and isolation of the causative organism. Treatment with antibiotics or sulphonamides should, if possible, be based on *in vitro* sensitivity testing. A multitude of organisms have been implicated, but *Pseudomonas aeruginosa, Escherichia coli* and *Pasteurella* spp. are common isolates. Other bacteria may be involved but rarely *Salmonella* spp. (McDonald 1980). Sequelae to bacterial infections can be rhinoliths or abscessation, especially of the sinuses.

1   **Sinusitis**

This is an infection of the sinuses, which may be unilateral or bilateral. It is usually the infraorbital sinus which is affected. The infection is located extraosseously in the area between the eye and the commissure of the mouth. Supraorbital sinusitis is a term used to describe a subcutaneous abscess in the supraorbital region, there not being a true supraorbital sinus (Arnall and Petrak 1982).

Mycoplasma is incriminated in poultry as a primary pathogen in sinusitis and has been isolated from birds of prey with respiratory disease (Cooper, 1978) but is rarely cultured from cage birds (McDonald 1980).

Treatment may involve lancing of these firm or fluctuating swellings and flushing out the infected and necrotic material from the sinuses. Infusion with antibiotic is indicated as is systemic antibiotics. Coles (1985) described the technique of infraorbital sinus injection with antibiotics (see Chapter 5). The authors also recommend concomitant vitamin A therapy and attention to the bird's environment, as there is some evidence of association with poor ventilation and suboptimum temperature/relative humidity.

2. **Rhinoliths**

    These are an amalgam of dust and dirt with nasal mucus which involves blockage of the external nares (Plate 18:4). These can be due to a bacterial infection but may also be associated with hypovitaminosis A. The resulting mass has a ball and valve effect that can obstruct breathing. This may be unilateral or bilateral. The rhinolith may also have a physical effect of enlarging the external nasal orifice which may make it easier to diagnose. Treatment is the removal of the mass by use of a needle. Recurrence is common so the underlying chronic sinusitis or hypovitaminosis A must be treated.

3   **Abscesses**

    These are commonly seen in lingual, palatine, submandibular or periocular sites, especially in the larger parrots. Treatment is by surgical removal of the inspissated pus and surrounding capsule, under anaesthesia. The wound should be sutured. Any underlying infections should be treated; they may be purely bacterial or associated with hypovitaminosis A. The role of other organisms, such as mycoplasmas is debatable.

VIRAL RESPIRATORY DISEASES

1. **Influenza**

    Some strains of influenza may be transmitted from humans to parrots and vice versa. During history taking it is wise to ask if a member of the family has also had a 'cold' recently. The clinical signs seen will vary, depending upon the health state of the bird prior to infection and the strain of virus involved.

2. **Paramyxoviruses**

    These are the viral infections of importance. They are highly contagious and affect most species of birds.

    Velogenic viscerotropic Newcastle Disease is the most virulent form (Clubb 1983, 1984; Fowler 1987) causing high morbidity in psittacines. Mortality rate can be high in young birds if the disease is peracute (Fowler 1987). In adults there is more variation, cockatoos and cockatiels showing a high morbidity and mortality, while macaws, parakeets and African grey parrots are less susceptible, and usually recover completely from the disease (Clubb 1983).

    The clinical signs in psittacines are mainly those described earlier as characteristic of respiratory disease, there being no pathognomonic signs or lesions (McDonald 1980, Clubb 1983, Fowler 1987). Early signs may be anorexia, depression, sometimes diarrhoea, coughing, sneezing and dyspnoea. Clubb (1983) mentioned that the head may also become oedematous. Deaths may occur 1 to 3 days after the onset of clinical signs.

    Although Fowler (1987) stated that the central nervous system is commonly affected, Clubb (1983) found that neurological signs are rare and only seen if the course of the disease is prolonged. Neurological signs seen include ataxia, incoordination, hyperexcitability, torticollis, opisthotonus, tremors and paralysis. In birds showing paralysis which survive, there may be persistence of the damage. It is possible that neurological signs may be seen in the absence of the respiratory or digestive signs.

    For more details, the reader is referred to Chapter 15.

3. **Avian Pox**

This has been reported (McDonald 1980) as a cause of blepharitis or sinusitis. In addition, lesions in the buccal cavity or pharynx may cause clinical signs similar to dyspnoea.

PSITTACOSIS (ORNITHOSIS or CHLAMYDIOSIS)

This disease is caused by *Chlamydia psittaci*, which is an obligate intracellular parasite. The clinical signs are often those of a febrile systemic illness but there may also be asymptomatic carriers. Psittacosis should always be suspected in a psittacine bird with more than a mild respiratory disease. This infection is a zoonosis and owners must be warned of this. The mortality rate in birds depends on the condition of the patient before the clinical signs appear and the species affected. Mortality is often 100% in parakeets, conures and Amazons but only 50% in cockatoos and even lower in budgerigars.

For further information on this disease, the reader is referred to Chapter 13.

FUNGAL RESPIRATORY DISEASES

These are usually due to *Aspergillus fumigatus* or *Candida albicans*. Other fungi may be involved but are rare.

1. **Aspergillosis**

Aspergillosis is only pathogenic under certain circumstances. The affected bird usually has a history of debilitation due to some other disease, immunosuppression, stress, malnutrition, prolonged antibiotic (Patgiri 1987) or corticosteroid therapy (Campbell 1986). Exposure to large numbers of spores — for example, in a damp aviary — may also increase the likelihood of infection.

Aspergillosis is predominantly a disease of the lower respiratory tract (Campbell 1986), especially the air sacs, probably due to the relative paucity of blood supply. Unlike pneumonia, air sacculitis can be present for some time and become extensive before clinical signs are shown (Coles 1985). Aspergillosis should always be suspected in the chronically ill bird with a respiratory disease which is unresponsive to antibiotics. Redig (1983) described the diagnosis and treatment of aspergillosis as one of the most difficult and yet frequently encountered problems of the avian practitioner.

Although acute disease may occur (Redig 1983), due to the inhalation of large quantities of spores by a healthy bird, aspergillosis is usually a chronic problem. Respiratory distress is usually only seen terminally and is associated with inflammation of the air sacs and blockage of the airways within the lungs (Redig 1983).

Diagnosis is usually based on isolation of the fungus or *post mortem* findings. Culture can be attempted using tracheal swabs plated onto Sabouraud's dextrose agar. Bronchoscopy may reveal plaques of *Aspergillus* at the tracheal bifurcation. Laparoscopy may also permit diagnosis; lesions may be seen in the air sacs and biopsied/swabbed as necessary. Serology may also be used for confirmation.

The *post mortem* examination shows lesions throughout the lungs and the air sacs; these usually appear as cotton-wool like mould, yellow/green caseated plaques or granulomatous nodules, depending on the severity and chronicity of the disease. Radiographs *ante mortem* may reveal these increased densities or nodules involving the lungs or air sacs (Campbell 1986; Cooper, 1978).

If diagnosed *ante mortem* treatment can be attempted with amphotericin B, ketoconazole, miconazole or other antifungal drugs, but usually this is unsuccessful.

Redig (1983) discussed methods of treatment which included: air sac aspiration and irrigation with 20 ml of 5 mg amphotericin B in sterile water; use of intratracheal amphotericin B 1 mg/Kg bid (in 2 to 3 ml of water) and amphotericin B intravenously 1.5 mg/Kg tid, but this may cause transient ataxia.

As this condition usually only occurs in the debilitated bird, levamisole 2 mg/Kg intramuscularly at 4 to 6 day intervals (Redig 1983) may be tried in order to stimulate the immune system.

2. **Candidiasis**

Candida usually affects the crop and the oesophagus and is seen as white plaques and patches. When the glottis is affected there is respiratory distress due to mechanical obstruction (McDonald 1980).

This is particularly a disease of young birds (Flammer 1986) where it results in the formation of an exudative white sheet over the mucosal surfaces.

Diagnosis is on the isolation or demonstration of *Candida* in impression smears or histological sections.

Oral/topical treatment with nystatin has been recommended (see page 181). Petgiri (1987) also advised reduction of carbohydrates and supplementation with vitamin A. Other drugs which may be used include amphotericin B (see page 181), griseofulvin and ketoconazole (see page 182). Chlorhexidine 10 ml/gallon of water for 10 days may also be helpful (Flammer 1986).

PARASITIC RESPIRATORY DISEASE

Parasitic causes of respiratory disease include trichomonads, the mites *Sternostoma trachaecolum* and *Cnemidocoptes pilae* and the nematode *Syngamus trachea.*

1. **Trichomoniasis**

This occurs mainly in budgerigars (see Chapter 7) where it may be seen as a creamy diphtheritic deposit in the mouth in its classic form; the condition may only be suspected by the accumulation of fluid in the pharynx and gurgling on respiration. Diagnosis is on aspiration and microscopy. One of us (ML) has found treatment with metronidazole 160 mg/Kg as a single dose very successful.

2. **Sternostoma trachaecolum**

This mite lives in the respiratory system of canaries and finches. It has also been reported from budgerigars but rarely other psittacines (McDonald 1980). Mortality is high. Diagnosis is by microscopy of tracheal aspirates or demonstration of the mites by transillumination of the trachea. Treatment is with ivermectin 200 μg/Kg (Sikarskie 1986) or levamisole. Lafeber (1973) described the use of malathion (10%) in 'Alevaire' for 1 hour at a rate of 40 ml/hr in an area of 1 cubic foot. An alternative approach is to place dichlorvos strips ('Vapona', Shell) in the bird room but these must be used with great caution.

3. **Cnemidocoptes pilae**

This mite can cause respiratory problems due to hypertrophy of the cere and physical blockage of the nares.

4. **Syngamus trachea**

This parasite is found in the upper respiratory tract. Infestation involves the ingestion of snails, earthworms or infected soil so the condition is usually only seen in an aviary bird or a solitary parrot which has recently originated from an aviary collection.

The clinical signs are described as a frenzied coughing and sneezing, head shaking and gasping (McDonald 1980).

Diagnosis is by detection of the parasite which is usually found in a 'Y' shape due to permanent copulation between the male and the female. This may be visible by transillumination or endoscopy, or eggs may be seen in faeces or tracheal washings. Treatment is with thiabendazole (50-100 mg/Kg for 7 days), oxfendazole (1 ml/Kg), ivermectin or levamisole.

NEOPLASTIC RESPIRATORY DISEASE

Tumours of the nasal and frontal sinuses are infrequently encountered (Altman 1986). When they occur they are usually squamous cell carcinomata. Respiratory problems arise due to the pressure and mechanical obstruction of the nares. Diagnosis is based on cytology or histology.

Neoplasia of the respiratory system is rare but should not be overlooked in differential diagnosis, especially when dealing with elderly birds.

NUTRITIONAL RESPIRATORY DISEASE

For further description of some of these problems and their treatments, refer to Chapter 18.

1. **Hypovitaminosis A**

    This has been implicated as a factor in most types of respiratory infection but its exact role is not easy to elucidate. It has been most commonly associated with sinusitis in parrots, the formation of abscesses, conjunctivitis and rhinoliths.

    Seeds fed to parrots contain little or no vitamin A; thus, parrots which are fed only on a seed diet are prone to this condition. Vitamin A deficiency should always be considered in any respiratory problem.

    Diagnosis of hypovitaminosis A is possible by taking a biopsy of oral lesions. It is also possible to make a diagnosis on the basis of blood levels.

    Treatment is with vitamin A, initially by injection and then orally, as well as inproving the diet.

2. **Iodine Deficiency**

    This is fully described in Chapter 18. Pressure on the trachea and the syrinx from the goitre may be responsible for respiratory signs.

MECHANICAL OBSTRUCTION

Foreign bodies may lodge in the external nares, choana or epiglottis and may cause persistent coughing, sneezing or nasal discharge. This should be suspected when there is a unilateral nasal discharge (Altman 1986). A good clinical examination will often show the offending item, usually a seed husk or splinter.

Cooper and others (1986) described respiratory distress associated with multiple papillomata in the buccal cavity resulting in mechanical obstruction of the glottis.

ALLERGIC

True asthma has been described (Altman 1986) as producing clinical signs similar to those seen with thyroid hyperplasia. The diagnosis is made retrospectively on the basis of response to corticosteroids. The term 'asthma' is used to describe a vast range of diseases, probably with many aetiologies, in their later stages (Arnall and Petrak 1982). Causes of true asthma are not known: there is no convincing evidence of an allergy.

APPROACH TO DIAGNOSIS

A general approach to diagnosis of respiratory disease in psittacine birds is as follows:-

1. **Observation** of the bird, preferably in its own environment before it is disturbed or alerted to human presence.

2. **Clinical examination.** While some examination can be carried out without restraining the bird, a full clinical examination can only be performed if the bird is handled. As little stress as possible should be caused to the bird and therefore the examination must be planned carefully taking full advantage of subdued light, ensuring that assistance and equipment are readily available so that the period of restraint is as short as possible.

    Although Arnall and Petrak (1982) believed that clinical examination in small birds was difficult, inexact and often unrewarding, advances in techniques and knowledge over the last few years have made clinical examination essential on the basis that any information gained may help in a tentative diagnosis, suggest what further tests should be performed and what line the treatment should follow.

3. **Aids to Diagnosis.** Standard techniques should be used. Auscultation can be of value in the identification and localisation of an abnormal sound (Altman 1986) but is technically easier in the larger birds.

    Radiography, which should be both ventrodorsal and lateral, may help to demonstrate changes in the respiratory system, the presence of foreign bodies etc, and is described in detail by Silverman (1977) and in Chapter 3.

    In selected cases, laparoscopy is of value, especially where a particular lesion has been localised by radiography (Altman 1986). Laparoscopy should be carried out under light general anaesthesia or, exceptionally, local analgesia. It provides an excellent way of locating and examining air sac lesions and at the same time permits the taking of biopsies, swabs and washings for further investigation (Cooper 1987).

    Tracheal swabs may be taken in an unanaesthetised parrot but care must be exercised when plunging the swab into the trachea since it may precipitate respiratory embarrassment or arrest in a bird with dyspnoea. In a lightly anaesthetised or sedated bird a tracheal wash using saline or an appropriate diluent or medium can be carried out. Likewise, swabs and aspirates from swollen sinuses, abscesses and other lesions, may be take.

    Other techniques which facilitate diagnosis, such as demonstration of *Syngamus* eggs or the identification of *Sternostoma* mites by transillumination, were mentioned earlier.

GENERAL PRINCIPLES OF TREATMENT AND NURSING

Any bird with moderate to severe respiratory problems should be hospitalised rather than sent home with medication added to water or having to return daily for re-examination, which can only result in further stress to an already compromised bird. It may also reduce the health risk to the owner (see later).

Useful guidelines to owners of birds with suspected respiratory disease were given by McWhirter (1987) who listed four important principles, these being i) minimise stress; ii) treat promptly and seek advice; iii) isolate affected birds and iv) provide good nursing care.

Where the aetiology is known and there is a specific treatment then the latter should be implemented promptly. In cases without a specific treatment or if the aetiology is unknown or uncertain then the treatment should be supportive and should involve:-

1. **Warmth**
    Keeping the bird warm (80°F or 27°C) will prevent chilling and reduce the energy requirement for thermoregulation. The use of an infrared lamp is recommended, but this should be used in conjunction with a thermometer so as not to overheat the bird.

2. **Subdued Lighting**
    This helps to minimise stress and relaxes the bird, especially prior to capture for medication. The bird should not be kept in darkness or it may not feed.

3. **Lower Perches**
    In birds with severe pneumonia or systemic disease, it is advisable to lower the perches in the cage. This has a dual function: a) it is less far for the bird to fall if it is having problems perching and b) it will make it easier for the bird to climb back on the perch. It is also important that the food and water containers are lowered to within easy reach.

4. **Weight**

Regular weighing will help in the monitoring of food intake. Crop tube feeding should be performed if the bird is not eating or is dehydrated. Birds with respiratory embarrassment will often not attempt to feed or drink as they are concentrating on breathing. The authors have found that a baby food such as Millupa (fruit variety) is usually more acceptable to a sick bird than is a normal seed mixture, and has the advantage of supplying both energy and fluid.

5. **Antibiotics**

The route of medication is important. Medication via the water is to be avoided as any alteration in the taste of the water may cause a bird with an already reduced intake to drink even less and dehydration results. It is also inexact and thus should be avoided, certainly in the single bird. Although there are risks involved in handling a bird the advantages of giving an adequate dose by a known route far outweigh any risk. Medication can be by crop tube, intramuscular injection or intratracheal injection.

The advantage of injection is that by using certain preparations the frequency of dosing may be reduced to as little as once a day, whereas crop tubing, for example using oral ampicillin mixtures, may have to be repeated as much as four to six times a day in order to produce adequate blood levels.

Some parrots will voluntarily take sweet mixtures, such as paediatric solutions of certain drugs, but this is the exception rather than the rule.

Intratracheal injection can be delivered via a catheter through the glottis. In larger parrots, a gag or sedation will facilitate this. Coughing will occur after administration but quickly subsides.

Nebulisation of antibiotics is advantageous (see Chapter 20) because the agent is more likely to reach the lower respiratory tract and the bird continuously inhales small droplets containing the antibiotic mixture. This is particularly useful in treating air sacculitis: if the droplet size is below 5 μm in diameter then it will saturate the air sacs (Coles 1985).

Suitable antibiotics for the treatment of respiratory diseases of bacterial origin are ampicillin, cephalexin, cotrimoxazole, oxytetracycline, doxycycline and tylosine (see Chapter 20).

6. **Vitamin A**

Hypovitaminosis A can be involved in respiratory conditions. It is wise to use Vitamin A routinely for treatment of respiratory cases together with antibiotics by injection or other routes.

7. **Other Medicants**

In addition to antimicrobial agents other drugs may be helpful. These include steroids, respiratory stimulants such as doxapram or even diuretics but care must be taken. Short acting corticosteroid formulations are particularly helpful in birds with airway obstruction or shock. Doxapram is a respiratory stimulant which can be used at 0.5 ml/Kg to stimulate breathing both in anaesthetised birds and those with respiratory embarrassment.

HEALTH HAZARDS TO HUMANS

The potential danger of psittacosis (chlamydiosis or ornithosis) has already been mentioned and appropriate precautions must be taken to reduce the danger of this to staff and owners. This is particularly important if *post mortem* examination is performed. Birds with suspect psittacosis should be hospitalised but, if psittacosis is suspect or is high on the list of differential diagnoses, appropriate warning should also be given to those involved in care and management. The use of a mask and other protective clothing is strongly recommended.

Other respiratory infections present less of a hazard than psittacosis but may pose a threat to humans — for example, influenza and possibly other viruses.

There is no doubt that certain strains of influenza virus can pass from birds to humans and vice versa. The epidemiological features of this transmission are under study at present and there are indications that, in addition to being infected, birds may serve as reservoirs and that variants of a virus may emerge as a result of bird to bird passage.

There are other possible hazards to humans who come into contact with psittacine birds. The most important of these is an allergic condition, commonly called 'budgerigar fancier's lung', which is associated with an Arthus reaction to feather, faecal material or other derivatives of birds (Hendrick *et al* 1978). It can occur in people in contact with birds other than psittacines, for example, pigeons and wild bird casualties. It should be noted that in these cases the bird itself is healthy; the allergy is to products of a *normal* bird. The symptoms in humans are those of respiratory disease, shortness of breath, narrowing of airways and in severe cases bronchospasm. The condition is usually noticed when the person is in close proximity with the birds or their products and symptoms decline or disappear when contact ceases.

In order to diagnose this condition definitively, standard immunological investigations must be performed and some hospitals in Britain specialise in these tests. The veterinary practitioner should be aware of this condition and be prepared to explain to his/her client the difference between this and infectious disease such as psittacosis. There is sometimes a lack of understanding of this point by members of the public and local health authorities.

Psittacosis and 'bird fancier's lung' provide an excellent opportunity for the veterinary surgeon to collaborate with his medical colleagues in order to help both the owner and the bird.

REFERENCES

ALTMAN, R. B. (1986). Non-infectious Diseases in Zoo and Wild Animal Medicine 2nd. Edition edited by M. E. Fowler. Pub. W. B. Saunders Co.

ARNALL, L. and PETRAK, M. L. (1982). Diseases of the Respiratory System in Diseases of Cage and Aviary Birds, 2nd. edition edited by M. L. Petrak. Pub. Lea and Febiger.

CAMPBELL, T. W. (1986). Mycotic Diseases in Clinical Avian Medicine and Surgery edited by G. J. Harrison and L. R. Harrison. Pub. W. B. Saunders Co.

CAVILL, J. P. (1980). Newcastle Disease in Aviary and Pet Birds. Vet Rec 25 (7) :6-9.

CLUBB, S. L. (1983). Viscerotropic Velogenic Newcastle Disease in Pet Birds in Current Veterinary Therapy VIII. Edited by R. W. Kirk. Pub. W. B. Saunders Co.

CLUBB, S. L. (1984). Velogenic Viscerotropic Newcastle Disease in Zoo and Wild Animal Medicine. Edited by M. E. Fowler. Pub. W. B. Saunders Co.

COLES, B. H. (1985). Avian Medicine and Surgery. Pub. Blackwell Scientific Publications.

COOPER, J. E. (1987). Veterinary Aspects of Captive Birds of Prey. The Standfast Press, Glos.

COOPER, J. E., LAWTON, M. P. C. and GREENWOOD, A. G. (1986). Papillomas in psittacine birds. Vet Rec **119**, 535.

COOPER, J. E. (1987). Veterinary work with non-domesticated pets III. Birds. Brit. Vet. J. **143**, 21-34.

FLAMMER, K. (1986). Oropharyngeal Diseases in Caged Birds in Current Veterinary Therapy IX. Edited by R. W. Kirk. Pub. W. B. Saunders Co.

FOWLER, M. E. (1987). Velogenic Viscerotropic Newcastle Disease in Companion Bird Medicine. Edited by E. W. Burr. Pub. Iowa State University Press.

HENDRICK, D. J., FAUX, J. A. and MARSHALL, R. (1978). Budgerigar-Fancier's Lung: the commonest variety of allergic alveolitis in Britain. Brit. Med. J. 2, 81-84.

LAFEBER, T. J. (1973). Respiratory Disease Vet. Clin. N. Am. 3, 199.

MCDONALD, S. E. (1980). Respiratory Disease in Psittacine Birds in Current Veterinary Therapy VII. Edited by R. W. Kirk. Pub. W. B. Saunders Co.

MACWHIRTER, P. (1987). Editor 'Everybird. A Guide to Bird Health'. Inkata Press, Melbourne.

PATGIRI, G. P. (1987). Systemic Mycosis in Companion Bird Medicine. Edited by E. W. Burr. Pub. Iowa State University Press.

REDIG, P. T. (1983). Aspergillosis in Current Veterinary Therapy VIII. Edited by R. W. Kirk. Pub. W. B. Saunders Co.

SIKARSKIE, J. G. (1986). The use of Ivermectin in Birds, Reptiles and Small Mammals in Current Veterinary Therapy IX. Edited by R. W. Kirk. Pub. W. B. Saunders Co.

SILVERMANN, S. (1977). Avian Radiographic Technique and Interpretation in Current Veterinary Therapy VI. Edited by R. W. Kirk. Pub. W. B. Saunders Co.

Chapter 9

THE UROGENITAL SYSTEM

J. E. Cooper, B.V.Sc., D.T.V.M., F.I.Biol., Cert.L.A.S., F.R.C.V.S.

M. P. C. Lawton, B.Vet.Med., Cert.V.Ophthal., M.R.C.V.S.

This chapter is divided into two parts. The first deals with disorders of the kidneys and associated structures, the second with reproductive diseases.

Diseases of the renal system are not uncommon in psittacine birds but in the past have often failed to be diagnosed clinically. Hasholt and Petrak (1982) summarised some of the available data and emphasised the difficulty of making a clinical diagnosis. Over the past 5 — 10 years improved diagnostic tests have helped permit the detection of renal disease in the live bird and, in some cases, methods of therapy have been devised and developed. Nevertheless, the subject is still one that requires more research and more published data.

In this first part particular attention is paid to pathological conditions of the kidney, but mention is also made of diseases which involve associated structures, such as the cloaca and reproductive tract.

It is important to remember that renal diseases may be:-

1. Primary — where the initial lesion is in the kidney(s), e.g. a renal tumour, or

2. Secondary — where the kidney becomes affected as a sequel to another pathological change e.g. micro-abscesses following a blood-borne infection.

In this chapter particular emphasis will be laid on the diagnosis and treatment of the former although many of the investigative techniques described are applicable to the latter.

ANATOMY AND PHYSIOLOGY

Psittacine birds have paired kidneys which are lobed and lie in a subvertebral position (Figure 1 — overleaf). They are drained by ureters which empty into the urodaeum of the cloaca. There is no bladder. A detailed description of the urogenital system is given by McKibben and Harrison (1986).

Birds are uricotelic and 60 — 80% of their excreted nitrogen is in the form of uric acid. Urates are visible in the droppings as white viscous material which becomes chalky when dry.

TYPES OF RENAL DISEASE

Hasholt and Petrak (1982) divided diseases of the urinary system into a) acute, b) chronic, and c) neoplastic. In this chapter a system is used which provides some information on the aetiology and/or pathogenesis of the condition. Renal diseases are divided into:-

a.	Infectious	d.	Traumatic	f.	Toxic
b.	Parasitic	e.	Neoplastic	g.	Uncertain
c.	Nutritional/metabolic				

It should be noted, however, that there is often overlap between these and one may progress to another.

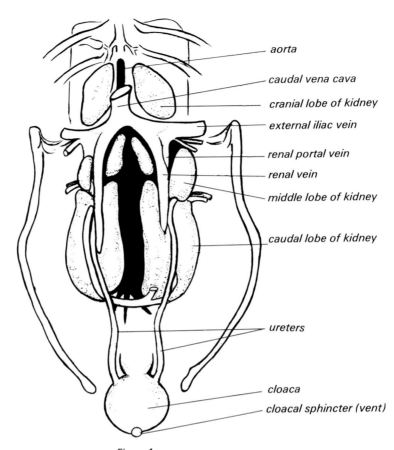

Figure 1
Anatomy of the Avian Renal System
Illustration by Mrs. D. Florio

Infectious

A number of organisms have been reported from nephritis in birds. In some cases they have been associated with acute inflammation, in others with chronic changes. Some bacterial infections of the kidney are a manifestation of more generalised disease e.g. *E.coli* septicaemia, while others are primarily e.g. purulent (ascending) pyelonephritis.

Fungi have also been incriminated in renal disease. For example, *Aspergillus* is not infrequently isolated from renal lesions *post mortem* but this is usually part of a more generalised mycotic infection.

Diagnosis of infectious renal disease is not easy. Clinical signs vary from apparent normality to depression, lethargy, straining and increased respiration rate. Careful history taking is important: purulent nephritis and ureteritis may follow cloacal damage.

Treatment may be attempted using appropriate anti-microbial agents. The use of hexamine, a urinary tract disinfectant, has been discussed by Hasholt and Petrak (1982). It is of doubtful value in birds and may even be contraindicated.

Cloacitis is not uncommon and may be a sequel to cloacal calculi. The clinical signs are similar. Swabs should be taken and appropriate antimicrobial therapy instigated — if necessary both parenterally and *per cloacam*. Fluid intake must be maintained.

Parasitic

A number of species of parasite have been reported from the kidneys of psittacine birds at *post mortem* examination. Again, many are also present in other organs and therefore these cannot usually correctly be described as causes of primary renal disease. Hasholt and Petrak (1982) described some of the features of *Encephalitozoon* infection. The clinical signs were fairly non-specific — lethargy, fluffing of feathers, anorexia, loose droppings and weight loss. Diagnosis was only made *post mortem*.

Nutritional/Metabolic

A number of factors may predispose to renal changes. There is evidence, for example, that a high protein intake may contribute to chronic renal disease, including interstitial nephritis and degenerative changes in the tubules and Bowman's capsules.

Similarly, psittacine birds which have received an incorrect calcium:phosphorus ratio may, in addition to effects on the skeleton and parathyroid glands, show foci of mineralisation in the kidney. The latter are not usually of any consequence *per se* but may be detected on radiography or *post mortem*. It is important to distinguish them from urate tophi in histological sections.

Calculi, usually composed of urates, may form in the cloaca or, more rarely, kidneys or ureters. The pathogenesis is not always clear but calculus formation may follow a period of water deprivation/dehydration or cloacitis. Cloacal stones may develop if a bird is recumbent for a few days, presumably because of stasis in the cloaca. Affected birds strain, produce abnormal droppings or show soiling round the vent. Cloacitis can be a sequel to calculi as well as predisposing to them. In such cases it is important to treat the cloacitis as well as dealing with the stones.

Calculi may be detected by radiography or cloacal examination. They can be removed manually (with the aid of a speculum or endoscope) or, if very large and hard, surgically. A novel way of treating kidney stones — by extracorporeal shockwave lithotripsy — has been described in a penguin (Machado *et al,* 1987) and could have applications in work with psittacines.

Gout may affect many organs of the body but is presumed to be renal in origin and the kidneys are often involved. Treatment can be attempted using allopurinol (Steiner and Davis, 1981) but this only prevents further formation of tophi and does nothing to treat those that are already present (see page 131).

Traumatic

The kidneys may be damaged during handling, laparoscopy or as a result of a traumatic episode.

As a general rule if the bird survives more than 24 hours then it makes an uneventful recovery. Acute effects before this stage may include collapse, signs of shock and a distended abdomen (blood). Diagnosis may be confirmed by laparoscopy or by aspiration of fluid from the body cavity. Treatment is symptomatic.

Neoplastic

Renal tumours are not uncommon is psittacine birds, especially budgerigars, and should always be considered in any differential diagnosis. Some e.g. renal adenocarcinomas, originate from the kidneys but others may be secondary (metastases) from sites elsewhere in the body especially lymphoproliferative disease.

Clinical signs vary but often the owner reports a distended abdomen and increased fluid intake associated with other, more non-specific, signs such as anorexia or lethargy. Renal adenocarcinomas are usually manifest as unilateral flaccid/spastic paralysis of the affected side. Full clinical investigation (see later) should confirm the presence of an intra-abdominal swelling and laparoscopy/laparotomy will help to distinguish the condition from others such as ovarian or testicular neoplasia, egg-binding etc. Renal cysts have been reported in psittacine birds (Hasholt and Petrak, 1982) and must also be considered in differential diagnosis: however, they are not usually associated with clinical signs.

Although diagnosis of a renal tumour may not present problems its treatment is usually less easy. Sometimes the whole lesion can be removed intact but often this is impracticable. (See Chapter 5).

Toxic

Toxins of various types may cause renal disease. Some drugs e.g. gentamicin, are specifically nephrotoxic (Phillips, 1986) while others e.g. certain sulphonamides, may cause tissue damage if a bird is dehydrated. Some aviculturists give salt (sodium chloride) to their birds: as Hasholt and Petrak (1982) stated, this can prove dangerous. Zinc is a potential hazard to psittacine birds: Reece *et al* (1985) reported deaths in peach-faced lovebirds *(Agapornis roseicollis)* associated with the ingestion of zinc from the galvanised wire of their enclosures. The birds' kidneys were enlarged and histological examination revealed a degenerative nephritis. Lead poisoning is associated with inclusion bodies in the renal tubules (Woerpel and Rosskopf, 1986) while changes in the kidney may also occur following ingestion of certain plants or chemicals such as propyleneglycol (antifreeze).

Uncertain

At the present time many cases must fall into this category, mainly because we know so little about the origins and development of renal disease in psittacine birds. Thus, it is possible that some of the chronic changes seen *post mortem* e.g. dilated tubules, fibrosis of the interstitium, may be sequelae to earlier infectious, parasitic or nutritional disease.

There is some evidence of allergic diseases of the kidney. Eosinophilic infiltrates, not apparently associated with parasites, are sometimes seen in kidneys on histopathological examination. Similarly, plasma cell and lymphocyte aggregates are seen from time to time. It is possible that these conditions are due to an allergic response but there are, as yet, no reliable data to substantiate this. Haemorrhagic lesions seen in the kidneys following the administration of certain contra-indicated drugs, e.g. procaine penicillin (Hasholt and Petrak, 1982; Hauser, 1960) are unlikely to be allergic in the immunological sense but may indicate an adverse reaction to these agents. Glomerulonephritis is frequently seen *post mortem* and an antigen-antibody complex may be involved.

Diagnosis

Diagnosis of renal disease in psittacine birds may be based upon a combination of the following:-

1. clinical signs
2. clinical examination
3. laboratory investigations

Each will be discussed in more detail.

Clinical signs

Birds with renal disease may show a variety of clinical signs (Coles, 1985). Some are non-specific e.g. anorexia, weight loss, while others, such as the production of watery droppings or ascites, may be strongly suggestive of kidney dysfunction. Observation of the sick bird can provide valuable information and owners should be encouraged to keep records of frequency of passing droppings, their appearance and any signs of discomfort or distress. Watery droppings may not be noticed by an owner or he/she attributes them to diarrhoea (See Chapter 7). For this reason it is often wise to hospitalise suspect cases. The bird can be observed and appropriate samples taken. A piece of greaseproof paper on the floor of the cage provides a simple way of collecting samples. As a general rule 'normal' droppings consist of dark (brown, yellow, sometimes green) faecal material around which there is a zone of yellow or yellowish-white urate material. The proportion of the two is probably not significant and it must be stressed that variation in appearance is not unusual, being related to a variety of factors including diet and frequency of caecal emptying.

Clinical examination

This must be carried out thoroughly and systematically. Manipulation of macaws and other large species will be facilitated if the patient is lightly anaesthetised. Ketamine hydrochloride (5mg/kg intramuscularly) is usually adequate and appears safe, even in birds with renal disease. Alternatively, a small dose of alphaxalone-alphadolone ('Saffan': Glaxovet) may be given intravenously or intramuscularly. Methoxyflurane is the inhalation agent of choice but must be used with caution in view of its nephrotoxic potential.

An important aspect of clinical investigation is careful palpation of the abdomen followed, in birds weighing 100g or more, by cloacal examination. A lubricated gloved finger can be inserted through the anus and moved dorsally in the cloaca in order to palpate the caudal part of the kidney. Any swelling, asymmetry or tenderness may be indicative of renal disease.

Important aids to clinical examination are radiography and laparoscopy/laparotomy. Plain lateral and dorso-ventral radiographs may demonstrate enlargement of a kidney or, alternatively, displacement of other organs. Contrast radiography can also be used. Barium may be administered *per os* or *per cloacam* or pneumocloacography performed. Krautwald (1987) reported on the use of water soluble iodine based contrast medium ('Urografin': Schering) given intravenously into the brachial vein and for examination of the kidneys advocated 800mg medium/kg bodyweight given slowly into the vein followed by radiography one minute later.

Laparoscopy is an excellent diagnostic aid using the site and technique recommended for surgical sexing (Chapter 6; Bush, 1981). Various types of endoscope may be employed, ranging from a sophisticated rigid arthroscope/cystoscope to the battery operated 'Focuscope' or even a simple auroscope.

Laparotomy should only be used if laparoscopy proves unsuitable or surgery is contemplated. Biopsies can be taken using a laparoscope or via a laparotomy.

Laboratory tests

These are increasingly proving useful in the detection of renal disease in birds.

Insofar as biochemical investigations are concerned a useful review paper is that by Lumeij (1987), working with pigeons, but it should be noted that his conclusions do not entirely concur with current thinking about psittacine birds. The following notes relate to the latter; Lumeij's comments are added where appropriate.

Uric acid estimations can be of value in assessing renal function. Either plasma or serum can be used and microtechniques permit the analysis of capillary tube samples. Normal values for psittacine birds lie between 2 and 15mg/dl. Values above 15 may be indicative of renal dysfunction but can also be associated with severe tissue damage. Care must always be taken to avoid contamination of samples with urates from the bird's body or environment.

Creatinine estimations appear to be of less value than uric acid. The normal blood value is 0.2mg/dl. In renal disease levels of 1 − 1.5mg/dl may be recorded. Lumeij (1987) suggested that plasma urea concentration might be a useful parameter for detecting prerenal failure in birds.

Haematological investigations may prove of value in diagnosis, especially in birds with infectious disease. Techniques are discussed by Hawkey et al (1982 and in this volume).

Laboratory tests on urates in the droppings may also prove of value in diagnosis. For example, crystals may be seen microscopically or blood (etc.) detected chemically. Urinalysis strips can be used in birds and will also assist in the diagnosis of non-renal diseases e.g. diabetes mellitus.

Post mortem examination

Some cases will be diagnosed at necropsy. While certain lesions e.g. tumours, are readily detected, careful examination of the kidneys and ureters is necessary to detect some changes: a hand lens may prove helpful. Material can be taken fresh for microbiological and parasitological examination and fixed (formol saline and/or glutaraldehyde) for light and electron microscopy. Touch preparations of the cut surface of the kidney can, if appropriately stained, provide valuable information.

Treatment

Specific methods of treatment are given under the appropriate disease but some general principles will be discussed here.

Therapy of renal disease may comprise 1) chemotherapy, 2) surgery, 3) attention to management, and 4) supportive care (nursing). Often a combination has to be used.

Care must be taken in the use of chemotherapeutic agents as some may prove toxic or harmful, especially in birds with impaired renal function. It is particularly important to ensure that fluid levels are maintained. These can be roughly assessed by skin testing and PCV estimations: saline is administered, if needed, subcutaneously, intravenously or by crop tube.

Surgery on the renal system can prove difficult. (Chapter 5).

Managemental changes usually involve altering the diet.

Supportive care, or nursing, is always vital when dealing with sick birds. The parrot with severe renal disease will die if it is allowed to become chilled, or is not given adequate fluid, regardless of how professional the diagnosis and specific the treatment.

REPRODUCTIVE DISEASES

Breeding problems

Due to importation restrictions and economic and conservation pressures, the successful breeding of psittacines is of utmost importance. For this reason an understanding of the possible problems associated with reproductive failure is vital. A useful review of the subject is provided by Rosskopf and Woerpel (1987).

Successful breeding should result in the production of a live and healthy chick or chicks. There are numerous reasons why this may not be achieved. Failure to mate, failure to ovulate, failure of the eggs to be fertilised are problems which must be ruled out. It is, of course, important that paired birds are of the opposite sex (see Chapter 6), fed a correct diet and subjected to the correct amount of daylight in order to rule out easily corrected but common problems. (See Chapter 21.)

Provided the birds are mating then it is reasonable to expect eggs to be laid. Failure to produce eggs, or difficulty in laying eggs, are common problems and may arise due to ovarian disease, failure of ovulation, infections of the reproductive tract, space-occupying lesions, such as tumours or egg binding, inflammation or physiological alterations (Reece, 1987).

Diagnosis will require a full case history, and careful examination and palpation, radiography and sometimes even laparotomy or endoscopy. A visit to the owner's premises can be of great value.

Enlarged abdomen

This is the commonest presenting sign associated with reproductive disease, and thus will be dealt with in some detail. The clinical signs associated with an enlargement of the abdomen, often irrespective of cause, are very similar (McMillan and Petrak, 1986).

1. Lameness

Any space-occupying mass in the abdomen may be associated with lameness or paresis; this is due to increased pressure on the sciatic nerve plexus (Blackmore and Cooper, 1982; Reece, 1987). Such signs are commonly seen in the case of renal or gonadal tumours (see Plate 9:1). Difficulty in perching may be purely due to altered centre of gravity.

2. Respiratory distress

The degree of increased pressure (and thus abdominal enlargement) will affect the severity of this clinical sign. Pressure on the air sacs is presumed to be responsible for difficulty in breathing and is usually more pronounced when fluid rather than a solid mass is involved (see Chapter 8).

3. Soiled vent

This common finding is mainly due to the vent being lifted dorsally and (often) opposed to the tail feathers following abdominal enlargement.

4. 'Sick bird syndrome'

General clinical signs of depression, weight loss, anorexia and fluffing up are exhibited.

5. Death

This may follow an increase in the abdominal pressure and respiratory embarrassment. Death may be sudden, due to shock or secondary infection.

Palpation of the enlarged abdomen will differentiate between a fluctuating mass which is fluid-filled, a solid space-occupying mass and a ventral abdominal rupture.

A solid mass is usually indicative of the presence of a tumour or an egg. If differentiation is not possible on palpation then radiography will be helpful. For the treatment of a retained egg, see egg binding. For a non-egg mass, laparotomy or laparoscopy may be required to reach a diagnosis and to attempt treatment.

For a fluid fluctuating mass, abdominal paracentesis is very useful; the type of fluid obtained may indicate the cause and should be subjected to laboratory investigation as well as gross examination. Cystic ovaries tend to exude a brownish yellow fluid which flows easily through a small gauge needle. Egg peritonitis yields a thick yellow to green/brown fluid with a very high protein content. Ascitic fluid is also associated with some neoplasms.

Ventral abdominal rupture is commonly seen in the obese budgerigar (Coles, 1985). It is also seen in the female bird that is overused for breeding. The ventral abdominal muscles are weakened by the constant egg laying and/or by infiltration of fat. The resultant stretching of the muscles results in separation, usually at the linea alba, and thus a resulting ventral rupture. Treatment can be attempted, and consists of repairing the defect with nonabsorbable sutures and reducing the weight of the bird.

Ovarian problems

An ovarian problem should be considered if mating is observed in mature birds but no eggs are produced. Diagnosis of an ovarian problem is difficult and may require exploratory surgery or laparoscopy. Treatment is even more difficult, and usually restricted to drainage or attempted removal of cystic structures.

Problems of the ovary include:-

1.   Ovarian cysts

This is a common problem (Altman, 1986) especially in the budgerigar. The cause is unknown, but usually secondary to neoplasia of the ovary (Blackmore and Cooper, 1982). Diagnosis is made by palpation of a soft fluctuating mass within the abdomen. Treatment can be attempted by abdominal paracentesis but this only gives temporary improvement. The use of testosterone (5mg methyltestosterone per week in food) has been reported (Blackmore and Cooper, 1982) as helpful. Surgical removal of the cyst can be attempted: diathermy is recommended.

2.   Gonadal tumours

Not uncommon and occur mainly in budgerigars (Blackmore and Cooper, 1982). There are numerous types of tumours which have been reported in the literature (see Table A); some result in hormonal changes which can bring about a change of colour of the cere to that of the opposite sex (Beach, 1962) and can be used as a useful diagnostic guide. Some of these tumours can become very large and thus the clinical signs are those commonly seen in any cause of an enlarged abdomen, although usually there is also weight loss and non egg-laying (see Plate 5:4). Surgical removal can be attempted (see page 61) and should the bird survive the surgery, the outcome will depend on what type of tumour was causing the problem. Altman (1986) considers metastasis rare while Reece (1987) does not consider surgery possible due to miliary nodules that are often implanted on the serosal surface.

TABLE A

Gonadal Tumours

Adenocarcinoma
Lymphoproliferative disease
Arrhenoma
Haemangiosarcoma
Theca cell tumour
Mixed cell tumour
Dysgerminoma
Teratoma
Fibroma
Fibrosarcoma
Myxofibroma
Leydig cell tumour
Seminoma
Sertoli cell tumour

---

3   Persistent egg-laying

This is usually a problem of the non paired pet bird; large clutches may be laid (see page 167). Persistent laying can predispose towards egg binding and calcium depletion (Altman, 1986); it also distresses the owner. Diagnosis is easy, being based on the large number of eggs produced. Treatment can be medical or surgical. Medical suppression is recommended (Coles, 1985) by intramuscular injection of medroxyprogesterone acetate (Promone-E; Upjohn or Perutex; Leo) at 0.25 to 1 ml depending on the bird's size. Surgical ovariohysterectomy is the treatment of choice (Altman, 1986; Nye, 1986), especially if egg binding becomes a subsequent problem (Rich, 1987).

4.   Oophoritis (Ovariitis)

This is inflammation of the ovary. It can lead to a congested and distorted ovary. This problem is thought (Reece, 1987) to be secondary to systemic disease. The clinical signs are of depression, anorexia, wasting and often death due to systemic infection. Treatment is with antibiotics, as indicated by the systemic disease.

5.   Ovarian haemorrhage

This has been reported (Reece, 1987) to be an occasional problem in ovulation or due to trauma. Diagnosis would be by exploratory laparotomy or laparoscopy and treatment only if indicated on the finding at surgery.

EGG BINDING

Egg-binding is a very common presenting clinical problem (Reece, 1987). Egg binding is the obstruction of the oviduct by an egg or material associated with egg peritonitis (Blackmore and Cooper, 1982; Altman, 1986).

The cause of egg binding is unknown but is thought to be due to atony or to spasm of the oviduct (Blackmore and Cooper, 1982; Turner 1985; Harrison, 1986; Nye, 1986). It may have a genetic basis (Harrison, 1986) as it is more prevalent in budgerigars and cockatiels. There are numerous factors which have been associated with egg binding such as calcium deficiency (Blackmore and Cooper, 1982; Turner, 1985; Harrison, 1986; Nye, 1986), obesity (Turner, 1985; Harrison, 1986; Nye, 1986), cold (Turner, 1985; Harrison, 1986), first clutch, egg oversize, age, tumours (Harrison, 1986) and salpingitis (Nye, 1986).

In all birds it is normal for the hen to appear rather depressed and lethargic as egg-laying becomes imminent (Cooper, 1978; Coles, 1985). The clinical signs of egg binding are associated with the length of time the bird has been egg-bound, and the position of the egg. There are four sites at which the egg is commonly found:-

1.   **Distal oviduct** ('vagina') is the most common site. The egg is usually intact and prolapsed through the cloacal opening but with mucosa still covering it (see Plate 9:2). Diagnosis is straightforward.

2.   **Distal uterus** ('shell-gland') is the next commonest site and usually related to calcium deficiencies. The clinical signs are those associated with an enlarged abdomen; there may be unsteadiness on the perch, with a tendency to squat, straining, sometimes with diarrhoea, often wagging of the tail and exhaustion. For differential diagnosis of straining, see Table B. Diagnosis is on clinical signs and the palpation of an egg transabdominally or *per cloacam*.

TABLE B

Differential diagnosis of straining

Egg binding	Nephritis
Cloacitis	Pelvic lipoma
Vent trauma	Enterolith
Enteritis	

---

3. **Mid-body of oviduct** (magnum) is more difficult to diagnose. The clinical signs are non specific, being those of a 'sick bird' and it is often not possible to palpate the egg transabdominally. This condition is usually diagnosed on a routine whole body radiograph of a sick bird, on endoscopy, or at necropsy.

4. **Abdominal/ectopic eggs:** here the bird is often found dead without any premonitory signs (Reece, 1987), or may be presented with clinical signs of egg binding, as seen at other sites (Harrison, 1986). This may well be due to uterine rupture (Harrison, 1986). Diagnosis is often made on laparotomy in order to differentiate it from egg binding in the mid-body of the oviduct.

Regardless of where the egg is stuck, it is important to assist the bird to pass it as soon as possible. If the blockage is in the pelvic area large blood vessels may be compressed and severe circulatory disorders may result as well as intestinal and ureteral blockage (Hasholt, 1966; Blackmore and Cooper, 1982). Treatment depends upon where the egg is and how sick the bird is when presented, but wherever possible the following regime should be tried:-

   a.   Clean out the vent area: often there is an accumulation of faeces and urates. If the egg is in the distal oviduct and thus presented, an incision over the mucosa and gentle separation from the eggshell with the aid of some lubrication is often all that is required. It may also be necessary to remove any prolapsed necrotic tissue.

   b.   If the egg is not presented through the cloaca, the bird should be placed in a hospital cage and warmed to minimum of 26°C (80°F) (Blackmore and Cooper, 1982; Altman, 1986; Nye, 1986). Intramuscular injection of calcium is also indicated, at 0.01 – 0.02 ml/g 1% calcium gluconate solution (Nye, 1986). Oxytocin may also be given – 0.3 – 0.5ml/kg (10iu/ml) intramuscularly (Coles, 1985). Most cases will respond to this treatment. The high incidence of soft shelled eggs, overbreeding and decreased peristalsis of the oviduct indicates an excessive drain on calcium reserves (Blackmore and Cooper, 1982); calcium injections will cause an increased peristaltic rate and usually the rapid expulsion of the eggs.

   c.   If after 48 hours the egg is not laid, surgical removal is required (Altman, 1986). Under general anaesthesia, the cloaca or oviduct is lubricated via a catheter. Sometimes it is necessary to incise through the wall of the oviduct to allow access to the egg. In the case of the distal uterine egg, gentle pressure on the anterior pole of the egg transabdominally, directing it in a caudal direction, should press the egg into the oviduct-cloacal opening. If the cloaca is dilated the egg will be seen. On further dilation of the cloacal-oviduct opening the egg should pass into the cloaca and thence out. (For more details, see page 59)

   d.   If it is not possible to remove the egg by c) the contents of the egg should be aspirated using an 18 gauge needle (Blackmore and Cooper, 1982; Rosskopf and Woerpel, 1984; Altman, 1986; Nye, 1986). The egg collapses by gentle pressure, and the shell is removed piecemeal. After this, the cloaca and oviduct should be catheterised and flushed with a balanced saline or Hartmann's solution to remove all egg material.

   e.   ) If it is not possible to aspirate and remove the egg *per cloacam*, exploratory laparotomy and salpingotomy should be performed. If the patient is a single pet bird thought should be given to performing ovariohysterectomy at the same time (see pages 60, 61).

After any of the more invasive procedures, it is wise to give postoperative antibiotics for five days, to discourage infection.

EGG PERITONITIS

Egg peritonitis is caused by the escape of the yolk material into the peritoneal cavity (Blackmore and Cooper, 1982, Harrison, 1986) and is common in all species of birds. Some 'egg' material proves to be fibrin on histological examination (Reece, pers. comm.) suggesting that the condition should be regarded as a heterophilic peritonitis/serositis rather than a true egg peritonitis. Often it appears to be sterile (Blackmore and Cooper, 1982) but this may reflect the techniques used rather than indicate that no organisms are involved. Secondary bacterial infection can occur (Harrison, 1986).

Egg peritonitis is usually associated with other reproductive problems, such as obstruction of the oviduct which prevents the ova from entering the infundibulum. The clinical signs are usually those of sudden death, but a sick bird with an enlarged abdomen may be presented. This is a particular problem in budgerigars, cockatiels and lovebirds (Harrison *et al.* 1986). The yolk material in the abdomen is yellow to green/brown and associated with generalised peritonitis with adhesions between the various organs and intestines (Blackmore and Cooper, 1982).

Treatment is not possible in many cases (Blackmore and Cooper, 1982) but may be attempted by drainage (a Penrose drain), irrigations and antibiotics (Harrison *et al.,* 1986).

EGG ABNORMALITIES

Abnormalities include shell-less eggs, double yolked eggs (due to double ovulation), eggs containing blood (due to haemorrhage at ovulation), and soft-shelled eggs (usually due to a calcium:phosphorus imbalance or absolute deficiency of calcium).

IMPACTED OVIDUCT

Impaction of the oviduct is often caused by inspissated egg material (Blackmore and Cooper, 1982). It can also become impacted as a result of excess secretion of mucin and albumen associated with cystic hyperplasia of the mucosa of the oviduct.

The clinical signs associated with impaction are less obvious than those seen in egg-bound birds, due to the smaller mass of the obstruction. It is unlikely to be diagnosed except at *post mortem* or laparotomy (Blackmore and Cooper, 1982).

Treatment can be attempted if the problem is diagnosed at laparotomy.

SALPINGITIS

This is probably a common problem (Reece, 1987). It is often encountered in association with egg binding or impaction of the oviduct. An ascending infection, usually due to *E. coli*, is the cause and this is often secondary to trauma or cloacitis.

The clinical signs are often vague, and may include depression, anorexia, weight loss, abdominal enlargement, usually peritonitis and sometimes a vent discharge. Salpingitis may cause cloacitis (vent gleet).

Treatment is by correction of the primary cause and the use of antibiotics.

PROLAPSED OVIDUCT

Prolapse of the oviduct usually involves the distal part which protrudes through the vent; sometimes the cloaca or rectum is also prolapsed. Diagnosis is based on the presence of the prolapse, without a palpable egg.

Prolapse of the oviduct is amost always associated with egg production (Blackmore and Cooper, 1982; Altman, 1986; Harrison, 1986; Reece, 1987). It may be due to excessive straining to pass a retained egg, overproduction or physiological hyperplasia of the oviduct.

The treatment and the prognosis depend on the length of time that the prolapse has been present and the degree of sepsis and trauma. If the prolapse is fresh and non-traumatised it should first be cleaned, ideally with a diluted povidone-iodine solution. Obstetrical lubrication is then applied and the prolapse corrected and retained by placement of a purse string suture for about three days, making sure that the bird can still pass faeces and urates. This procedure is best performed under general anaesthesia or sedation. Oxytocin will contract the oviduct and help to retain it. If the prolapse is very contaminated or traumatised then it will be necessary to debride or even carry out amputation. The use of antibiotics is recommended.

REFERENCES

ALTMAN, R. B. (1986). Non Infectious disease. In 'Zoo and Wild Animal Medicine' 2nd edition, edited by M. E. Fowler. W. B. Saunders, Philadelphia.

ARNALL, L. and KEYMER, I. F. (1975). 'Bird Diseases'. Baillière Tindall, London.

BEACH, J. E. (1962). Diseases of budgerigars and other cage birds: A survey of *post-mortem* findings. Part II. Veterinary Record **74**, 62-68.

BLACKMORE, D. K. and COOPER, J. E. (1982). Diseases of the reproductive system. In 'Diseases of Cage and Aviary Birds' 2nd Edition, edited by M. L. Petrak. Lea and Febiger, Philadelphia.

BUSH, M. (1981). Diagnostic avian laparoscopy. In Cooper, J. E. and Greenwood, A. G. (editors) 'Recent Advances in the Study of Raptor Diseases'. Chiron Publications, Keighley.

COLES, B. H. (1985). 'Avian Medicine and Surgery'. Blackwell Scientific Publications. Oxford.

COOPER, J. E. (1978). 'Veterinary Aspects of Captive Birds of Prey'. Standfast Press, Glos.

HARRISON, G. J. (1986). Reproductive medicine. In 'Clinical Avian Medicine and Surgery' edited by G. J. Harrison and L. R. Harrison. W. B. Saunders, Philadelphia.

HARRISON, G. J., WOERPEL, R. W., ROSSKOPF, W. J. and KARPINSKI, L. G. (1986). Symptomatic therapy and emergency medicine. In 'Clinical Avian Medicine and Surgery' edited by G. J. Harrison and L. R. Harrison. W. B. Saunders, Philadelphia.

HASHOLT, J. (1982). Diseases of the female reproductive organs of pet birds. Journal of Small Animal Practice **7**, 313.

HASHOLT, J. and PETRAK, M. L. (1982). Diseases of the urinary system. In Petrak, M. L. (editor) 'Diseases of Cage and Aviary Birds' 2nd edition. Lea and Febiger, Philadelphia.

HAUSER, H. (1960). Tödlicher Streptopenicillinschock bei Papageien mit Lugenmykose. Monatsschr. f. Vet. Med. **15**, 632.

HAWKEY, C. M., HART, M. G., KNIGHT, J. A., SAMOUR. J. H. and JONES, D. M. (1982). Haematological findings in healthy and sick African grey parrots *(Psittacus erithacus).* Veterinary Record **111**, 580-582.

KRAUTWALD, M-E, (1987). Radiographic examination of the urinary system of birds with organic iodinated contrast media. Proceedings of the 1st International Conference on Zoological and Avian Medicine, Hawaii.

LOTHROP, C., HARRISON, G. J., SCHULTZ, D. and UTTERIDGE, T. (1986). Miscellaneous diseases. In Harrison, G. and Harrison, L. (editors) 'Clinical Avian Medicine and Surgery'. W. B. Saunders, Philadelphia.

LUMEIJ, J. T. (1987). Plasma urea, creatinine and uric acid concentrations in response to dehydration in racing pigeons *(Columba livia domestica).* Avian Pathology **16**, 377-382.

MACHADO, C., MIHM, F., BUCKLEY, D. N., STOLLER, M. L., ZOMOW, M. H. and THÜROFF, J. (1987). Disintegration of kidney stones by extracorporeal shockwave lithotripsy in a penguin. Proceedings of 1st International Conference on Zoological and Avian Medicine, Hawaii.

McKIBBEN, J. S. and HARRISON, G. J. (1986). Clinical anatomy. In Harrison, G. and Harrison, L. (editors) 'Clinical Avian Medicine and Surgery'. W. B. Saunders, Philadelphia.

McMILLAN, M. C. and PETRAK, M. L. (1986). Clinical significance of abdominal enlargement in the budgerigar *(Melopsittacus undulatus).* Exotic Animal Medicine in Practice. The Compendium Collection. Veterinary Learning Systems, New Jersey.

NYE, R. R. (1986), Dealing with the egg-bound bird. In 'Current Veterinary Therapy IX' edited by R. W. Kirk. W. B. Saunders, Philadelphia.

PHILLIPS, I. R. (1986). Parrots encountered in practice: a survey of one hundred and twelve cases. Journal of Small Animal Practice **27**, 189-199.

REECE, R. L. (1987). Reproductive diseases. In 'Companion Bird Medicine' edited by E. W. Burr. Iowa State University Press, Ames.

REECE, R. L., SCOTT, P. C., FORSYTH, W. M., GOULD, J. A. and BARR, D. A. (1985). Toxicity episodes involving agricultural chemicals and other substances in birds in Victoria, Australia. Veterinary Record **117**, 525-527.

RICH, G. A. (1987). Ovariohysterectomy in an egg bound cockatiel. Companion Animal Practice **1:2**, 48-49.

ROSSKOPF, W. J. and WOERPEL, R. W. (1984). Egg binding in caged and aviary birds. Veterinary Medicine/Small Animal Clinician **79**, 437.

ROSSKOPF, W. J. and WOERPEL, R. W. (1987). Pet avian obstetrics. Proceedings of the 1st International Conference on Zoological and Avian Medicine, Hawaii.

STEINER, C. V. and DAVIS, R. B. (1981). 'Caged Bird Medicine'. Iowa State University Press, Ames.

WOERPEL, R. W. and ROSSKOPF, W. J. (1986). Heavy-metal intoxication in caged birds. Exotic Animal Medicine in Practice. The Compendium Collection. Veterinary Learning Systems. New Jersey.

Further Reading
University of Sydney (1981). Refresher Course for Veterinarians. Proceedings No. 55. Refresher Course on Aviary and Caged Birds. February 16-20, 1981. Sydney, New South Wales, Australia.

Chapter 10 — SKIN, FEATHERS, BEAK, CERE AND UROPYGIAL GLAND

W. T. Turner B.Vet.Med., M.R.C.V.S.

The skin of birds is similar to that of mammals in that it consists of an outer, thin epidermis with an underlying thicker dermis but differs from that of mammals in that it is thin, inelastic and covered in feathers. The feathers grow in tracts called pterylae separated by featherless spaces, apteriae. Avian skin is attached only loosely to underlying muscle and contains few glands but many delicate intradermal muscles. These originate and insert on feathers and provide the means by which erection and ruffling of the feathers can occur. In addition, in certain sites there are also dermo-osseus muscles which originate on bones and insert onto feathers. This is the means by which crests and hackles are raised.

Beak, cere, glands, claws, footpads and feathers are all skin or integumental derivatives.

Three main types of feathers are distinguished:-
1. Contour feathers which are so named because they sheathe the body, wings and tail and give the bird its shape.

2. Plumules or down feathers which lack a definite shaft beyond the quill: these form the covering of nestlings and also underline the contour feathers of the adult. Sometimes they also cover the apteriae or featherless areas — see below.

3. Filoplumes are hairless degenerative feathers consisting of a slender shaft which terminates in a tiny tuft of barbs. Filoplumes are always associated with contour feather follicles. They can be further modified to form bristles, as occurs in the budgerigar where they form the eyelashes.

The number of contour feathers is fairly constant for each tract or pteryla for each species. Depending on the type of bird, down feathers may be associated only with the pterylae or cover the entire bird, being found also in the intervening spaces or apterae.

The static air space between the feathers can be accurately regulated by the bird and this, together with the insulating properties afforded by the feathers, helps to maintain the high body temperature of the bird. In addition the strength of the contour feathers acts to protect the bird against mechanical injury.

The water repellent property of feathers depends on several factors of which the amount of oil from the preen gland is of minor importance. Structure and network of the feathers and intricate interlocking of the barbules is of far greater importance. The uropygial or preen gland does secrete an oily substance which the bird spreads on to its feathers and scales during the preening process but this acts mainly as a lubricant and serves to decrease the wear on the feathers, particularly the contour feathers.

Disintegration of the tips of the so-called powder down feathers produce a fine powder that also helps to waterproof, lubricate and preserve the feathers and is also spread during the preening process.

PREENING
Careful maintenance of the feathers is important to ensure flight and also insulation and waterproofing properties. At one time it was considered that part of the preening process involved the spreading of the secretion of the preen or uropygial gland onto the surface of the feathers but it is now known that

103

feathers can be maintained in good condition even if the preen gland has been excised. Of greater importance is the careful interlocking of the barbules of the feathers which regular preening ensures.

Feathers develop with a keratin sheath (pin feathers) and it is essential that this feather case is removed during preening to allow further development of the feather. Birds wearing collars, e.g. to prevent feather picking) cannot carry out this essential process and therefore it has to be done for them if the normal process of feathering is to continue. Spraying or misting with water will often encourage birds to preen the pin feathers.

Preening appears to be a habit acquired from the parents and therefore hand reared birds may have to be encouraged to undertake the task; misting the feathers with a water spray helps as does the use of damp cotton wool smoothed along contour feathers.

AVIAN DERMATOLOGY

Problems involving avian skin are usually reflected in clinical signs evident in the overlying feathers. However, unfeathered skin may be involved in independent disease processes unassociated with the feathers. Dermatology is one of the most challenging areas of day-to-day clinical evaluation and avian dermatology; particularly, disorders of the feathers is one of the most frustrating areas for the avian practitioner and owner alike, not to mention the bird itself.

Examination of the skin of the bird can be undertaken in the featherless spaces between the pterylae or feather tracts or in the very young bird before it has acquired its contour feathers.

Dermatitis may be secondary to disease affecting other body systems. For example, infection of the periorbital or paranasal area is often associated with chronic respiratory disease, and irritation of the cloacal skin often follows bouts of diarrhoea or soiling by the bird.

The wing web across the leading edge of the wing (propatagium) is the most usual site for bacterial infections which often lead to self mutilation. Healing in this area may result in loss of elasticity which in turn can lead to a recurrence of signs due to the irritation caused by the stretching and tearing of the skin. Treatment may even involve radical resection under general anaesthesia but this will of course affect flight.

Care should be taken when applying drugs topically to birds to avoid the oily preparations which can rapidly spread over the feathers and destroy their insulating properties. Aqueous solutions or powders are preferable.

Lacerations
Free flying pet birds often suffer trauma and laceration of the skin from other predator pets within the family, cats, dogs, etc.

Infection
Deep puncture wounds are especially prone to infection with *Pasturella spp.* Parenteral and topical broad spectrum antibiotics should be considered in all cases involving puncture wounds.

Wounds involving the crop often result in fistula formation, up to two weeks later. The crop and overlying skin should be sutured in separate layers using synthetic absorbable suture materials.

Burns
Small psittacines, cockatiels, lovebirds etc. when free may fly into fires, gas rings etc. The resultant burns can be quite extensive. The bird should be treated initially for shock; a warm atmosphere (25–30°C) with high humidity is beneficial. The skin should be cleansed and a corticosteroid/antibiotic cream applied. Systemic corticosteroid may be necessary. If required, the skin should be sutured.

Neoplasia
Tumours involving the integument are particularly common in the budgerigar and some may occur when the bird is barely one year of age. Lipomata, fibromata and adenomata are the most common

superficial tumours. Adenomata and adenocarcinomata are particularly common around the uropygial gland. Swelling in this area must be investigated and neoplasia differentiated from simple impaction of the gland with or without infection.

Papillomata occur in the larger parrots. There is always the possibility of haemorrhage with these tumours for although the outer surface may dry and fall off, the tumour irritates the bird and self trauma may take place. Cautery using a silver nitrate stick is often effective if the tumour is small.

Xanthomata occur mainly in budgerigars. They are of characteristic yellow colour and may occur as mere thickening of the skin or as discreet yellow, tumour-like masses.

FEATHERS

Feather picking
Feather picking by the bird itself is a common problem which presents a daunting diagnostic and therapeutic challenge. This problem is discussed fully in Chapter 19.

Bullying
If a bird's feathers are being picked by a bully this can be differentiated from self mutilation since the feathers of the head are also involved. In fact, the back of the head is the most common site for such attacks. This is particularly a problem in cockatiels and cockatoos.

Poor quality feathers
Caged birds are dependent on their owners for food and therefore malnutrition is one of the greatest contributory factors in feather disorders (see Chapter 18).

Unsatisfactory housing and hygiene will result in damaged, dirty feathers.

Humidity plays an important part in the appearance of feathers. If the environment is too dry, poor feather growth may result. In summertime, most birds enjoy daily spraying with tepid water; a small hand-held plant spray is an ideal implement.

The thyroid glands, gonads and adrenal glands are all associated with normal feather growth. A behavioural problem leading to self-plucking and to excessive feather growth may for example result in thyroid exhaustion so that even if the fundamental problem is overcome there is inadequate feather growth.

Damaged feathers
Frequently birds are kept in accommodation which is too small for them. This results in battered, dirty looking feathers due to impact with the wire sides of the cage every time the bird moves.

Broken feathers will not normally regrow until the next moult but forcible extraction will stimulate new feather growth in a short time (4 − 6 weeks).

Stress (or fault) lines and colour breaks.
Stress or fault lines occur where the barbules fail to hook together due to malformation. This results in a structural weakness to the feather vane (see Plate 18:1).

Colour breaks are bands of abnormal colour (for example, a yellow band on a blue feather).

Nutritional deficiencies are considered to be responsible for many of these abnormalities but other causes such as liver disease or lead poisoning should be taken into consideration.

Moulting
Moulting is a normal means by which birds change their plumage. In their natural environment various species generally moult at specific seasons of the year. Cage birds however, exist under varying

environmental conditions and these factors may influence the moulting cycle. Many parrots are tropical birds and moult single feathers throughout the year.

During a moult the bird is under considerable nutritional and physiological stress and the supply of animal protein — a raw chop bone to a large parrot — and replacement of the drinking water with 50% milk and water ensures an increased level of nutrition during the moulting period. Heavy moulting is often associated with puritis so careful examination is necessary to differentiate between this and ectoparasite infestation. Birds with broken feathers should have these removed in order to stimulate new feather growth which takes from 4 − 6 weeks in the healthy bird.

Feather cysts

Feather cysts are more common in canaries than psittacines. They may occur in any species as the result of trauma when the feather is growing within its follicle. The feather curls within the follicle and as it grows the follicle becomes enlarged and bulges from the surface of the skin. (See Plate 5:2). The wall of the follicle becomes thickened and a cheesy exudate forms within. An acute inflammatory reaction may follow and the bird is then attracted to the area. Pecking can cause extensive haemorrhage. Psittacine feather cysts are usually solitary.

Surgical treatment of feather cysts is discussed on page 52.

Psittacine beak and feather disease syndrome

This condition has been variously called beak rot, non responsive dermatitis, Cockatoo feather picking disease or adrenal gland insufficiency. Psittacines other than cockatoos have been reported to be affected and recent work has shown that it does occur in the wild as well as in captive birds. Affected birds show a progressive deterioration in the quantity and quality of normal plumage and eventually lose contour feathers over most areas of the body. The replacement feathers usually show retained feather sheaths and blood within the shafts of the feathers as well as being short and deformed. Lesions also include changes in colour, growth with progressive elongation and development of fault lines. Changes in the beak include overgrowth and deformity, transverse fracture lines and alteration in colour and glossiness (See Plate 10:1)

There appears to be no evidence of adrenal, thyroid or other endocrine gland insufficiency in the birds studied. Diagnosis depends upon microscopic examination of developing feathers. Intracytoplasmic inclusion bodies are found in cells of the epidermis, feather sheaths or feather pulp. Virus particles have also been demonstrated by direct electronmicroscopy and it appears these may be members of the parvovirus family (McOrist et al 1984). The clinical abnormalities are due to a dystrophy induced within the epidermis of the feathers, the beak and the claws due to multifocal necrosis of epidermal cells. Atrophy of the thymus and burse of Fabricus seen in some affected birds indicated immunosuppression and death can often be due to secondary bacterial invasion.

French Moult

Pass and Perry (1985) have conducted exhaustive studies into psittacine beak and feather disease syndrome and are of the opinion that, in Australia, French Moult has identical lesions and the conditions are synonymous. In other parts of the world the pathogenisis appears less clear. Budgerigar fledgling disease has been attributed to a papovavirus. Obviously, further studies are needed to clarify the relationship between viruses and French Moult. A multifactorial aetology is feasible. In Britain and the United States, French Moult refers to a condition seen in budgerigars, cockatiels and lovebirds in which feather replacement is significantly delayed following loss of primary feathers. Young budgerigars appear to be most commonly affected and clinical signs can vary considerably. In chronic cases most of the flight and contour feathers in the active growing stage are lost and these birds are known as creepers or crawlers since they are unable to fly. The feathers are often mis-shapen and stunted and when shed often contain blood within the quill which may be due to increased capillary fragility. Genetic factors do not appear to be involved but the incidence of the disease increases as the breeding season progresses. There is no specific treatment but mildly affected birds may recover provided a high nutritional level is maintained. Badly affected birds should be culled. In view of the evidence that a high level of vitamin A in the diet may increase the percentage of affected young, Taylor, (1982) suggested that diets containing high levels of vitamin A should be avoided.

Ectoparasites

External parasites are relatively rare in pet birds especially in caged birds. Nevertheless, the sale of avian ectoparasite sprays continues to increase. Practically every feather picking bird will have been subjected to a thorough spraying by the owner before being presented to the veterinarian. Unfortunately, this action will further dry out and irritate the underlying skin, thus furthering the bird's discomfort and pruritis.

Lice

Many species of biting lice (order *Mallophaga*) can be found on both domestic and wild birds but they are of little problem to the average pet bird. They are more of a problem on passerine than psittacine birds. They can be successfully and safely treated with Bromocyclen ('Alugan', Hoechst) either in powder or spray form.

Bugs (order *Hemiptera*)

The bugs that are parasitic on birds belong mainly to the family *Cimicidae*.

Fleas

Fleas rarely attack cage birds although domestic poultry often serve as hosts.

Ticks and Mites (order *Arachnida*)

This order includes some of the most important and most pathogenic ectoparasites found on cage and aviary birds. Ticks, especially soft ticks (order *Metastigmata*, family *Argasidea*) are occasionally found on caged birds.

Mites, (order *Mesostigmata*) present most problems. *Dermanyssus gallinae*, the red mite, can be found on budgerigars. In addition there are many non-pathogenic feather mites. *Dermanyssus spp.* only attacks the host at night and therefore control should involve removing birds from their cages during the day and thoroughly cleaning the cage, using either BHC or bromocyclen ('Alugan', Hoechst) as a spray. The latter is a safer product (see chapter 20).

THE BEAK

The horny beak or rhamphotheca replaces the lips and teeth found in mammals. It is a hard, keratinised, epidermal structure covering the rostral parts of both the upper and lower jaws. It consists of dermis, which is closely attached to the periosteum of the jawbones, and the overlying epidermis, which is modified with an extremely thick stratum corneum. The cells of the stratum corneum contain free calcium phosphate and crystals of hydroxyapatite which, together with the keratin present, gives the beak its characteristic hardness and strength.

In psittacines, as well as some other species, the skin at the base of the upper bill is swollen and sometimes pigmented (e.g. male budgerigars). It is highly sensitive and is known as the cere. Both upper and lower beaks and also the cere are well supplied with sensory nerve endings from the trigeminal nerve. The external nares or nostrils open through the cere. In all the parrot family, the upper beak is massive and curved whereas the lower is much smaller and roughly horseshoe shaped.

Beak Abnormalities

Simple overgrowth is probably the most common beak abnormality presented in general practice. This may be due to malocclusion, or insufficient normal wear and honing. It may also be due to localised disease such as a neoplasm or a sign of liver disfunction or metabolic bone disease. Most usually it is the upper beak which is affected but due to the problems of malocclusion which occur frequently in psittacines, both upper and lower beaks may be affected. Regular and careful trimming using heavy scissors or nail clippers will help. Rasping with an emery board is beneficial. It should be remembered that the beak, or rhamphotheca, is a living structure and is continually growing towards the tip. If there are any abnormalities in the growth rate, overgrowth and/or deformities may occur. Surgical correction of beak abnormalities is discussed in Chapter 5.

Deformities of the beak are a component of the Psittacine beak and feather disease syndrome (see page 106).

In budgerigars and some of the other small psittacines (cockatiels) infection with *cnemidocoptes pilae* can result in gross beak overgrowth and deformity. The mite lives entirely within the skin of the host feeding on keratin. Transmission may be direct from parent to fledgling or indirect by rubbing the head on parts of the cage or other objects. Recent evidence supports the theory that transmission may be to the young bird by the parent before feather growth has occurred and while the bird is still immunologically incompetent. Infestation with cnemidocoptic mange does not appear to be highly contagious; often only one or two members of a flock are affected.

In the early stages the mite burrows into the skin in the region of the cere and at the base of the beak. (See Plate 10:2). Later the whole beak will be found to be honeycombed with minute holes caused by the mites burrowing into the keratinised epithelium. This in turn may interfere with the growth of the beak, particularly the upper mandible, and so lead to deformity. In advanced cases the commisures of the mouth also show lesions. The skin around the eyes, the vent and the legs and feet, are areas that are also susceptible although in the budgerigar it is the head which is usually affected. Sometimes horny outgrowths occur, resembling keratomata. Puritis is seldom a marked feature although Oldham and Beresford-Jones (1954) reported feather picking in a parakeet with a confirmed infection.

Diagnosis can be confirmed by examination of scrapings and identification of the mite. Differential diagnosis is needed in budgerigars since the disease may occasionally be confused with neoplastic changes involving the cere and beak, e,g, osteocarcomata and fibrosarcomata.

Treatment with a mineral oil application using a cotton tipped applicator is safe and effective in the long term. Quicker results can be obtained using a 10% emulsion of Benzylbenzoate applied at once/twice weekly intervals. This is potentially toxic, however. Mason (1980) reported the use of Oterna ear drops (Glaxovet) which contain 0.1% betamethasone, 0.5% neomycine sulphate and 5% monosulphuram. This preparation has been used by the author with no sign of toxicity. Elimination of the mite will prevent further damage to the beak but the already existing deformity is irreversible.

Candidiasis ('beak rot')
Infection of the junction between the epithelium lining the oral cavity and the horny tissue of the beak by candida albicans causes an accumulation of soft necrotic material at this site. Bizarre abnormalities of the mandible result. Nystatin, gentian violet or chlorhexidine may be used for treatment.

Nutritional Deficiencies
Imbalance of vitamins A and D and calcium can sometimes lead to osteodystrophies involving the beak, frequently called 'rubber beak' by the layman. The loss of rigidity of the beak leads to malnutrition and death unless forced feeding is undertaken. Supplementation of the diet with calcium and vitamins A and D is the treatment of choice. Candidiasis may sometimes be a sequel to this.

Tumours
Keratomata, osteosarcomata and fibrosarcomata have all been recorded involving the beak of psittacines particularly budgerigars.

Haemorrhage from the beak
Haemorrhage may occur during beak trimming or as a result of trauma. Silver nitrate, ferric chloride or other styptic solutions may be used but care should be taken to avoid the bird swallowing the chemical.

CERE

The fleshy, highly sensitive skin at the base of the upper beak is known as the cere. This can be useful in the budgerigar as a means of determining sex, since it is blue coloured in the adult male and brown in the adult female. Male budgerigars undergoing hormonal imbalance may show alteration in colour of the cere, the so-called 'sex change' phenomenon.

In ageing hen budgerigars the cere often undergoes brown hypertrophy. This is a normal occurrence and requires no treatment unless the excess tissue is interfering with the external nares in which case the excess tissue can be gently removed.

The organ is susceptible to infestation with Cnemidocoptes spp. mites, and powderiness or loss of bloom should be carefully investigated.

As a result of respiratory disease the cere may lose its plumpness, become atrophied and the nostrils distorted. Rhinoliths may also form in the external nares causing further distortion. These can usually be removed by gentle manipulation, sometimes without anaesthetic (see page 55).

Budgerigars and other psittacine birds may occasionally develop abscesses involving the cere. These appear as whitish, hard swellings, distorting the surface of the organ. Lancing and curettage is the treatment of choice particularly if the abscess is occluding the nostrils. Care must be taken to control haemorrhage which sometimes can be copious. General anaesthesia is preferable. Haemorrhage can usually be controlled using silver nitrate or ferric chloride solution. White blood cells of birds do not contain lysosomes and therefore the pus is always of a semi-solid, cheesy consistency. Depending on the value of the bird, bacteriological investigation and antibiotic sensitivity testing may be worthwhile. The cavity should be left open for drainage and packed with an appropriate antibiotic powder.

UROPYGIAL OR PREEN GLAND

Although the composition of the secretion of the uropygial gland varies in different species of birds it usually contains a complex of water repellent waxes, lipids and proteins. The gland is well developed in the budgerigar but absent in parrots of the Amazon species in which epidermal glands appear to perform the same function. Coles (1985) comments that removal of the preen gland does not seem to have any adverse effects. It is a bilobed gland lying dorsally near the tip of the tail; each lobe is drained by a duct which opens on a uropygial papilla which is surmounted by a circlet of feathers. In the budgerigar it is known that this circlet of feathers acts as a wick for receiving the secretion which during preening is transferred on to the beak and then in turn onto the feathers. The secretion helps to keep the feathers, beak and skin supple and in good condition. It is also important in preventing the growth of micro-organisms and helps to waterproof the feathers.

Enlargement of the gland can occur as the result of infection, abscessation, blocking of the duct and neoplasia (See Plate 5:3). Bleeding from the tail in the budgerigar almost invariably involves the preen gland in the author's experience. The haemorrhage may be due to simple feather picking or neoplasia involving the gland. Surgical excision using electro cautery can be undertaken with reasonable success.

REFERENCES

ALTMANN, R. B. (1977) Parasitic Diseases of Cage Birds. Current Vet. Theory (VI) p. 682.

ARNALL, L. and KEYMER, I. F. (1975) Bird Diseases. Ballière Tindall, London.

BEACH, J. E. (1962) Diseases of Budgerigars and other Cage Birds. Vet. Rec. **74** 10, 63, 134.

COLES, B. H. (1985) Avian Medicine and Surgery. Blackwell, Oxford.

COOPER, J. E. (1984) A Practical Approach to Cage Birds. In Practice **5,** 29.

ENSLEY, P. (1979) Caged Bird Medicine and Husbandry. Vet Clinics of North America **9** 499.

HARRISON, G. J. and HARRISON, L. R. (1986) 'Clinical Avian Medicine and Surgery'. W. B. Saunders Philadelphia.

HARRISON, G. J. (1984) Feather Disorders. Vet. Clinics North America 14.2 179.

JACOBSON, E. R., CLUBB, S., SIMPSON, C., WALSH, M., LOTHROP, C., GASKIN, J., BAUR, J., HINES, S., KOLLIAS, G. V., DOULOS, P. and HARRISON, G. (1986) Feather and Beak Distrophy in Cockatoos. Clinico-Pathologic Evaluations J.A.V.M.A. **189** 999.

KING, A. S. and McLELLAND, J. (1984) Birds, Their Structure and Function. Baillière Tindall, Eastbourne.

LAFEBER, T. J. (1971) Feather Disorders of Common Caged Birds. Current Vet. Therapy (VI) p. 371. W. B. Saunders, Philadelphia.

LAFEBER, T. J. (1977) Feather Disorders of Common Caged Birds. Current Vet. Therapy (VI) p. 675. W. B. Saunders, Philadelphia.

McORIST, S., BLACK, D. G., PASS, D. A., SCOTT, P. C. and MARSHALL, J. (1984) Beak and Feather Dystrophy in Wild Sulpher Crested Cockatoos (Cacatua gabrita). J. Wildlife Dis. **20:**120.

MASON, K. (1980) The Treatment of Scaly Face and Scaly Legs in Budgerigars. Australian Vet. Journal **56** 400.

OLDHAM, J. N. and BERESFORD JONES, W. P. (1954) Observations on the Occurrence of Cnemidocoptes pilae in Budgerigars and a Parakeet. Brit. Vet. Journal **110** 29.

PASS, D. A. and PERRY, R. A. (1984) The Pathology of Psittacine Beak and Feather Disease. Australian Vet. Journal **61,** 3, 69

PASS, D. A. and PERRY, R. A. (1985) Psittacine Beak and Feather Disease, an Update. Australian Vet. Practit. **15,** 55.

PETRAK, M. L. (1982) Ed. Diseases of Cage and Aviary Birds (2nd Edition). Lea and Febiger, Philadelphia.

STEINER, C. V. and DAVIES, R. B. (1981) 'Caged Bird Medicine'. Iowa State University Press, Ames.

TAYLOR, G. T. (1982) 'Diseases of Cage and Aviary Birds', (2nd Edition). Ed. Petrak, M. L. p. 361.

TURNER, T. (1985) 'Manual of Exotic Pets' p. 106. BSAVA Publications.

COLOUR PLATES

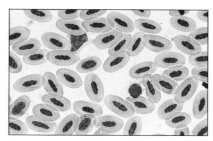

PLATE 4:1 Blood from a healthy green-winged macaw showing normal red cells, a typical lymphocyte and a typical thrombocyte. It is usual for lymphocytes to appear deformed by close contact with other cells. The thrombocyte has irregular (partially activated) cytoplasm.

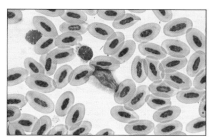

PLATE 4:2 A typical monocyte, a thrombocyte and a disintegrating red cell nucleus from a healthy macaw.

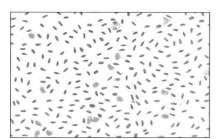

PLATE 4:3 A low power view of psittacine blood showing a number of disintegrating nuclei from disrupted red cells.

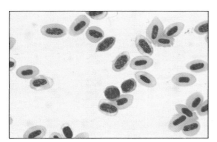

PLATE 4:4 Mature red cells and immature red cells (erythroblasts) in various stages of maturation from a healthy budgerigar.

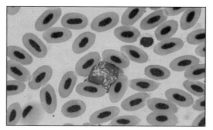

PLATE 4:5 A typical heterophil with a bilobed nucleus and brick red, spiculate cytoplasmic granules from an African grey parrot.

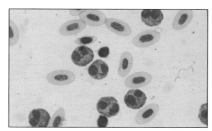

PLATE 4:6 An increased number of heterophils in a macaw with acute respiratory infection. The nuclear structure and cytoplasmic granules are relatively normal but the cells appear condensed.

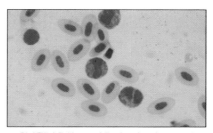

PLATE 4:7 Heterophils showing decreased nuclear lobulation (left shift) from the same macaw with respiratory infection.

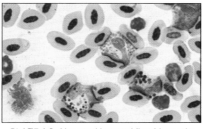

PLATE 4:8 Abnormal heterophils with poorly lobed nuclei and abnormal cytoplasmic granules from an Amazon parrot with acute respiratory infection.

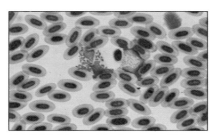

PLATE 4:9 A heterophil and an eosinophil from a healthy budgerigar. The heterophil has brick red, spiculate granules and the eosinophil has smaller, round, brightly eosinophilic granules.

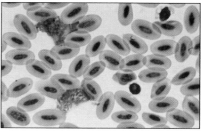

PLATE 4:10 A heterophil and an atypical eosinophil with blue-staining granules from a healthy lesser sulphur-crested cockatoo.

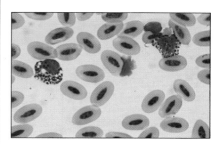

PLATE 4:11 Typical basophils and two disintegrating red cell nuclei from the same sulphur-crested cockatoo.

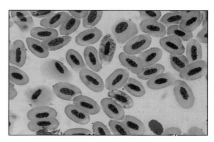

PLATE 4:12 Two red cells containing *Haemoproteus handai* parasites from a Moluccan cockatoo.

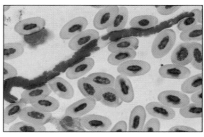

PLATE 4:13 A microfilarian from a Moluccan cockatoo.

Plate 5:1
Xanthoma in a budgerigar *(Melopsittacus undulatus)*. These tumours may easily be confused with multilocular abscesses.

Plate 5:2
Feather cyst in a Blue Headed parrot *(Pionus menstrous)*.

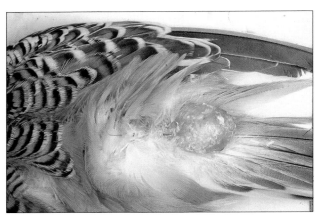

Plate 5:3
Adenocarcinoma of the uropygial gland in a budgerigar *(Melopsittacus undulatus)*.

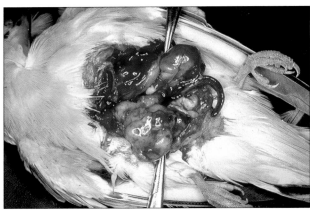

Plate 5:4
Seminoma in a budgerigar *(Melopsittacus undulatus)*.

Plate 5:5
Cataract in an African Grey parrot *(Psittacus erithacus)*.

Plate 5:6
Abscessation of the periorbital sinuses of an African Grey parrot *(Psittacus erithacus)*.

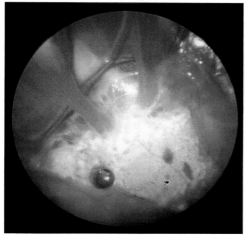

Plate 6:1
Laparoscopy: General view of the thorax/abdomen showing lung tissue and muscle bundles. The gonads lie to the right.

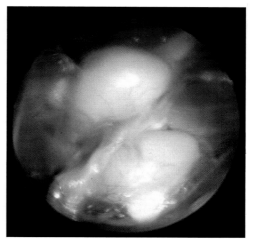

Plate 6:2
Laparoscopy: The paired testes, with a section of kidney lying above them.

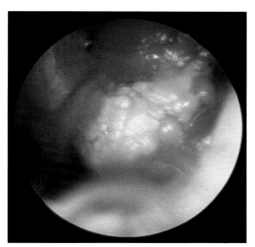

Plate 6:3
Laparoscopy: The mature ovary showing follicles, with a section of kidney above.

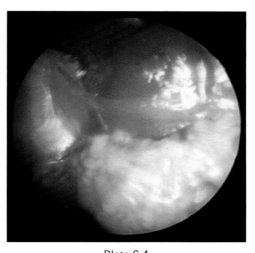

Plate 6:4
Laparoscopy: The immature ovary where follicles have not yet developed.

Plate 8:1
Psittacosis in an oranged tipped Amazon parrot. Note how the bird is fluffed up, has the eyes closed and is mouth breathing. A bird in this condition often has problems perching.

Plate 9:1
A budgerigar with an abdominal mass showing paresis of
the left leg.

Plate 9:2
An egg bound budgerigar with an egg presented at the
cloaca.

Plate 10:1
Cockatoo beak
and feather
syndrome
(Cacatua
sulphurea)

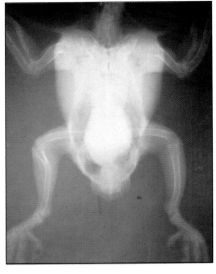

Plate 12:1
Radiograph of an
African grey
parrot (Psittacus
erithacus)
showing
distortion of the
skeleton due to
metabolic bone
disease.

Plate 10:2
Cnemidoceptic Mange

Plate 12:2
Young African grey parrot (Psittacus erithacus) affected
with metabolic bone disease.

Plate 12:3
Blue-eyed cockatoo *(Cacatua ophthalmica)* showing deformation of the upper and lower beaks caused by metabolic bone disease.

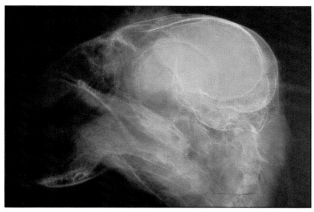

Plate 12:4
Radiograph of the head of a Blue-eyed cockatoo *(Cacatua ophthalmica)* affected with metabolic bone disease.

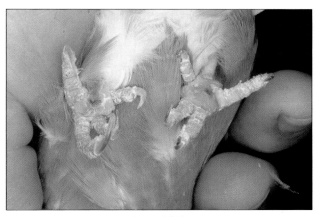

Plate 12:5
Feet of budgerigar *(Melopsittacus undulatus)* showing bumblefoot abscesses.

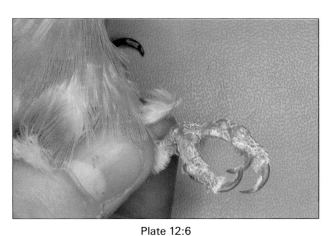

Plate 12:6
Budgerigar *(Melopsittacus undulatus)* showing tophi on the feet caused by deposition of urate crystals.

Plate 12:7
Swelling of the foot of a budgerigar *(Melopsittacus undulatus)* caused by an aluminium marking band.

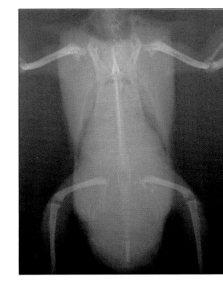

Plate 12:8
Radiograph of a budgerigar *(Melopsittacus undulatus)* showing polyostotic hyperostosis.

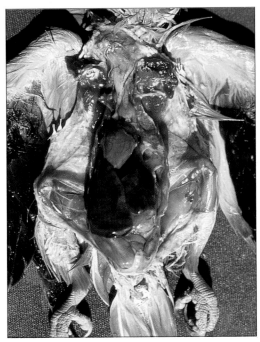

Plate 13:1
Opened carcase of Amazon parrot
(*Amazona sp*) with psittacosis, showing
enlarged dark liver.

Plate 13:2
Liver showing surface haemorrhages
caused by psittacosis.

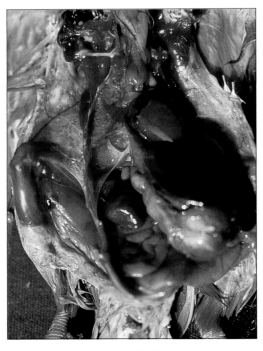

Plate 13:3
Liver displaced to show enlarged spleen
due to psittacosis.

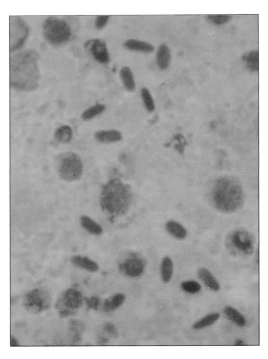

Plate 13:4
Ziehl-Neelsen stained liver impression smear
showing *Chlamydia psittaci* inclusion bodies.

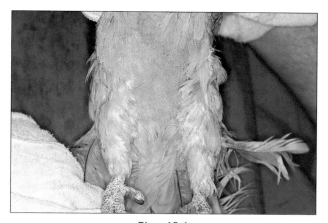

Plate 18:1
An Amazon parrot showing fret lines, deformed feathers and poor feather quality due to nutritional deficiencies.

Plate 18:2
The budgerigar on the left is suffering hypothyroidism and is assuming the typical posture. The bird on the right is a normal for comparison.

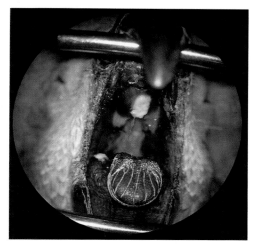

Plate 18:3
A typical choanal abscess in an African grey parrot on a Vitamin A deficient diet. Note also the lingual abscess on the left of the tongue.

Plate 18:4
A yellow fronted Amazon with a rhinolith totally blocking the right nostril.

Plate 18:5
An anaesthetised African grey parrot prior to the surgical removal of a periorbital abscess which proved sterile on culture.

Plate 19:1
A bored macaw showing a totally bald body, but a fully feathered head. Any bird so presented should be considered a behavioural problem.

Plate 19:2
An African grey parrot showing normal feather regrowth two months after the initial placement of the collar. This author prefers riveting the collar as shown as birds appear to accept it more readily.

Plate 19:3
An African grey parrot wearing an Elizabethan collar in the 'reversed' position.

Plate 19:4
Trauma to the back of the head caused by a cage mate.

Chapter 11

THE CARDIOVASCULAR SYSTEM

J. E. Cooper B.V.Sc., D.T.V.M., F.I.Biol., Cert. L.A.S., F.R.C.V.S.

In this chapter emphasis is laid on primary conditions of the cardiovascular system; only brief mention will be made of clinical or pathological conditions (e.g. infection, poisoning, metabolic disturbances) in which, *inter alia,* changes in the heart, blood vessels, blood and lymphatics may be seen. It must be remembered that there are few disease processes which do not impinge in some way or another on the cardiovascular system.

Before discussing the diseases of the cardiovascular system a brief resumé of its anatomy and physiology is desirable. The structure and constituents of the blood are discussed in Chapter 4 and will not therefore be covered in any detail here. Brief mention is made later of the lymphoid and lymphatic systems.

ANATOMY AND PHYSIOLOGY

Insofar as the anatomy of the cardiovascular system is concerned, the heart of psittacine birds is relatively large. It is conical in shape and has four chambers — two atria and two ventricles — and a right aortic arch. Harrison (1986) provides an excellent description of the heart and main blood vessels of the Amazon parrot. The veins are thin and the right jugular — which can be used for blood sampling — is usually larger than the left. Birds have a renal portal system, receiving venous blood from the legs and elsewhere, as well as an arterial supply from the aorta. In theory this renal portal system should prove a complication — for example, an injectable anaesthetic given into the leg muscles may be detoxified by the kidney — but in practice no such effect is usually observed.

The heart rate of psittacine birds can be very high. Arnall and Keymer (1975) give values ranging from 120—200 beats per minute (African grey parrot) to 240—600 (budgerigar).

In the past, relatively little work has been carried out specifically on the cardiovascular system of psittacine birds. However, some surveys of cardiac and other pathological conditions have included birds of the order Psittaciformes. Examples are given in Fiennes (1982) and elsewhere. In aviculture circles a number of diseases are considered to be associated with some dysfunction of the heart or blood vessels (Coffey, 1975). Thus, such terms as 'apoplexy', 'fainting' and 'vertigo' are not infrequently used (Arnall and Keymer, 1975). However, as has been emphasised elsewhere (Cooper, 1978), the exact meaning and significance of such descriptions remain uncertain. Some are likely to involve the cardiovascular system but further research is needed to elucidate this.

Information of relevance to parrots is to be found in publications dealing with the diseases of other species of bird — for example, in the paper by Cooper and Pomerance (1982) which describes some pathological lesions of the heart of birds of prey. Arnall and Keymer (1975) and Wallach and Boever (1983) discuss circulatory disturbances in companion birds, including members of the Psittaciformes, and there is a section on cardiovascular disease in Rübel and Isenbügel (1985). However, in many books the subject is not indexed and there is only scant information in the text. It seems likely that this reflects lack of knowledge and the difficulty of diagnosis rather than indicating that cardiovascular diseases are rare.

In this chapter the clinical and *post-mortem* investigation of cardiovascular disease in parrots will be described. Specific conditions will be discussed, with particular reference to pathogenesis, diagnosis and treatment.

CLINICAL EXAMINATION

Observation should precede handling and clinical examination. Clinical signs may be less readily seen when the bird is alarmed or being restrained. However, once the parrot is in the hand, auscultation should take place immediately. The practitioner should familiarise himself with normal heart sounds by routine examination of birds submitted for other reasons. He should also check the normal appearance of mucous membranes: there is considerable variation, even within species, and some varieties e.g. lutinos, may show a blue colouration even when in good health. Light anaesthesia, using ketamine (5 – 15 mg/kg bodyweight) or methoxyflurane, will greatly facilitate examination. It will minimise the risk of injury to the handler, reduce fear and apprehension in the bird and make auscultation easier.

Clinical signs of a cardiovascular disorder may be similar to those seen in respiratory disease — coughing, dyspnoea, cyanosis, syncopy, lethargy and 'seizures'. The practitioner should be aware that pneumonia or air sacculitis is often accompanied by pericarditis or other cardiac changes.

On auscultation the clinician should check a) whether the cardiac rhythm is normal in terms of clarity and frequency and b) if any murmurs are present. Both sides of the stethoscope should be used: the diaphragm tends to be more sensitive to murmurs. A healthy bird has two heart sounds: the first is the longer. The high heart rate of many species, especially when being handled, can make interpretation difficult.

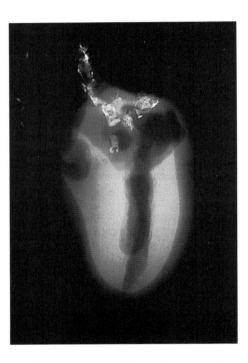

Plate 11:1
Post mortem radiograph of the heart and aorta of a thirty year old Amazon parrot showing mineralisation of the blood vessels.

Radiography can be of value in diagnosis. Careful positioning of the patient is essential (Cooper and Kreel, 1976) and both dorso-ventral and lateral views are required. Whole-body radiographs should be taken of small birds. Important points to note are a) the size and position of the heart, and b) (particularly easily seen in lateral radiographs) the size and appearance of the great vessels. The heart is normally visible in ventro-dorsal radiographs as a triangular or cone-shaped soft tissue density in the midline (see Plate 3:2). Laterally it appears elliptical. Mineralisation of blood vessels may be visible: a hand lens is recommended to detect these and other subtle changes (See Plate 11:1). Additional points which may aid diagnosis are the appearance of the lung fluids and the size of the liver. A very useful but little known work on the radiological examination of the larger parrots is the Dissertation by Rübel (1985).

The greatest aid to the investigation of cardiovascular disease is electrocardiography. ECG(EKG) equipment is used routinely in many North American avian practices but relatively infrequently in this country. Nevertheless, in view of the financial and sentimental value of many of the birds submitted for examination it may soon be considered a standard means of monitoring birds during surgery or other veterinary procedures.

ECG will help in the detection of cardiac arrhythmias and disturbances of the conduction system. In recent years there has been an upsurge of interest in avian electrocardiography and normal data are now available for certain species (Miller, 1986; Zenoble and Graham, 1979, 1981).

As was mentioned earlier, a number of other pathological conditions are relevant to the cardiovascular system — for example anaemia — and routine venepuncture in order to obtain blood for haematological and biochemical tests (and in some cases for bacteriological culture) should be considered a standard part of clinical examination.

POST MORTEM EXAMINATION

Many cases of cardiovascular disease will only be diagnosed *post mortem.* The practitioner should be prepared to examine birds that die or to submit them elsewhere. Gross lesions of the heart and blood vessels can usually be detected readily but the *post mortem* examination has to be thorough and a hand lens may prove necessary. The person performing the necropsy must be familiar with the normal appearance of the cardiovascular system. Appropriate samples may need to be taken for subsequent light (and possibly even electron) microscopy.

The heart should be observed *in situ* before it is removed from the body. If it is large enough (e.g. macaws) it can be dissected and the chambers examined. In small birds, however, histological examination alone is likely to yield more useful results.

Samples for histology are probably best taken following the technique described by Cooper and Pomerance (1982). The heart is removed *in toto* and then, following examination with the naked eye or a lens, is trimmed in two planes — a transverse section of the base of the great vessels and a longitudinal section through the ventricle(s). *Post mortem* investigation of the blood vessels will require careful dissection and this may prove time-consuming and difficult. In a freshly dead bird the escape of unclotted blood from the vessels will hamper dissection and may mask pathological changes. It is preferable to allow 2 — 4 hours to elapse following the death of the bird and then to dissect the vessels which contain clotted blood. An alternative approach, not usually practicable in veterinary practice but which ensures optimum material for laboratory investigation, is for the bird to be perfused with buffered formol saline or glutaraldehyde. This technique should certainly be considered if a valuable bird is involved and the owner or the veterinary surgeon requires comprehensive pathological reports on underlying lesions.

TYPES OF CARDIOVASCULAR DISEASE

There are various ways of classifying cardiovascular disease but the following modification of Fiennes (1982) provides a useful framework:-

1. Diseases of the heart
   Pericarditis
   Myocarditis
   Endocarditis
   Other non-inflammatory changes (parasitic lesions, neoplasia, 'round heart disease', congenital and developmental abnormalities, e.g. ventricular septal defects, diseases of the conduction system).

2. Diseases of the blood vessels
   Arteritis
   Non-inflammatory changes (degenerative and sclerotic lesions, thrombosis, embolism).

3. Diseases of the blood (anaemia, neoplasia).

4. Diseases of the lymphatic system (neoplasia).

5. Diseases associated with changes in the circulatory system but not primarily cardiovascular in nature.
   Haemorrhage (agonal, terminal; associated with shock, dietary disorders, injury or organic diseases)
   Oedema

The above will be discussed briefly, with particular reference to clinical diagnosis and treatment.

DISEASES OF THE HEART

These are not uncommon in psittacine birds, but are often only detected *post mortem*. Pericarditis can be concomitant to respiratory infection, especially air sacculitis, and abnormal heart sounds may be detected on auscultation. Hydropericardium may be suspected if heart sounds are very muffled. Sometimes it is a feature of infective cardiac disease but often is terminal to circulatory disorders or other diseases e.g. pneumonia. In cases of visceral gout (see Chapter 9) urates may be deposited in the pericardium. They are not usually detected in the live bird but may be observed during laparoscopy.

Myocarditis may be due to an infection or a toxic factor. It is difficult to diagnose in life but an altered ECG pattern may be an indication. Hypertrophy of the heart is sometimes seen *post mortem*. Fiennes (1982) describes it in birds which fly to great heights or long distances and Arnall and Keymer (1972) state that 'an energetic bird will have a proportionately larger heart than a more sluggish one'. The condition can also be pathological — for example, following a chronic debilitating disease. In the larger parrots such hypertrophy may sometimes be suspected on auscultation: there is tachycardia and an arrhythmia may be evident. Arnall and Keymer (1975) describe heart sounds in some cases as 'unusually loud and sloppy'.

Endocarditis is not uncommon in birds, including psittacines. Again it is generally only detected *post mortem*: the valves are usually involved.

Parasites are sometimes seen in the heart muscle. They may only be an incidental pathological finding but can be of significance. Keymer (1982) points out that 'aberrant type' *Leucocytozoon* is becoming more common in psittacines and can be responsible for illness lasting 24 − 48 hours, followed by death in nestlings.

Cardiac neoplasms are rare. It should be possible to detect (or suspect) such a lesion clinically but treatment is unlikely to be of any avail.

A condition resembling 'round heart disease' (toxic heart degeneration) has been described in psittacine birds by Miller (1987). Congenital and developmental abnormalities are poorly documented, probably because relatively few birds are subjected to a thorough pathological examination after death.

Rupture of the heart is sometimes diagnosed at *post mortem* examination. The atria are usually affected and the condition is generally attributable to pathological changes elsewhere in the body.

DISEASES OF THE BLOOD VESSELS

The commonest cause of arteritis in birds is frost-bite. Parrots kept in outside aviaries may develop dry gangrene of digits; the latter usually slough. The condition should be suspected if during (or following) cold weather a bird shows locomotory disturbances, pecks at its feet or has discoloured digits.

Non-inflammatory changes in the blood vessels are not uncommon but are usually only detected *post mortem*. Fiennes (1982) lists arterial diseases he encountered among various Orders of birds. Atheroma was seen in a number of psittacines. Medial calcification ('arteriosclerosis') is also sometimes seen in aged parrots *post mortem*. The aetiology of both conditions is unclear but dietary factors may be involved. Obesity may be significant in the case of atheromatosis, while calcium/phosphorus/vitamin imbalances are likely to be associated with medial calcification. Birds with such lesions may show no clinical signs, the arterial changes only being detected on pathological examination, but severe cases may cause sudden death. Sometimes mineralisation of blood vessels can be detected in the live bird by radiography.

Dilated, distorted, 'varicose' veins are sometimes seen in birds, especially canaries. They are not common in parrots and when they do occur the cause is often obstruction to venous return — for example, by a subcutaneous lipoma.

In addition to the above, a number of lay terms are used by aviculturists and some of these may refer to cardiovascular disorders. Examples are given by Arnall and Keymer (1975). 'Apoplexy', for example, describes a condition characterised by inco-ordination, loss of consciousness and circulatory collapse. Some cases recover but the majority die, often within a few minutes. *Post mortem* examination may reveal haemorrhage in the brain but it is important to distinguish this from intra-osseous haemorrhage, which is a common agonal (terminal) sign in birds (Cooper, 1978). Arnall and Keymer (1975) are quite unequivocal about 'apoplexy': they state that 'the cause lies in the circulation' and suggest that it is associated with a 'generalised rise in blood pressure, injury, degenerations in the blood vessel walls or because of some abnormal effect of nerves on blood vessels in various organs'.

Therapy of 'apoplexy' and other conditions of doubtful aetiology can only be supportive (see later — non-specific treatment).

TREATMENT

Specific therapy of cardiovascular disease depends upon the cause.

Inflammatory conditions can be treated using antimicrobial agents coupled, where appropriate, with corticosteroids.

There is no specific therapy for visceral gout (see Chapter 9)

Parasitic lesions present problems. In the first instance it is not always clear whether parasites detected *post mortem* are the cause of illness or death. A variety of anthelmintic and antiprotozoal agents may kill parasites but dead organisms in the tissues may evoke a severe inflammatory reaction. If therapy is to be attempted care must be taken; it is wise in the first instance to restrict treatment to a small number of birds in case an adverse response occurs.

Treatment of anaemia, haemorrhage and oedema is covered elsewhere in this book.

Corticosteroids and benzodiazepines can be useful in controlling certain atrial and ventricular arrhythmias (Miller, 1987). Digoxin has a half-life of one day in sparrows *(Passer domesticus)* (Miller, personal communication). A dose of 0.02mg/kg bodyweight once a day for five days will produce a plasma concentration of 1.6 nanograms/ml — and this is within the therapeutic range for mammals. Such a dosage regime can be tried in psittacine birds but the client must be warned that the drug is not licensed for the species and advised that the treatment of heart disease in birds is still in its infancy. Other standard anti-arrhythmic drugs, such as procainamide, propanolol and quinidine may have a part to play in avian work but still have to be evaluated.

Insofar as non-specific treatment is concerned, birds in which cardiovascular disease is suspected should be subjected to as few stressors as possible. Every effort must be made to minimise disturbance due to noise or movement. Subdued lighting may calm the bird. The patient should also not exert itself too much — for instance by prolonged flying or climbing. Careful design of the cage/aviary or re-arrangment of the 'furniture' will help in this respect.

If a parrot is seriously ill — for example, following 'apoplexy' — supportive treatment is indicated. The bird should be kept warm, in the dark or subdued light, and fluids administered by the oral, subcutaneous or intravenous routes. Corticosteroids and glucose may be of value.

CONCLUSIONS

There is an urgent need for a more scientific and systematic approach to the diagnosis of cardiovascular disease in psittacine birds. The veterinary surgeon can play a part by collating data on clinical cases, by ensuring that birds are subjected to *post mortem* and laboratory investigation and by reporting his findings.

REFERENCES.

ARNALL, L. and KEYMER, I. F. (1975). 'Bird Diseases'. Baillière Tindall, London.

COFFEY, D. J. (1975). Ailments. In 'Encyclopedia of Cage and Aviary Birds' by C. H. Rogers. Pelham, London.

COOPER, J. E. (1978). 'Veterinary Aspects of Captive Birds of Prey'. Standfast Press, Glos.

COOPER, J. E. and KREEL, L. (1976). Radiological examination of birds: report of a small series. Journal of Small Animal Practice **17**, 799-808.

COOPER, J. E. and POMERANCE, A. (1982). Cardiac lesions in birds of prey. Journal of Comparative Pathology **92**, 161-168.

ENSLEY, P. K. and HATKIN, J. (1979). Congestive heart failure in a greater hill mynah. Journal of the American Veterinary Medicine Association **175**, 1010-1013.

FIENNES, R. N. T-W. (1982). Diseases of the cardiovascular system, blood and lymphatic system. In 'Diseases of Cage and Aviary Birds' edited by M. L. Petrak. 2nd edition. Lea and Febiger, Philadelphia.

KEYMER, I. F. (1982). Parasitic diseases. In Petrak, M. L. (editor) 'Diseases of Cage and Aviary Birds'. Lea and Febiger, Philadelphia.

McKIBBEN, J. S. and HARRISON, G. J. (1986). Clinical anatomy. In 'Clinical Avian Medicine and Surgery' edited by G. J. Harrison and L. R. Harrison. W. B. Saunders, Philadelphia.

MILLER, M. S. (1987). Electrocardiography. In 'Clinical Avian Medicine and Surgery' edited by G. J. Harrison and L. R. Harrison. W. B. Saunders, Philadelphia.

MILLER, M. S. (1987). Do pet birds get heart disease? How do we diagnose and treat birds with heart disease? Paper presented at World Veterinary Association Congress, Montreal, August 1987.

PECKHAM, M. C. (1984). Vices and miscellaneous diseases and conditions. In 'Diseases of Poultry' edited by M. S. Hofstad *et al*. 8th edition. Iowa State University Press, Ames.

RÜBEL, A (1985). 'Röntgenuntersuchungen bei Inneren Erkrankungen von Grossen Psittaziden'. Dissertation, University of Zurich.

RÜBEL, A. and ISENBÜGEL, E. (1985). Papagein. In 'Krankheiten der Heimtiere' edited by K. Gabrisch and P. Zwart. Schlütersche, Hannover.

STEINER, C. V. (1980). The cardiac-racing phenomenon in parakeets. VM/SAC **76**, 250.

WALLACH, J. D. and BOEVER, W. J. (1983). 'Diseases of Exotic Animals'. W. B. Saunders, Philadelphia.

WALLACH, J. D. and FLIEG, G. M. (1969). Frostbite and its sequelae in captive and exotic birds. Journal of the American Veterinary Medical Association **155**, 1035-1038.

ZENOBLE, R. D. and GRAHAM, D. L. (1979). Electrocardiography of the parakeet, parrot and owl. Annual proceedings of the American Association of Zoo Veterinarians, 42-44.

ZENOBLE, R. D. and GRAHAM, D. L. (1981). Electrocardiography in the parakeet and parrot. Compendium on Continuing Education **3**(8), 711-714.

Chapter12

THE MUSCULO-SKELETAL SYSTEM
INCLUDING THE FEET

B. H. COLES B.V.Sc., M.R.C.V.S.

METABOLIC BONE DISEASE

An imbalance in the absorption of calcium, phosphorus and Vitamin D is common in parrots and results in a variety of disease conditions. The disease produced will depend on a number of factors including the age of the bird, the level of malnutrition, the length of time the condition has been allowed to progress and the presence of any concurrent disease. The metabolic bone diseases seen in parrots are osteoporosis, osteomalacia, rickets and secondary nutritional hyperparathyroidism.

Aetiology

Captive parrots are prone to this group of diseases because of their customary diet of high oil-bearing foods such as sunflower seed and peanuts. Some parrots become habituated to a very narrow range of diet and will eat only sunflower or hemp seeds. All species of birds tend to be conservative in their choice of food and eat only those foods with which they are familiar. The calcium:phosphorus ratio in the following seeds is:- sunflower 1:7, millet 1:6, maize 1:37 and peanuts 1:35. The ideal ratio for absorption is between 1:1 and 2:1. In the alimentary canal the excess of phosphorus ions leads to the formation of insoluble calcium phosphate. Moreover, the high oil content of these foods results during digestion in the production of long chain fatty acids and glycerol, which in turn leads to the formation of insoluble calcium soaps reducing further the availability of calcium. Furthermore, formation of insoluble calcium soaps interferes with the absorption of fat soluble Vitamin D_3.

Vitamin D_3 is changed in the liver into the intermediary metabolyte 25-hydroxycholecalciferol. This, in turn, is further hydroxylated in the kidney to active metabolytes which influence the absorption of calcium from the alimentary canal. Consequently, diseases of the bowel, liver or kidney may indirectly contribute to metabolic bone disease.

Other factors which may adversely affect the absorption of calcium ions include the presence of internal parasites and the existence of any chelating substance such as oxalates, phytic and acetic acids and also the tetracycline antibiotics.

An imbalance in the absorption of calcium and phosphorus leads ultimately to a lowered blood calcium level which in turn results in the emergence of one of the metabolic bone diseases. Which clinical condition develops will depend to some extent on whether the parrot is a growing immature bird or an adult.

The basic structure of avian bone is similar to that in mammals and consists of a lattice work of hydroxyapatite crystals intimately associated with a mesh of collagen fibrils together with the proteinaceous material osteroid. The hydroxyapatite crystals are composed of calcium and phosphorus ions together with small amounts of other ions such as sodium, potassium, magnesium, manganese, zinc and copper. The whole is a dynamic structure with the mineral constituents kept in constant equilibrium with those in the blood. Those cells within the osteoid known as the osteoblasts and osteoclasts are constantly maintaining this balance by either building up or breaking down the bone structure. In the fledgling, if there are insufficient total mineral constituents present in the blood or their proportions are incorrect, inadequate mineralisation of the growing bone will take place. In the adult bird, if the level of calcium ions in the blood falls below normal these will be withdrawn from bone.

Clinical signs in immature birds

Immature birds with metabolic bone disease have bone which is soft and easily crushed between the fingers or cut with a knife. In a normal avian long bone the cortex is dense, hard and porcelain-like.

Radiographically, the cortex is very thin and there is an overall loss of density which approaches that of the soft tissues. An increase in the trabecular pattern of the bone and in the amount of osteoid may be seen. Distortion of the bone and folding fractures are often found, Plate 12:1.

Distortion of the long bones in the wings and legs can sometimes be palpated. Usually the bird does not perch properly or the wings are not held in the normal position, Plate 12:2. All parts of the skeleton including the ribs, the sternum, the ilium, ischium and pubis can be affected. If the thoracic cage collapses the bird develops a hunchbacked appearance. The premaxillae and mandible may also be affected so that the upper and lower beak do not oppose each other properly and prehension of food is faulty, Plates 12:3 and 12:4.

Clinical signs in adult birds

In the adult bird, which has started life with a normally shaped and properly mineralised skeleton, inadequate calcium intake leading to a lowered blood calcium level, results in a response by the parathyroid glands. These enlarge, often equalling the neighbouring thyroids in size, and produce more parathyroid hormone. This influences the osteoclasts to withdraw calcium from the skeleton resulting in osteoporosis and osteomalacia, a condition known as nutritionally induced secondary hyperparathyroidism. To some extent the influence of the parathyroid hormone is counterbalanced by calcitonin, a hormone produced by the ultimo branchial glands which lie adjacent to the parathyroids.

Initially, when the level of calcium in the blood is normal but there is increased activity within the bone to maintain this level, blood alkaline phosphatase levels will be raised. The normal serum calcium level in parrots is 73-96 mg/litre; this may fall below 50 mg/litre in severe cases.

The condition may develop very slowly over many years and only becomes critical when reserves of calcium in the bone are exhausted. Then the blood calcium level falls and a reduction in appetite, regurgitation, intermittent soft droppings, polydipsia, weakness, lethargy, poor feather growth and chewing at the plumage may be seen. If the blood calcium level falls further the bird will show slight muscle twitching which later develops into tonic and clonic muscle spasms. These may first start with apparent uncontrollable flapping of the wings. Alternatively, the bird may sway drunkenly on the perch, then topple over and may even hang upside-down. The hypocalcaemic bird becomes hypersensitive and any of the above signs can be triggered off by sudden noises or the sudden opening of a door or switching on of a light. Birds in such a condition will die quickly.

Other body systems may also be affected. The proliferation of osteoid and fibrous tissue beneath the periosteum and endosteum to support the weakened bone may lead to a reduction in the diameter of the medullary cavity. The consequent reduction in haematopoietic tissue may result in anaemia. If the parathyroids overreact and produce a state of prolonged hypercalcaemia, microlyths may form in the kidney tubules because the renal threshold for calcium ions has been exceeded. Birds fed solely on a diet of high oil-bearing seeds are often excessively fat which increases weight on the weakened skeleton and damages the cardio-vascular system.

Treatment

Having confirmed that the condition is primarily caused by malnutrition and is not due to a primary disorder of the parathyroids, the liver or kidneys, therapy is directed towards stabilising the condition by achieving a balanced diet. Little can be done for an already distorted skeleton or any fractures. In fact, any attempt at orthopaedic surgery on these fragile bones is liable to result in further fractures.

If the bird is hyperaesthetic or exhibiting muscle spasms, immediate treatment with a slow intravenous injection of calcium borogluconate should be given until the hyperaesthesia abates. At the same time an intramuscular injection of diazepam (0.6 mg/Kg) or midazolam may be given.

Calcium lactate tablets can be given at a dose of 150 mg daily for thirty days. Lactose aids the absorption of calcium ions.

Attempts should be made to encourage the parrot to take a greater variety of foods rather than just the high oil-bearing seeds. Most species of birds are reluctant to try food items other than those with which they are familiar and parrots are no exception. It is often difficult to wean them off their habitual diet.

A variety of pulses can be tried and these can be made into a mash. If some of this is scraped onto the lower beak and the bird acquires the taste, it may begin to take this food. Parrots are individuals; some may take readily to a new food, others may persistently reject any unfamiliar food placed in the mouth. Great patience and persistence are required. Mashed potato and peanut butter can be tried and although not suitable as a permanent item for the diet, they can be used as temporary carriers for more suitable food items. When the bird has become used to the desired additives then the amount of carrier item is slowly reduced.

Fruits often contain a good calcium to phosphorus ratio (e.g. apple 1:1. grapes 1.2:1). Unfortunately fruits contain a lot of water and very little solid so that a great deal of fruit would need to be consumed to satisfy the bird's calcium requirements. To some extent this can be overcome by using dried fruits. Fruit juices can also be added to the drinking water and milk can be given once or twice a week. Birds often learn about new food items by watching other birds and parrots will do likewise. If a parrot on a restricted diet can be introduced to one on a normal diet, this ploy will sometimes work providing the two birds are compatible in temperament and are supervised when first introduced.

Feeding the bird at set times during the day, rather than having a routine of *ad lib.* feeding, will sometimes make a bird more eager for its food.

Parrots should have access to calcium carbonate in the form of oyster shell grit or cuttle fish bone. However, it is important that a comprehensive vitamin and mineral supplement should be offered such as S.A. 37 (Intervet) or Vionate (Ciba-Geigy Agrochemicals). This can be mixed in mash or sprinkled onto the cut surface of fruit but will not be taken if mixed with dry seed. These vitamin and mineral supplements are important to ensure adequate levels of Vitamin D_3 and trace elements such as manganese and magnesium.

It is also good practice to expose all birds to a source of ultra violet light for one or two hours each day. A number of light sources emitting a broad spectrum of radiation, including ultraviolet, are commercially available.

It is not a good practice to use tetracylclines in treating any concurrent disease, since they adversely affect the absorption of calcium.

Perosis

This condition of growing birds results in malformation of the cartilagenous and bony structures of the intertarsal joint. The flat tendon of the gastrocnemius muscle, which runs across the posterior surface of the joint, slips medially, resulting in a lateral rotation of the tarso-metatarsal bone. Sometimes ulceration of the integument over the caudal surface of the joint will result in a pododermatitis similar to that described under bumblefoot.

Perosis has been well documented in poultry and is not uncommonly seen in both domestic and wild ducks and geese. Although the disease has not been generally recognised in parrots, Smith (1979) reported having seen it. Also, similar distortions of the tarsal joint have occasionally been seen by the author which have resulted in functional deformities of the claws and these conditions probably have a similar aetology. Undoubtedly, the disorder is less liable to occur in parrots because it is related to the weight of the bird and the length of the tarso-metatarsal bone. Both of these factors are smaller in parrots than in poultry.

A deficiency of manganese is usually considered to be the major cause of the condition. Manganese activates a number of enzymes concerned in the formation of muco-polysaccarides and chondroitin sulphate, both of which are involved in the formation of bone, cartilage and tendon. However, Altman (1982) lists the following other factors which may contribute to the formation of perosis: sub optimal levels of choline, biotin, pantothenic acid, nicotinic acid, pyridoxine, folic acid and zinc. Deficiencies of these substances can occur when substandard seed is fed.

The two bones adjacent to the intertarsal joint, the tibial tarsal and the tarso-metatarsal, are both rapidly growing bones in the young bird. Also, these bones are the only bones in the appendicular avian skeleton that have true epiphyseal secondary centres of ossification. (In the long bones of the wing ossification at the end of the bone proceeds directly from the one centre of bone formation in the metaphysis. There is no cartilagenous epiphyseal disc as in mammals). Because cartilage is relatively unstable when under compression, there is a tendency for abnormal rotation of the leg to take place in this area.

Treatment
Once distortion has taken place very little can be done. Therapy can only be directed towards stabilising the condition and introducing a more varied diet with added supplements as already described for metabolic bone disease.

CONGENTITAL DEFORMITIES
Various deformities are seen from time to time but many are not brought to the notice of the veterinary practitioner. These abnormalities may be luxations of the various joints, twisted claws or splayed legs. Some of these disorders are similar to the conditions already described under perosis, although they are seen at the time of hatching. They may, in fact, be nutritionally based rather than genetic in origin.

BUMBLEFOOT (PODODERMATITIS) AND ASSOCIATED ARTHRITIS
The condition is well documented in poultry (e.g. Gordon 1977) and is not uncommonly seen in raptors as described by Cooper (1978). Harrison (1986) described it as being common in the budgerigar, Plate 12:5. It is occasionally seen in parrots although it rarely proceeds to the gross septic condition as seen in raptors.

It starts as a penetrating wound of the planter surface of the foot and can progress to infect the interphalangeal, metatarso-phalangeal and intertarsal joints. The condition is often associated with poor hygiene. Wounds may also be caused by flakes of iron oxide rust picked up by the bird walking on a rusted iron grill at the bottom of the cage, or clinging to the rusted mesh of an aviary, as happens in raptors (Forbes 1987). A contributory factor in psittacines may be a lack of Vitamin A which is important for the health of the integument. Heavy, obese birds are also more prone to this condition.

Bacteria commonly involved are *E.coli* and *Staphylococci* but other organisms such as *Proteus* and *Pseudomonas* may also infect the wound. Janovski (1966) suggested the possibility of a delayed hypersensitivity reaction to *E.coli* if the birds are continuously exposed to this organism. Harrison (1986) also says that birds which do not respond to antibiotics may have an immune mediated reaction.

Whatever the aetiology, the condition can be progressive, leading to a sero-fibrinous and purulent arthritis which is usually unilateral. Because of this, all cases should be routinely X-rayed to enable an accurate prognosis to be made. The joint is swollen and there is obvious pain with the bird attempting to take the weight off the leg, sometimes resting against a corner of the cage.

If untreated the infection may ascend the leg to affect the intertarsal joint or even the stifle. Septicaemia with anorexia and weight loss can also be a sequel. In a badly affected case the phalanges become gangrenous and may be sloughed. Radiography may show a degenerative arthritis with an increase in the joint space and an obvious lysis of bone together with proliferative bone changes around the joint.

Treatment
This usually consists of lancing, curretting and draining the infected area. At the same time swabs are taken for culture and antibiotic sensitivity testing. It is a wise precaution to give antibiotics by injection at the time of surgery when there is a risk of a transient bacteraemia.

When the results of antibiotic sensitivity testing become available a more appropriate antibiotic can then be used for a course of treatment extending over a minumum of five days. Bandaging the feet after surgery to protect the wound is good practice. However, some parrots will remove the dressing so that an Elizabethan collar may have to be used and even then this is not always effective.

The perches and surroundings must be kept scrupulously clean. Harrison (1986) states that in mild cases the use of a padded perch soaked in Chlorhexidene has resulted in healing. However, if there is any sign of any allergic reaction to the Chlorhexidene this should be stopped immediately.

OSTEOMYELITIS
Although seen in other species of bird, particularly ducks, this condition is rarely seen in psittacines. It is most likely to occur if the bird should sustain a compound fracture or after bone surgery. On radiography, there is an increase in bone density with an associated periosteal proliferation and swelling of surrounding soft tissue. Differentiation from neoplasia may be difficult radiographically and can best be achieved by needle biopsy. A swab for bacteriology can be taken at the same time as the biopsy.

NON-INFECTED DEGENERATIVE ARTHRITIS

This is occasionally seen in old parrots particularly if confined throughout life. It can also occur subsequent to trauma. There is a swelling and sometimes distortion of the joint. Movement may be restricted. Radiographic changes may show collapse of the joint space and periarticular proliferation of bone together with soft tissue swelling. There is no associated bumblefoot and bacteria cannot be cultured from the lesion. If the joint is sufficiently swollen it may be possible to extract a small amount of joint fluid for cytology. Normal synovial fluid contains few cells but that from a degenerating joint may contain large numbers of mono-nuclear cells. This examination together with bacteriology and radiotherapy should help to confirm the diagnosis.

ARTICULAR GOUT

Birds, like reptiles, produce uric acid as the end product of nitrogen catabolism. Uric acid is produced in the liver and excreated by the kidney but it is less soluble than urea produced by mammals. In the domestic fowl only 10% of the urates are in aqueous solution, 18% are protein bound whilst the rest is in an ultrafiltrable colloidal state. Approximately 65% of the blood carried urates are secreted by the renal tubules, supplied with blood from the renal portal system (King 1984) and the rest is excreted by glomerular filtration. The kidney can only excrete a certain maximum amount of urate; should disease affect the kidney or the level of urates rise above the renal threshold then urates will rapidly precipitate in the body. This will occur on any tissue surface normally exposed to the body's fluids and produce the condition called gout. Dehydration, high protein diet and primary kidney disease are all contributory factors. However, dehydration or high protein diet by themselves will not experimentally produce gout. The crystals of uric acid are deposited in most of the joints and within tendon sheaths although they rarely seem to be found in the hip or shoulder joints. Gout is seen in poultry, waterfowl, raptors and psittacines, particularly in the budgerigar, lovebirds and conures. The nodules of uric acid or tophi are white or cream in colour and are most readily seen subcutaneously over the intertarsal and digital joints of the feet, Plate 12:6. Pain is caused by mechanical irritation of the crystals and movement in the joint is restricted. The bird will exhibit a shifting lameness or attempt to hang on to the sides of the cage with the beak, so taking weight off the leg. There is often loss of bodily condition, not only because of the pain but also because the internal organs are infiltrated with uric acid crystals. Urates themselves are not toxic, they are normally deposited in the allantois of the egg by the developing embryo. Also, the disease initiating the gout may be responsible for loss of condition. In the early stages the tophi over the joints may be confused with a bumblefoot abscess. Confirmation of diagnosis can be gained by incising the lesion and carrying out a muroxide test on the contents. One drop of concentrated nitric acid is added to the material which is then evaporated to dryness over a source of heat. If a drop of ammonia is then added a purple colour will appear if uric acid is present. A microscopical examination of the extracted material will show needle-like crystals. Birds with gout show elevated uric acid levels of over 200-300 mg/litre. The normal level lies between 20-150 mg/litre.

Treatment

The best that can be done is to adjust the diet and increase the water consumption by giving plenty of fruit and fresh green food. The protein content of the food should be reduced by stopping the use of pulses, meat, cheese and hard-boiled egg. Scooping out the contents of the tophi has little therapeutic value since it is the uric acid crystals within the joint which cause the trouble. Allopurinol ('Zyloric', Calnic-Wellcome Foundation Ltd. or 'Aluline', Steinhard Ltd.) reduces the level of uric acid in plasma by decreasing its production in the liver by means of the inhibition of the enzyme xanthine oxidase, which catalyses purines to uric acid. The tablet is administered crushed in drinking water at a dosage of 40 mg/Kg. The use of Allopurinol has had a variable success, probably because it is aimed at the result of the disease rather than the initiating cause. At best, birds can rarely be kept alive for more than a few months and euthanasia may be the most humane solution.

DRY GANGRENE OF THE FEET

This may be seen, particularly in the budgerigar, as the end result of constriction by a metal marking ring (Plate 12:7). The birds are banded by breeders for recording purposes and subsequently often sold to the pet trade as surplus to breeding and showing requirements. At first, there may be irritation and bruising of the skin under the ring. This may lead to swelling and impairment of the venous return from the foot and the ring may eventually become embedded in swollen tissue.

A similar condition can occur in the larger psittacine as a result of twine or human hair becoming twisted around one or more digits. If the hair is embedded in the depth of the lesion, it will not be obviously seen. In any case, the owner often does not notice the budgerigar's foot or the parrot's toe until it is too late and the tissues have become dry and necrotic.

Treatment

Special cutters are available for removing leg bands or canine nail clippers can be used. When attempting removal of a leg band, great care must be exercised in trying to cut through the ring. It is very easy for the metal band to suddenly twist, fracturing the metatarsus. Whatever instrument is used for cutting, the ring must first be gripped firmly to stop it twisting. It is difficult to do this with the fingers and it is easier to use a pair of artery forceps or, better still, a pair of canine tooth forceps. The hollowed ends of these instruments facilitate gripping of the ring. In any case two persons are required, one to hold the bird and the other to cut the ring.

Harrison (1986) suggests using the tip of a hypodermic needle bent to form a small hook to pick up a constricting fine hair embedded in a wound.

FROST BITE

A dry gangrene of the digits commonly results from frost bite in parrots kept outside aviaries and many birds are seen which have lost claws. The birds often cling to the wire netting of the aviary when the temperature of the metal may be several degrees below freezing. Often the anterior two toes are affected first because when hanging on to the wire these digits take the bird's weight and are in firmer contact with the metal. Sometimes, freezing is so rapid the bird can become sealed to the wire and in trying to free itself tears the skin. There is intense pain and irritation and the bird may be brought to the veterinarian as an acute case, having lost some of the terminal digits. The rest of the phalanges may be a shredded mess of skin, tendon and bone oozing blood as a result of self trauma.

Treatment

This is directed towards arresting haemorrhage and attempting to salvage what tissue remains. Often the skin of the whole foot is swollen. A topical cortico-steroid and antibiotic preparation should be used and the foot bandaged to give protection and prevent further self-trauma.

THE CLAWS

A horny claw encloses the terminal phalanx of each digit. The dorsal and lateral walls of the claw are made of very hard, highly keratinised plates while the ventral wall is composed of the softer ventral plate. The dorsal plate grows faster than the ventral and hence the claw adopts its characteristic curved shape.

Elongated claws lacking the natural curve are commonly encountered. Such claws are susceptible to trauma which may result in considerable haemorrhage and therefore should be regularly clipped or amputated.

PRIMARY NEOPLASMS OF THE MUSCULO-SKELETAL SYSTEM

Osteomata and chondromata of the skeletal system as well as osteogenic sarcomata and chondrosarcomata have been reported by Arnold (1958), Beach (1962), Blackmore (1965) and Frost (1961) to occur in the budgerigar. Petrak and Gilmore (1982) and Harrison (1986) also describe bone tumours in other psittacines. Rhabdomyomata and rhabdomyosarcomata have also been reported by some of the above authors.

The lesion is often first indicated by the bird picking at the affected area so that the overlying skin becomes ulcerated. There is usually found to be swelling of the affected bone which can easily be mistaken for a fracture.

Radiographically there is usually osteolysis within the bone with new bone laid down at the periphery of the lesion but bone neoplasms can be difficult to distinguish from other bone conditions such as osteomyelitis. Apart frrom radiography, biopsy and bacterial culture must be used to differentiate these conditions. Sometimes there is an elevation in serum alkaline phosphatase. However, too much reliance should not be placed on this level as there appears to be considerable seasonal and interspecies variation (Barron, 1980). Also it is impossible to differentiate the exact type of tumour from the radiograph.

Most authors report that tumours arise near to joints. Of the four primary bone neoplasms seen by the author in birds, three have been at the distal end of the femur and one at the proximal end of the humerus.

Treatment

Amputation of the affected limb can be effective in limiting the progress of the disease providing the bird is not too disabled to be able to perch.

PATHOGENIC POLYOSTOTIC HYPEROSTOSIS

An increase in medullary bone or hyperostosis occurs normally in female birds a short time before egg laying commences. In the domestic fowl spicules of bone begin to grow out from the endosteal surface of the cortical bone about two weeks before egg laying begins. These spicules continue to grow throughout the egg laying period but seldom entirely fill the medullary cavity. The formation of medullary bone is under the influence of oestrogens and androgens which also induce increased absorption of calcium and phosphorus from the alimentary canal (King, 1984). Reabsorption of the medullary bone and redistribution of the minerals to the shell gland at the time each egg is laid is believed to be due to a temporary fall in the level of circulating oestrogen. The parathyroid hormone may also influence this process.

Localised increases in bone density, not associated with egg laying, are not uncommonly seen on the radiograph of budgerigars (Plate 12:8). They are sometimes also seen in radiographs of other psittacines, particularly cockatiels. Beach (1962) reported this condition in budgerigars associated with ovarian cysts. In a recent random survey of budgerigar X-rays taken by the author over the last five years, 14.28% showed this condition. Any female bird with an enlarged abdomen and showing a hyperostosis on radiography, almost certainly has ovarian cysts, even if there is no history of egg laying. Schlumberger (1959) was able to reproduce the condition using stilboestrol implants. The condition occurs in all the long bones where a definite increase in bone density throughout the bone and obliteration of the normal architecture can easily be recognised. In the healthy egg laying female a remnant of the medullary cavity can usually be recognised in both the tibiotarsal bone and the femur. The humerus usually just shows an increased trabecular pattern

The author has seen at least two cases of polyostotic hyperostosis in male budgerigars due to neoplasia of the gonads.

FRACTURES AND LUXATIONS

These are not often seen in captive parrots but they can occur, not only as a result of trauma but also because of metabolic bone disease, primary bone tumours and invasion of bone by soft tissue tumours. More discussion of fractures and luxations occurs in Chapter 5.

REFERENCES

ALTMAN, R. B. (1982) Diseases of the skeletal system, p 384: in Diseases of Cage and Aviary Birds, ed. M. L. Petrak, 2nd Edition. Lea and Febiger, Philadelphia.

ARNOLD, L. (1958) Experiences with cage birds. Vet. Rec. 70, pp120-128.

BARRON, H. W. (1980) Die Aktivitäts messung einiger Enzye in Blutplasma B.Z.W. — Serum verschiedener Vogel Spezies. University of München.

BEACH, J. E. (1962) Diseases of budgerigars and other cage birds. A survey of post-mortem findings. Vet. Rec. 74, pp 10-15, 63-68 and 134-140.

BLACKMORE, D. K. (1965) The pathology and incidence of neoplasms in cage birds. Journal of Small Animal Prac. 6: pp 217-233.

CAMPBELL, T. W. (1986) Neoplasia p 502: in Clinical Avian Medicine and Surgery. Ed. Harrison, G. J. and Harrison L. R. W. B. Saunders Company, Philadelphia.

COOPER, J. E. (1978) Veterinary Aspects of Captive Birds of Prey. pp 98 — 111. Standfast Press, Saul. Gloucestershire.

FORBES, N. A. (1987) Personal communication.

FROST, C. (1961) Experiences with Pet Budgerigars, Vet. Rec. 73, pp 621-626.

GORDON, R. F. and JORDON, F. T. W. (1977) Poultry Diseases, pp 55, 244. Baillière Tindall, London.

HARRISON, L. R., FLAMMER, R. and HARRISON, G. J. (1986) Choosing a bird, p 5: in Clinical Avian Medicine and Surgery, Ed. Harrison, G. J. and Harrison L. R. W. B. Saunders Company, Philadelphia.

HARRISON, G. J. (1986) Disorders of the integument, pp 520, 522. In Clinical Avian Medicine and Surgery, Ed. Harrison, G. J. and Harrison L. R. W. B. Saunders Company, Philadelphia.

JANOVSKI, M. D. (1966) Arthropathy associated with Escherichia Coli septicaemia in cage birds. J.A.V.M.A. No. 148, pp 1517-1522.

KING, A. S. (1984) Birds their structure and function, (1) p 184 (2) pp 73, 74. Baillière Tindall, London.

PETRAK, M. L. and GILMORE, C. E. (1982) Neoplasm, p 619; in Diseases of Cage and Aviary Birds, ed. M. L. Petrak, Lea and Febiger, Philadelphia.

SCHLUMBERGER, H. G. (1959) Polyostotic hyperostosis in the female Parakeet. Am. J. Path. 35: pp 1 — 23.

SMITH, G. A. (1979) Parrot disease as encountered in veterinary practice. In The husbandry and medicine of the parrot family — the proceedings of a B.V.Z.S./Parrot Society meeting, Regent's Park, London. Eds. A. G. Greenwood and J. E. Cooper.

Chapter 13

PSITTACOSIS

W. L. G. Ashton M.V.Sc., M.R.C.V.S.

HISTORY

In 1876 an astute physician in Germany noted that a flu-like illness affecting some of his patients appeared to be connected with a disease of parrots. During the next twenty years a number of similar incidents were reported, including one in Paris in which 16 out of 48 affected people died. Following these outbreaks the disease in humans and parrots was recognised as a distinct clinical condition and given the name psittacosis (Shaughnessy 1955). Between 1929 and 1932 many outbreaks of psittacosis with a 20 per cent mortality rate were diagnosed in humans in Europe and America. These incidents were clearly linked to the large number of parrots being imported to satisfy the demand for pet birds (Meyer 1969).

The growing concern about psittacosis resulted in investigation of the problem by a number of workers. The disease was shown to be an infection and the causal agent given the name Psittacosis lymphogranuloma venereum (PLV) agent. For many years there was a disagreement over the nature of this agent and how it should be classified. At various times it was considered to be a large virus, a rickettsia or a small bacterium and assigned to a number of different bacterial groupings such as *Bedsonia, Miyagawanella* and *Microbacteria.* Eventually it was shown to be a small intracellular bacterium containing RNA and DNA with a distinctive life cycle that distinguished it from both viruses and *Rickettsia.* It was finally classified as a member of the bacterial genus *Chlamydia* and given the name *Chlamydia psittaci* (Page 1968).

TAXONOMY AND NOMENCLATURE

The genus *Chlamydia* consists of two groups of bacteria, Group A, represented by *Chlamydia trachomatis* which can cause trachoma and genital infections in humans, and group B comprising strains of *Chlamydia psittaci*. The general term chlamydiosis is used to describe infection in any animal by any species of *chlamydia.* Psittacosis is still the term commonly used to describe the disease caused by *Chlamydia psittaci* in man or parrots, while ornithosis is the name given to the disease in non-psittacine birds. A variety of other diseases in domestic animals can be caused by *Chlamydia psittaci*. These include Enzootic abortion in sheep, pneumonia and arthritis in cattle, sheep and pigs, and conjunctivitis in cats. These strains of *Chlamydia psittaci* have a greater degree of host specificity than those affecting birds. However, there have been cases of spread of the organism from aborting sheep to humans with resultant illness and death.

LIFE CYCLE

Chlamydia psittaci exists outside the cell as highly infective elementary bodies, 300 nm in size. These are taken into the host cell by phagocytosis where they reorganise into reticulate bodies 1000 nm large, then multiply by binary fission and develop in the cytoplasm to form characteristic microcolonies or inclusion bodies comprising both reticulate and elementary bodies. The organism persists in the spleen of birds with latent infection.

EPIDEMIOLOGY

Chlamydia psittaci is endemic in many parrot populations in the wild. Latent infection is common and apparently healthy parrots can carry and excrete large numbers of infective particles continuously or intermittently for long periods. When such infected birds are subjected to the stress of capture and transit, clinical disease is often precipitated. If such carrier birds are mixed with large numbers of other susceptible birds in crowded quarantine premises, there is ample opportunity for spread of infection. Infection with *Chlamydia psittaci* has been reported in over 90 species of wild birds (Meyer 1965), and in this country infection is endemic in pigeons. Many outbreaks of psittacosis in this country are in home-bred birds and contact with indigenous infected birds is a likely origin of these cases. Large numbers of infective particles are excreted in the faeces of infected birds and dried faeces can remain infective for many months. Inhalation is probably the main route of infection and there is no evidence that vertical transmission occurs via the ovaries.

CLINICAL SIGNS

Birds infected with *Chlamydia psittaci* can appear clinically healthy or show a wide range of clinical signs. In the acute phase of severe disease there is marked depression, ruffled feathers, loss of appetite, respiratory distress with rapid breathing or gasping, an oculo-nasal discharge and watery diarrhoea. (See Plate 8:1.) These are non-specific signs seen in a number of acute febrile systemic bird diseases. A high mortality is often a feature of the acute form of the disease. If the bird survives this phase it will lose condition rapidly and characteristically there will be intermittent diarrhoea with watery scour alternating with viscous droppings. The pathogenicity of strains of *Chlamydia psittaci*, and the susceptibility of different parrot species, can vary considerably. Affected birds may thus show any combination of the above signs which can vary from mild to severe. Psittacosis can also be present as a localised kerato-conjunctivitis without any other systemic signs of disease. The disease is often complicated by intercurrent infection such as salmonellosis and aspergillosis.

DIAGNOSIS

As the clinical signs are not specific and vary considerably in severity, diagnosis of psittacosis in the live bird is difficult. However, psittacosis should always be considered as the possible cause of non-specific disease in a recently purchased parrot, particularly if there is a high mortality in the contact birds. In respect of a differential diagnosis of Newcastle disease, there is more likely to be central nervous disturbance with Newcastle disease, and an oculo-nasal discharge is more likely with psittacosis. Serological tests and virus isolation are expensive and time consuming and a tentative diagnosis of psittacosis often has to be made on the basis of the history and clinical signs. A diagnosis can be supported by a complement fixation test for which at least 0.5 ml of blood and preferably 1 ml is required. A titre of 1 in 8 or higher is positive and will indicate that the bird has been infected with *Chlamydia psittaci*, but not necessarily that the current clinical signs are due to psittacosis. Active infection is confirmed by a four-fold rise in titre in paired blood samples taken ten days apart. However, as infected birds can be carriers and excretors for long periods, a single positive titre is significant. If only one blood sample is taken, sampling should be delayed until the bird has been showing clinical signs for at least four days to allow time for complement fixing antibodies to develop. Unfortunately, African Grey parrots *(Psittacus erithacus)* and budgerigars *(Melopsittacus undulatus)* produce CF antibody irregularly and the test is not diagnostically reliable in these species (Arnstein and Meyer 1982).

Absolute confirmation of psittacosis would depend on isolating and identifying the causal agent. This is excreted in the faeces and a sample or a cloacal swab should be sent for cultural examination in the correct transport medium. A monoclonal antibody-based ELISA has been developed for detection of feline *Chlamydia psittaci* (Wills *et al.* 1986) which may well have a future application for the diagnosis of chlamydiosis in parrots.

POST MORTEM EXAMINATION

A diagnosis of psittacosis can usually be confirmed by examination of the carcase of an affected bird. In view of the considerable risk to human health, carcases should be handled with the greatest care. Before examination, the carcase should be soaked in a suitable disinfectant such as a mixture of 1 in 40 Lysol and 1 in 500 Teepol. If the carcase is sent to a laboratory it should, after soaking in disinfectant, be placed in a stout polythene bag with a bandage roll breather in the neck. The bag should then be dipped in the disinfectant solution, clearly labelled to show it contains a parrot carcase, and a biohazard label attached. The bag containing the carcase should then be placed in a strong wooden or metal case or a container approved by the Post Office. The inner bag should be surrounded by enough absorbent material such as cotton wool or sawdust to prevent leakage. The outside of the package should be marked, 'Pathological Specimen — with care'.

Post mortem examination of a bird that might have died from psittacosis should always be done in a microbiological safety cabinet meeting British Standard (BS) Specification 5726. This lays down requirements for air flow and filtration of extracted air.

The carcase of a bird dying in the acute phase of psittacosis has a septicaemic appearance with the subcutaneous blood vessels injected and prominent. The liver and spleen are swollen, dark, tense and friable, with surface haemorrhages often giving the surface of the organs a mottled appearance. (Plates 13:1, 13:2 and 13:3). A serositis with a clear or dirty exudate in the body cavities and strands of fibrin adhering to the surfaces of the abdominal viscera may also be present. There is sometimes a tracheitis, fibrinous pericarditis and usually an enteritis with the mucosa of the small intestine thickened and injected. In subacute and chronic cases there may be consolidation of the lungs, white or necrotic foci in the liver and spleen, and a diffuse air sacculitis with caseous deposits adhering to the air sacs. In such cases the loss of condition may be marked by atrophy of the muscles over the sternum.

A diagnosis of chlamydiosis can be confidently made by demonstrating the infective particles of inclusion bodies in stained liver or spleen smears. The smears should be made by lightly touching the intact surface of the liver and spleen with a clean, grease-free, glass slide. These smears should then be heat fixed and stained by a suitable procedure such as modified Ziehl-Neelsen or Machiavello's stain and examined under oil immersion. The infective particles appear in the cytoplasm as discrete, reddish-brown bodies varying slightly in size (Plate 13:4). Sometimes the cell wall bursts releasing the infective particles which then appear between the cells. A satisfactory diagnosis in respect of psittacosis can usually be made if such stained smears are carefully examined for 15 minutes.

The gross post mortem signs are not pathognomonic and similar changes are seen in birds dying from salmonellosis, reovirus infection, Pacheco's disease and *Pseudomonas* infections.

ISOLATION OF CHLAMYDIA PSITTACI
The definitive test for psittacosis is however isolation and identification of *Chlamydia psittaci* in tissues from the carcase or from the faeces. The organism will not grow on solid media but will multiply in tissue culture, in the yolk sac of chicken embryos or when injected intraperitoneally into mice. All strains will grow in the commonly used mammalian cell lines, and L929 mouse fibroblasts or McCoy cultures are eminently suitable for isolation purposes. Tissue culture is now the method of choice for isolating *Chlamydia psittaci* with subsequent identification of the agent by direct fluorescent antibody staining (Bevan *et al.* 1978).

THE DISEASE IN HUMANS
Psittacosis is a very unpredictable disease but can be extremely contagious. There are many accounts of serious illness and death in humans following the briefest contact with infected parrots. On the other hand people working in quarantine premises and pet shops sometimes remain healthy despite regular close contact with infected birds. Without question a bird infected with *Chlamydia psittaci*, even though it appears clinically healthy, can be a considerable health hazard to anyone in the same room.

In humans, psittacosis presents as anything from a mild flu-like illness to a severe generalised infection with cerebral, renal and haematological complications. The illness often starts with chills, fever and a frontal headache. An unproductive cough is often present and occasionally there is diarrhoea. If untreated the disease may progress to severe mental confusion, renal failure and death (Hillas Smith 1984).

TREATMENT
It has been shown repeatedly that tetracyclines are the most suitable drugs for control of psittacosis and chlortetracycline is normally considered the drug of choice. Clinical signs will usually disappear after a few days treatment. However, to eliminate latent infection it is necessary to continue treatment for up to 45 days. Work in America and Germany (Arnstein, Eddir and Meyer 1968; Luthgen, Bretschneider

and Wachendorfer 1979) has shown that for treatment to be completely effective it is necessary to maintain the birds' blood levels of chlortetracycline at over 1 microgram per millilitre continuously for long periods. These workers showed that the following treatment regimes were necessary for complete control of Chlamydia psittaci in parrots.

Type of Bird	Concentration of chlortetracycline in the feed (ppm)	Length of continuous treatment in days
Small e.g. budgerigar	500	30
Medium e.g. cockatiel	2,400	45
Large e.g. Grey parrots Amazon parrots cockatoos	5,000	45

Treatment of parrots with chlortetracycline in the water is unsatisfactory as many psittacine species do not drink sufficiently often to maintain a therapeutic blood level continuously for the required period. As chlortetracycline may be bound by calcium ions, the antibiotic should not be mixed with a calcium containing feed supplement. It has been found in Germany that an intramuscular injection of doxycycline every 5 days for 45 days at a rate of 75 mg/kg is also effective, and offers an alternative treatment regime to oral therapy (Wachenforfer, Luthgen, Traub and Bretschneider, 1982). Due to the varying nutritional requirements, physiological differences and appetites, it is difficult to persuade some species of parrots to take in sufficient concentrations of the drug for the required period. It is therefore essential to add the drug to a feed that meets the requirements of the individual species and is acceptable. In some countries proprietary feeds impregnated with chlortetracycline specifically for treatment of psittacosis are available. These consist of pelleted concentrates, peeled impregnated millet, oats and sunflower seeds. Medicated egg feed has also been found acceptable to some species and a liquid feed is needed to treat nectar or fruit eating parrots such as lories or lorikeets. A home-made mash, suitable for treatment of larger psittacines, can be made by cooking maize, rice and water in a ratio 2:2:3 until a soft, but not mushy, consistency is obtained (Arnstein and Meyer 1982). Chlortetracycline is then added to obtain a concentration of 5 milligrams per gramme of cooked feed. The mash should be prepared daily and a small amount of brown sugar and favourite seeds added to improve palatability.

To prevent reinfection a strict regime of daily cage or aviary cleaning and disinfection should be adopted during the treatment period and a vitamin supplement given to reduce the likelihood of enteric disturbances resulting from prolonged oral antibiotic therapy.

If a valuable bird is so ill with psittacosis that it refuses to eat, tetracycline should be given daily by intramuscular injection for 5 days and then the antibiotic should be continued in the feed for the required period.

CONTROL ON IMPORTATION OF PARROTS

The Importation of Birds, Poultry and Hatching Eggs Order of 1979 controls the import of parrots into this country. This order requires imported parrots to be licensed into approved premises where they must spend at least 35 days under veterinary supervision. Sentinel unvaccinated chickens are placed in the same air space as the imported parrots. Birds dying in quarantine are sent to a Veterinary Investigation Centre for post mortem examination. All batches of parrot carcases are screened for *Chlamydia* by examination of stained impression smears of liver and spleen. If chlamydiosis is diagnosed the quarantine period may be extended until the birds have been effectively treated. The imported birds would not be slaughtered unless there were evidence that the disease presented a real risk to poultry health, as shown by transmission of disease to the sentinel chickens. These controls prevent infected batches of birds from being split up and widely distributed immediately after being subjected to the traumas of capture and transit. The period in quarantine allows the birds to get over stresses in a favourable environment. It is, however, still possible for an infected bird to be released from quarantine and subsequently develop clinical signs of disease or infect contact birds.

MANAGEMENT OF PSITTACOSIS

If psittacosis is suspected the owner of the bird should be warned of the danger to himself, his staff and family. In view of the human health hazard and the difficulty of treatment, euthanasia of the affected bird and contact birds should be seriously considered. If it is decided to treat the bird, a blood and/or faeces sample should be taken and sent for complement fixation test and/or cultural examination. The bird should be isolated and managed so that dust from dried faeces and other debris from the bird are kept to a minimum. To reduce the risk of aerosols of infective particles, dampened sawdust or sand should be used on the cage or aviary floor and strict attention paid to cleaning and disinfection. When attending a bird suspected of having psittacosis protective clothing that includes gloves and a face mask should be worn. If the bird dies, the carcase should be sent for post mortem examination. If psittacosis is confirmed by laboratory tests the future of the affected and contact birds should again be discussed with the owner and euthanasia recommended.

If it is decided to continue treatment every effort should be made to ensure that it is continued for the required length of time at the correct dose rate. Although psittacosis is not a notifiable disease, State Veterinary Service Staff from the Ministry of Agriculture will investigate any cases referred to them to determine if there is any risk to contact poultry. They will also give advice in respect of diagnosis, treatment and the hazards to human health. A laboratory service for birds suspected of dying or being affected with psittacosis is also available from Ministry of Agriculture Veterinary Investigation Laboratories.

REFERENCES

ARNSTEIN, P., EDDIE, B. and MEYER, K. F. (1968) American Journal of Veterinary Research **29**, 2213.

ARNSTEIN, P. and MEYER, K. F. (1982). In Diseases of Cage and Aviary Birds. 2nd Edition, Ed. M. C. Petrak, Lea and Febiger, Philadelphia.

BEVAN, B. J., CULLEN, G. A. and READ, W. M. F. (1978). Avian Pathology 7:203.

HILLAS G. SMITH (1984). Personal communication.

LUTHGEN W., BRETSCHNEIDER, J. and WACHENDORFER, G. (1979) Deutsche Tierarztliche Wochenschrift 86 (ii) 426.

MEYER, K. F. (1965). In Viral and rickettsial infections of man. 4th Edn. Editor Horsfall, F. L. and Tamm I, London. Pitman Medical Publishing Co. Ltd.

MEYER, K. F. (1969), Archives Environmental Health 19:461.

PAGE, L. A. (1968). International Journal of Systemic Bacteriology 18 (1) 51.

SHAUGHNESSY, H. J. (1955). In diseases transmitted from Animals to Man. 4th Edn. Editor Hull, T. G., Publisher Charles C. Thomas, Springfield, Illinois, USA.

WACHENDORFER, G., LUTHGEN, W. TRAUB, C., and BRETSCHNEIDER, J. (1982) Tierarztliche Limschau **37** (3) 177.

WILLS, J. M., MILLARD, W. G. and HOWARD, P. T. (1986) Veterinary Record 119 No. 17 418.

Chapter 14

PACHECO'S PARROT DISEASE AND REOVIRUS-ASSOCIATED HEPATITIS

W. L. G. Ashton M.V.Sc.,M.R.C.V.S.

PACHECO'S PARROT DISEASE (PSITTACINE HERPES HEPATITIS)

HISTORY

In 1930 a disease of parrots was described in Brazil by Pacheco and Bier. It could not be transmitted to mice or canaries and thus appeared to be distinct from psittacosis. It was later shown to be a herpes virus infection and became known as Pacheco's parrot disease (Pacheco and Bier 1930, Rivers and Schwentker 1932). The features of the disease were high mortality and striking and characteristic necrotic lesions in livers and spleens. During the last fifteen years Pacheco's disease has been reported from many parts of the world, often causing heavy mortality in collections of parrots.

EPIDEMIOLOGY

The disease usually occurs in recently purchased parrots or soon after the introduction of a new bird to the aviary. A feature of this herpes virus infection is the occurrence of long-term latent infection, and carrier birds. The stress of a sudden change in the aviary management or a sharp drop in temperature can be the factors that precipitate clinical disease.

A herpes virus infection with heavy mortality and necrotic liver lesions has been described in pigeons in this country (Cornwell and Wright 1970). Herpes virus infections have also been described in birds of prey and there is evidence that the herpes virus can be transmitted from pigeons and birds of prey to parrots (Cavill 1982), (Mare 1975).

The available evidence suggests that airborne spread of the virus does not readily occur and that infection is transmitted from bird to bird mainly by faecal contamination of food or water.

CLINICAL SIGNS

Affected birds are frequently found dead or die within a few hours of the first sign of ill health, and an outbreak often starts with the sudden death of a single bird. The clinical signs are not consistent or specific and there is usually only anorexia, depression and progressive weakness. Occasionally there is yellow diarrhoea, ataxia and tilting of the head (Panigrahy and Grumbles 1984).

POST MORTEM FINDINGS

In typical cases there are well defined necrotic foci in the liver and spleen. They are yellow or white in colour, and can be seen on the surface and throughout the parenchyma. Sometimes the necrotic areas in the liver coalesce giving the whole surface a yellow mottled appearance. The tissue between the areas of necrosis is pale, with petechial haemorrhages often visible. Excess yellow gelatinous material is sometimes present in the pericardial sac, with haemorrhages on the epicardial surface of the heart. The mucosa of the small intestine is usually tense and injected. Unfortunately, focal splenic and hepatic necrosis is not invariably a feature of Pacheco's disease. In one report the only visible abnormality was intense reddening of the small intestinal mucosa (Randall *et al.* 1979), and in some cases no gross lesions can be found at *post mortem* examination (Panigrahy and Grumbles 1984).

HISTOLOGICAL EXAMINATION

Microscopic examination of haematoxylin and eosin-stained sections of the liver lesions will show loss of normal structure due to the necrotic foci. Some infiltration of lymphocytes and histocytes will be present at the margin of the abdominal tissue together with various stages of hepatocytic degeneration. The characteristic finding in Pacheco's disease, however, is margination of the chromatin in the nuclei of the hepatocytes and eosinophilic and/or basophilic intranuclear inclusion bodies.

ISOLATION AND IDENTIFICATION OF THE VIRUS

The causal herpes virus will grow in chicken embryos and also in chicken embryo fibroblasts. When ten day-old chicken embryos are inoculated via the allantois they die within seven days and show stunting and haemorrhages. The herpes virus also causes a cytopathic effect in chicken embryo fibroblast monolayers (Panigrahy and Grumbles 1984). Particles, with the characteristic morphology of herpes viruses, may then be demonstrated in tissue culture by electron microscopy.

DIFFERENTIAL DIAGNOSIS

A reovirus-associated hepatitis of parrots has been described in which the clinical signs and gross post mortem lesions are similar to those seen in Pacheco's disease (Ashton *et al.* 1984). Microsporidium infection has been reported as the cause of heavy mortality in love birds (Agapornis sp) in this country. The main post mortem findings were liver and kidney abnormalities with some of the livers swollen and mottled (Randall *et al.* 1986). An acute systemic disease of love birds, with congested mottled livers found in some affected birds, has also been associated with a papavo-like virus infection (Pass 1985). Infection with some *Salmonella typhimurium* phage types may also result in a bacterial hepatitis with focal necrosis (Randall 1986). Multifocal hepatic necrosis with intranuclear inclusion bodies found on examination of a cockatiel *(Nymphicus hollandicus)* has been associated with an adenovirus infection (Scott *et al.* 1986).

CONCURRENT INFECTION

It is axiomatic that any other infection of parrots could co-exist with herpes virus infection but aspergillosis is probably the most likely complication.

CONTROL

Pacheco's disease will not respond to treatment with antibacterial agents and no vaccines are commercially available in this country. To protect a collection of psittacines from this disease, all newly purchased birds should be isolated for at least four weeks before being introduced to the aviary. Unfortunately, due to the fact that a long latent phase can occur this does not guarantee complete protection. However, the stress of movement and a change of feed and management associated with purchase is likely to trigger off clinical disease in such a carrier bird. It has been suggested (Panigrahy and Grumbles 1984) that the faeces of newly purchased parrots should be tested for the presence of herpes viruses. This would be time consuming and expensive and need sophisticated laboratory facilities, and in most cases it is not a practical proposition. However, such a procedure might be considered to protect particularly rare and valuable parrot collections.

REFERENCES

ASHTON, W. L. G., RANDALL, C. J., DAGLESS, M. D. and EATON, T. M. (1984) Veterinary Record **114**, 476.

CAVILL, J. P. (1982). In Diseases of Cage and Aviary Birds, 2nd Edition, Ed. Petrak, M. C., Lea and Febiger, Philadelphia.

CORNWELL, H. J. C. and WRIGHT, N. G. (1970) Journal of Comparative Pathology, 80, 221

MARE, C. J. (1975) Journal Zoo Animal Medicine, 6, 6.

PACHECO, G. and BIER, O. (1930) Comptes Rendus Societe di Biologiee Sao Paulo 105, 109.

PANIGRAHY, B. and GRUMBLES, L. C. (1984) Avian Diseases 28 No. 3,808.

PASS, D. A. (1985) Australian Veterinary Journal, 62 No. 9, 318.

RANDALL, C. J., DAGLESS, M., JONES, G. R. and MACDONALD, J. W. (1979) Avian Pathology, 8, 229.

RANDALL, C. J., LEES, S., HIGGINS, R. J. and HARCOURT-BROWN, N. H. (1986) Avian Pathology, 15, 223.

RANDALL, C. J. (1986) Personal Communication.

RIVERS, T. M. and SCHWENTKER, F. T. (1932). J. Exp. Medicine 55, 911.

SCOTT, P. C., CONDRON, R. J. and REECE, R. L. (1986) Australian Veterinary Journal, 63 No. 10, 337.

REOVIRUS-ASSOCIATED HEPATITIS OF PARROTS

INTRODUCTION
A disease of parrots has been described that is very similar to Pacheco's parrot disease, but which is caused by a reovirus infection. Features of this condition are high mortality and necrotic foci in the liver as the predominant gross *post mortem* lesion (Ashton *et al.* 1984, Meulemans *et al.* 1983). Orthoreoviridae were isolated from 15 out of 28 lots of parrots that died over a two-year period shortly after importation into Belgium. Enteritis and hepatitis with congestion and necrotic foci in the livers were the main lesions found on *post mortem* examination. A reovirus was also isolated from the livers of parrots that died shortly after importation into this country from Zaire. The affected birds had died after a short illness and at autopsy striking and consistent necrotic lesions in the livers were found. No intranuclear inclusion bodies suggestive of Pacheco's disease could be found in haematoxylin and eosin-stained sections of the livers and no elementary bodies of the type associated with psittacosis could be seen on examination of liver and spleen impression smears stained with a modified Ziehl-Neelsen method. In 1985 Graham showed conclusively that reoviruses can cause liver disease in parrots. He isolated a reo-like virus from a parrot that died after showing signs of diarrhoea and loss of condition and which at *post mortem* had necrotic foci in the liver. He then reproduced the clinical signs and post mortem lesions by experimentally infecting two healthy parrots with the reo-like virus. Kochs postulate was fulfilled when he again isolated the virus from the carcases of the experimentally infected birds (Graham 1987).

CLINICAL SIGNS
Anorexia and depression are consistent clinical signs; some affected birds have a watery diarrhoea and others lose condition rapidly. Affected birds usually die within five days of the first sign of illness and the group mortality is likely to be between 10 and 30 per cent.

POST MORTEM FINDINGS
The carcases of birds dying of this condition are dehydrated, with the body muscles dark in colour and dry. The livers are enlarged and discoloured due to the presence of irregular pale areas of necrosis. These can be well defined but sometimes are confluent giving the liver a blotchy yellow appearance. The spleens are usually enlarged and thickening and reddening of the mucosa of the small intestine is a consistent finding. Occasionally there is excess clear gelatinous material in the pericardial sac and abdomen, congestion of the lungs and an air sacculitis.

MICROSCOPIC EXAMINATION
Histological examination of the liver lesions confirm the presence of necrotic areas irregularly distributed throughout the parenchyma. These comprise rounded foci of hepatocytes that have undergone coagulative necrosis. There is some leucocytic infiltration of the zones of necrosis and also leucocytic infiltration of the sinusoids of the surrounding liver tissue. No inclusion bodies are present in the nuclei of the hepatocytes.

CULTURAL EXAMINATION
Inoculation of liver tissue into the allantois of ten day-old chicken embryos or into the yolk sac of six day-old embryos, produces death of the embryos at 3-7 days post inoculation. Inoculation of chicken kidney cells or chick embryo fibroblasts produces a cytopathic effect with syncytial formation three days after inoculation. Particles with the morphology of reoviruses can be demonstrated when infected tissue culture cells are examined by electron microscopy.

CONCLUSION
This hepatitis has many features in common with Pacheco's parrot disease but is a distinct clinical entity, caused by a reovirus.

REFERENCES
ASHTON, W. L. G., RANDALL, C. J., DAGLESS, M. D. and EATON, T. M. (1984) Veterinary Record **114**, 476.

GRAHAM, D. L. (1978) Avian Diseases **31** No. 2 411-418.

MEULEMANS, G., DEKEGEL, D., CHARLIER, G., FROYMAN, F., VAN TILBURG, J. and HALEN, P. (1983) Journal of Comparative Pathology **93**, 127.

Chapter 15

NEWCASTLE DISEASE

W. L. G. Ashton M.V.Sc., M.R.C.V.S.

INTRODUCTION

Newcastle disease is a viral infection that is potentially the most important and destructive single disease of birds. It can cause up to 100 per cent mortality in a susceptible population and will spread rapidly both within an aviary and between separate groups of birds in the same locality. Newcastle disease virus (NDV) has been isolated from over 100 species of birds, 35 of which are parrots (Luthgen 1981), and it is probable that all avian species can be infected. However, the disease can present in a variety of forms depending on the pathogenicity of the strain of virus involved and the susceptibility of the infected species of bird. Some, such as ducks and geese, have considerable natural resistance to clinical disease while others, such as chickens, pigeons and most species of parrots, are very susceptible.

HISTORY

The name 'Newcastle' refers to Newcastle-on-Tyne where an outbreak was described in 1926 (Doyle 1927) and shown to be due to a filterable virus distinct from the Fowl Plague agent. A small flock of chickens was affected which had been fed waste food from ships plying with the Far East. A disease of poultry that was undoubtedly Newcastle disease was also described at this time in Java. For many years in this country any form of Newcastle disease or Fowl Plague was known as Fowl Pest.

CLASSIFICATION

Newcastle disease virus (NDV) contains ribonucleic acid, has a helical structure and a lipid-containing envelope, and is classified as a myxovirus. This family of viruses is further divided into an influenza group which contains the causal agent of Fowl Plague and a paramyxovirus group. There are nine serologically distinct avian paramyxoviruses and NDV is identified as paramyxovirus I. Isolates of NDV are morphologically and structurally indistinguishable, but their pathogenicity in birds can vary considerably producing a variety of different forms of clinical disease of varying severity. Group 3 paramyxoviruses have also been isolated from parrots dying in quarantine premises. Encephalitis and high mortality have been associated with such infections and mortality in budgerigars can be caused by infection with group 5 paramyxoviruses (Alexander 1986).

PATHOGENICITY

The pathogenicities of strains of Newcastle disease virus vary. Those of mild pathogenicity are referred to as lentogenic, those of moderate pathogenicity as mesogenic and highly pathogenic strains as velogenic. A study of a number of strains of Newcastle disease virus isolated from parrots showed that they were velogenic and did not differ antigenically from strains isolated from poultry (Luthgen 1981).

CLINICAL SIGNS

Infected birds may show no signs of disease or may show a range of clinical signs from mild to severe. In outbreaks of velogenic Newcastle disease the first signs are likely to be marked dullness, depression, ruffled feathers and a sudden loss of appetite. This is quickly followed by respiratory distress with rapid breathing, gasping and gurgling. Signs of central nervous system disturbance are often prominent with inco-ordination, head shaking or nodding, twisting of the neck and paralysis. Sometimes there is excess salivation with froth and strands of saliva visible at the beak commisures. There is usually diarrhoea with the droppings having a greenish watery appearance and containing prominent white urate deposits. There is no response to treatment with antibacterial agents and death usually occurs within three days of the onset of clinical signs. Newcastle disease should always be suspected in cases of sudden illness in parrots with heavy mortality.

Certain clinical signs may predominate depending on the tropism of the strain of the virus or on the species of bird affected. It has been reported that when parrots from South America develop Newcastle disease central nervous signs predominate. However, when species from South East Asia are affected enteric signs are the main clinical feature (Luthgen 1981).

POST MORTEM FINDINGS
Frequently no visible abnormalities can be seen on post mortem examination. Carcases may, however, have a septicaemic appearance with subcutaneous oedema and haemorrhage, the livers and kidneys dark and swollen, the lungs oedematous and the spleen enlarged. Tracheitis is the most consistent post mortem finding. The lining of the trachea is usually diffusely reddened and in some cases blood stained exudate may be present. Blood splashes may be present on the air sacs and haemorrhages in the mucosa of the proventriculus and small intestines and on the serosal surfaces of the intestines. There may be a haemorrhagic enteritis with the intestines distended with fluid and the mucosa of the small intestine thickened and congested.

DIAGNOSIS
In many outbreaks of velogenic Newcastle disease a diagnosis can confidently be made on th basis of the history and clinical signs. There is usually a history of the birds being recently imported or purchased and the sudden onset of severe disease with respiratory distress, inco-ordination and diarrhoea is very suggestive. However, if there is no history of recent purchase and the clinical signs are vague and only moderately severe, laboratory tests will be needed to establish a definite diagnosis. In the live bird a haemagglutination inhibition (HI) test on a serum sample can be of value. Haemagglutination anti-bodies are often present within two days of the appearance of clinical signs (Cavill 1982). However the definitive test for confirmation of Newcastle disease is isolation and identification of the causal virus.

NDV will grow readily when infected tissue is injected into the allantois of a ten day-old chicken embryo. If the velogenic strain of virus is present the embryo will be killed within 48 hours and the virus can be detected in allantoic fluid. The presence of a haemagglutinating virus can be demonstrated by showing that the allantoic fluid will agglutinate chicken red blood cells and Newcastle disease virus can be identified by the fact that agglutination is inhibited by specific Newcastle disease immune serum. Fluorescent antibody tests can also be used for rapid virus identification. Suitable tissues for virus isolation are pieces of trachea, lungs or intestine, and if no carcase is available, virus can be isolated from cloacal swabs taken from birds showing clinical signs of disease. Newcastle disease virus will also grow on tissue culture both in avian and many mammalian cell lines.

DIFFERENTIAL DIAGNOSIS
In mild or subacute Newcastle disease the clinical signs may be vague and non-specific, with affected birds showing only depression, respiratory distress and perhaps diarrhoea. These signs could also be due to psittacosis, salmonellosis, Pacheco's disease, reovirus infection and aspergillosis. Newcastle disease can also be complicated by concurrent infection with aspergillosis or salmonellosis.

TRANSMISSION
The usual way that Newcastle disease virus spreads within an aviary is by aerosol. Infected birds can transmit virus within 48 hours of exposure and before showing clinical signs of disease. The virus leaves the respiratory tract in expired air and can remain airborne for long periods (Hanson 1972). Airborne spread from one group of infected birds to another in the vicinity can thus occur. Vertical transmission through the egg has not been proven but eggs laid by diseased birds may be infected with the virus causing death of the embryo. The introduction of an infected bird is, however, the most likely way Newcastle disease virus will be introduced into a previously disease-free aviary. There have been claims (Lancaster and

Alexander 1975) that parrots can harbour Newcastle disease virus for long periods without showing clinical signs of disease. Other authorities believe that a long-term carrier state does not occur and infected parrots that do not die are free of the virus four weeks after clinical signs have disappeared (Luthgen 1981).

CONTROL

In this country the primary defence against Newcastle disease is by preventing its entry into the country in imported birds or poultry products. The importation of Birds, Poultry and Hatching Eggs Order 1979 prohibits the landing in Great Britain without a licence of any live bird. Parrots and other captive birds can, however, be licensed into this country into Ministry of Agriculture approved quarantine premises where they spend at least 35 days under veterinary supervision. Unvaccinated sentinel chickens are placed in the same air space as the imported parrots as a Newcastle disease check. Birds dying in quarantine are sent to a Veterinary Investigation Centre for post mortem examination which includes screening for NDV by egg embryo inoculation. If NDV was isolated the birds in that quarantine premises would not be released. The quarantine premises are secure buildings with filters to prevent escape of infective particles into the surrounding air. Despite these controls it would be a wise precaution for any aviculturist to isolate any purchased birds for at least four weeks before introducing them into his aviary.

VACCINATION

Live and inactivated vaccines of proven efficacy in chickens are available to control Newcastle disease. These are used successfully on a large scale in most countries for the protection of domestic poultry. Live vaccines are cheap and simple to use and can be given in the drinking water, by eye or nose drop or by spray. As parrots drink intermittently, water application is considered less reliable than other application routes for these species. A lentogenic live vaccine given by spray and repeated two to three weeks later should provide satisfactory lasting immunity. However, to protect cockatoos and parakeets in the Jurong Bird Park, Singapore, from a continuing threat from velogenic Newcastle disease, it was found necessary to spray the birds with a lentogenic live vaccine every month (Chew and Liow 1974). Use of the live lentogenic vaccine in the face of clinical disease will also increase the chance of survival of birds not already infected (Luthgen 1981). A machine such as a Turbair vaccinair or a Vulcan 6:Era that generates aerosol droplets that have an initial diameter of up to 60 microns which evaporate down to less than three microns is recommended as suitable for vaccinating parrots. The live vaccine should be diluted in 500 ml distilled water and given at the rate of five chicken doses per parrot. The vaccine should be sprayed over a period of 6-8 minutes with the sprayer between 0.5 and 1.5 metres distance away from the birds (Luthgen 1981, Gough and Allan 1973).

A formalised strain of Newcastle disease virus in an oil adjuvant vaccine and given by intramuscular injection is a very potent vaccine when given to chickens. Unfortunately, such inactivated vaccines do not appear to be so effective in parrots. When Grey parrots *(Psittacus erithacus)* and budgerigars *(Melopsittacus undulatus)* were injected with an inactivated vaccine there was no evidence of production of haemagglutination-inhibitory antibodies. In the same trial 75 per cent of the vaccinated budgerigars died when challenged with a pathogenic strain of virus (Luthgen 1981). The use of Newcastle disease vaccines in this country is dependent on the current government policy for control of Newcastle disease and whether suitable vaccines are licensed. When the country is free of Newcastle disease, vaccine of psittacine birds is probably not necessary. However, if the situation deteriorated and a collection of valuable psittacine birds was at risk from outbreaks of Newcastle disease in poultry in the vicinity, then vaccination should be considered.

EPIDEMIOLOGY

The movement of parrots has undoubtedly been an important factor in the spread of Newcastle disease, both within and between countries. For the past twenty years the national poultry flocks in a number of countries with intensive poultry industries have been put at risk from infected parrots. There are many accounts of the isolation of Newcastle disease virus from parrots shortly after importation from South America and South East Asia (Roepke 1973, Cavill 1974, Cullen and Allan 1974, Lancaster and Alexander 1975 and Luthgen 1981). Newcastle disease is almost certainly endemic in wild psittacine populations in these areas. Newcastle disease virus was isolated from 54 of 302 importations of psittacine birds into Holland (Smit 1975), and from 1.4 per cent of 1,847 psittacine birds examined in California in 1972 and 1973 (Pearson and McCann 1975). The origin of the disastrous outbreaks of Newcastle disease in poultry in California in 1971 was considered to be parrots imported from South America. Control of this disease epizootic in which nine million chickens were destroyed, cost the United States Department of Agriculture 56 million dollars (Hanson 1972, Utterback 1972, Walker, Heron and Mixson 1973).

The potential spread of Newcastle disease from imported parrots was vividly illustrated during the 1971 California epidemic when it was found that one importer had distributed 176 consignments of captive birds exposed to Newcastle disease to pet shops in 35 different states (Walker *et al.* 1973). In England in 1975 the owner of a battery flock of chickens imported 20 parrots from the Far East and put them in an aviary alongside one of his poultry sheds. All the imported birds died and a few days later clinical Newcastle disease was confirmed in his poultry. Within a week two other cases of the disease were confirmed in two neighbouring flocks. The origin of the outbreaks of velogenic Newcastle disease in East Anglia in 1970 was never clearly established but it is possible that the virus could have been introduced into the country with captive birds. Outbreaks of Newcastle disease in poultry in Holland and Canada have also been linked to the importation of parrots (Lancaster and Alexander 1975, Roepke 1973).

CONCLUSION

In this country Newcastle disease in parrots is likely to be encountered by any veterinary surgeon who regularly examines recently imported birds in quarantine. It is hoped that it will not be seen again in parrots outside quarantine or remain a very rare occurrence in such birds. However, it is a very important disease because of its potential for spread to poultry and the devastating losses it could cause to the national poultry flock. For this reason any veterinary surgeon who suspects Newcastle disease should notify the local Divisional Veterinary Officer. Advice on the diagnosis of the disease in parrots and a laboratory post mortem service is also available from the Ministry of Agriculture Veterinary Investigation Laboratories.

REFERENCES

ALEXANDER, D. J. Personal Communication.

CAVILL, J. P. (1982) In diseases of Cage and Aviary Birds 2nd Edition Ed. Petrak, M. L., Lea and Febiger, Philadelphia.

CAVILL, J. P. (1974) Veterinary Record **94** , 226.

CHEW, M. and LIOW, T. M. (1974) Avian Diseases 18 (1) III.

CULLEN, G. A. and ALLAN, W. H. (1974) Veterinary record **94**, 447.

DOYLE, T. M. (1927) Journal of Comparative Pathology and Therapeutics **40,** 144.

GOUGH, R. E. and ALLAN, W. H. (1973) Veterinary Record **93**, 458.

HANSON, R. P. (1972a) In Diseases of Poultry 6th Edition. Ed. Hofstad, M. S., Calnek, B. W., Helmboldt, C. F., Reid, W. M. and Yoder, H. W. Ames Iowa State University Press.

HANSON, R. P. (1972b) Proceedings of the 76th Annual Meeting of the US Animal Health Association, No. 5, p 276.

LANCASTER. J. E. and ALEXANDER, D. J. (1975) Monograph No. 11 Canada Department of Agriculture.

LUHGEN, W. (1981) Fortschritte der Veterinarmedizin 31 Verlag Paul Parey, Berlin and Hamburg.

PEARSON, G. L. and McCANN, M. K. (1975) Journal of the American Veterinary Medical Association, **167**, 610.

ROEPKE, W. J. (1973) 4th European Poultry Conference, London, p 579.

SMIT, T. (1975) Tijdschrift voor Diergeneeskunde 100 (6) 309.

UTTERBACK, W. (1972) Proceedings of the 76th Annual Meeting of the US Animal Health Association No. 5 p 280.

WALKER, J. W., HERON, B. R. and MIXSON, M. A. (1973) Avian Diseases 17 (3) 486.

Chapter 16

TUBERCULOSIS AND PSEUDOTUBERCULOSIS

I. F. Keymer, Ph.D., F.R.C.Path., F.I.Biol., F.R.C.V.S.

At post-examination these bacterial infections can sometimes be confused on the gross appearance of the lesions. They are both zoonotic infections. However, there the resemblance ends.

TUBERCULOSIS

Mycobacterium avium is the usual cause of tuberculosis in birds and it is likely that all species are susceptible. However, psittacines, especially the larger parrots, are unusual by also being susceptible to *M. tuberculosis* the human type (Stableforth, 1929), *M. bovis* (Fox, 1923) and atypical Mycobacteria (Britt *et al.* 1980). Since the first report by Stableforth, *M. tuberculosis* has been isolated from the larger psittacines on at least three occasions (Ackermann *et al.,* 1974; Hinshaw, 1933; Woerpel and Rosskopf, 1984).

All types of tuberculosis are now rare in psittacines in captivity, although previously *M. avium* may have been much more common because Francis, (1958) quoting Fröhner in 1893 found 25 per cent of 700 psittacines to be infected. In a necropsy survey Fox (1923) recorded 5.4 per cent of 698 psitticines to have tuberculosis. These percentages are both high compared with more recent surveys, e.g. 0.08, per cent of 1047 psittacines recorded by Keymer *et al.* (1982) and 0.35 per cent of 69 found by Montali *et al.* (1976).

The diagnosis of tuberculosis in psittacines has frequently been based entirely on the presence of acid fast organisms associated with lesions and without isolation and identifcation of the *Mycobacterium* sp. involved. Strictly speaking, such cases should be termed mycobacteriosis (Panigrahy *et al.* (1983); Riddell and Atlinson (1981).

Tuberculosis in budgerigars and other parakeets is extremely rare.

CLINICAL SIGNS

These can be very variable in *M. avium* infections and depend to a large extent on the organs which are mainly affected. Gradual loss of weight, over a period of months, debility and emaciation invariably occur. They are frequently associated with diarrhoea. Especially in the earlier stages, the appetite may remain good. Dsypnoea may eventually develop. The feathers are often ruffled and Burr (1982) stated that these may have a dull brownish colour 'which also affects the pigments of the skin'. Sometimes complete loss of feathers may occur (Burr, 1982).

When *M. tuberculosis* is the cause, the lesions are always superficial, affecting the skin and natural orifices rather than systemic. This is probably because this organism has a very limited growth, temperature range between 35° and 39°C, Boughton (1969). The skin lesions usually take the form of nodules or horny growths on the palpebral conjunctiva, and sides of the face, sometimes extending over the top of the head and to the commissures of the mouth (Keymer, 1977). In the early stages the lesions are soft and bleed easily but later become caseous. The superficial epithelium becomes thickened and forms scabby layers. When the crown of the head is affected the lesions may perforate the bone. Nodular lesions may also occur in the buccal cavity (Hutyra *et al.* 1938). Stableforth (1929) found an eyelid lesion to be caseous in nature. Slight, unilateral, exophthalmos, conjunctivitis and dorsal chemosis were recorded by Woerpel and Rosskopf (1984). Their parrot, a yellow-naped Amazon *(Amazona ochrocephala)* also had a unilateral, mucopurulent nostril discharge, an oral abscess near the left choanal slit and oedema of the left foot.

POST MORTEM FINDINGS

According to Peavy *et al.* (1976) tuberculosis lesions in psittacines are most frequently found in the intestine, liver, spleen and bone marrow. However, they may also occur in the lungs. Indeed, in other species any tissue may become infected. In all species of birds the lesions are whitish, caseous and necrotic and may be either discrete or partially confluent. They can vary in size from minute foci to large masses displacing all organ tissue. Calcification does not normally occur. Not infrequently lesions in the liver, spleen and kidneys are associated with amyloidosis. Nodular, visceral lesions can sometimes be confused with neoplasia (Panigrahy *et al.* 1983) or coligranulomata. Small focal lesions can be mistaken for pseudotuberculosis or salmonellosis. Granulomatous lesions in the lung sometimes resemble aspergillosis.

BACTERIOLOGICAL EXAMINATION

Examination of smears made from the lesions and stained with Ziehl-Neelsen will usually reveal the presence of numerous acid fast organisms when the causal agent is *M. avium*. If other *Mycobacteria* spp. are involved organisms may be difficult to find. Mycobacteria are slow growing organisms and need special media. Affected tissues, therefore, should be submitted for laboratory examinations.

DIAGNOSIS

This is made on the basis of the history, clinical signs, post-mortem findings and the demonstration of acid fast organisms associated with characteristic lesions on histological examination. Ideally the Mycobacteria should be cultured and typed to confirm the diagnosis. In the live bird diagnosis is more difficult and depends on culturing the organisms from lesions of the skin, buccal cavity or excreta. There is no reliable tuberculin or agglutination test for psittacines. Schroder (1981) has discussed in some detail the diagnosis and prevention of tuberculosis in birds in zoos.

EPIDEMIOLOGY AND PREVENTION

Overcrowding, lack of sunlight, malnutrition, increased or decreased humidity, and poor hygiene are all predisposing causes (Arnall and Keymer, 1975). As the disease is relatively common in gallinaceous birds such as free-range poultry, game birds and peafowl, enclosures and aviaries previously inhabited by such species should never be used for psittacines. Contact with wild birds either direct or indirect should be avoided, because many species, especially woodpigeons *(Columba palumbus)* can be infected and excrete the organisms. The disease is most likely to be acquired by ingestion of food contaminated with excreta of tuberculous birds.

There is evidence that *M. tuberculosis* in psittacines may be acquired from infected humans (Stableforth, 1929; Hutyra *et al.* 1938). The possibility of this type of infection should therefore be considered in any parrot showing skin lesions that has recently been imported from a country where human tuberculosis is prevalent.

TREATMENT

Euthanasia is recommended because treatment is unlikely to be effective. In exceptional circumstances when a very rare, endangered species is involved and a long-standing infection is not suspected it might be worthwhile considering the use of rifampicin ('Rifadin', Merrell Pharmaceuticals Ltd.). If skin lesions are present the treatment should be combined with their surgical removal. In such an event, however, the owner should be warned of the possible zoonotic implications.

REFERENCES

ACKERMANN, L. J., BENBROOK, S. C. and WALTON, B. C. (1974) *Mycobacterium tuberculosis* infection in a parrot *(Amazona farinosa)*. American Review of Respiratory Diseases **109**, 388-390.

ARNALL, L. and KEYMER, I. F. (1975). Bird Diseases. An Introduction to clinical diagnosis and treatment of diseases in birds other than poultry. Baillière Tinsall, London and TFH Publications, Inc. Ltd. Neptune, New Jersey, U.S.A. 528 pp.

BROUGHTON, E. (1969). Tuberculosis caused by *Mycobacterium avium.* The veterinary Bulletin. **39**, 457-465.

BRITT, J. O. Jr., HOWARD, E. B. and ROSSKOPF, W. J. (1980) Psittacine tuberculosis. Cornell Veterinarian **70**, 218-225.

BURR, E. W. (1982). Diseases of Parrots. T. F. H. Publications, Inc. Ltd., Neptune, New Jersey, U.S.A. 318 pp.

FOX, H. (1923) Disease in Captive Wild Mammals and Birds. Philadelphia, J. B. Lippincott, Co. 665 pp.

FRANCIS, J. (1958) Tuberculosis in Animals and Man — A Study in Comparative Pathology. London, Cassell and Company Ltd. 357 pp.

HINSHAW, W. R. (1933). Tuberculosis of human origin in an Amazon parrot *(Amazona sp.)* American Review Tuberculosis. **28**, 273-278.

HUTYRA, F., MAREK, J. and MANNINGER, R. (1938). Special Pathology and Therapeutics of the Domestic Animals. Vol. 1. p. 673.

KEYMER, I. F. (1977). Diseases of Birds other than Domestic Poultry, p.224. In Poultry Diseases, Ed. R. F. Gordon, Ballière Tindall, London.

KEYMER, I. F., JONES, D. M., PUGSLEY, S. L. and WADSWORTH, P. F. (1982). A survey of tuberculosis in the Regent's Park Gardens of the Zoological Society of London. Avian pathology, **11**, 563-569.

MONTALI, R. J., BUSH, M., THOEN, C. O. and SMITH, E. (1976). Tuberculosis in captive exotic birds. Journal American Veterinary Medical Association **169**, 920-927.

PANIGRAHY, B., CLARK, F. D. and HALL, C. F. (1983). Mycobacteriosis in psittacine birds. Avian Diseases, **27**, 1166-1168.

PEAVY, G. M., SILVERMAN, S., HOWARD, E. B., COOPER, R. S., RICH. L. J. and THOMAS, G. N. (1976). Pulmonary tuberculosis in a Sulfur-crested Cockatoo. Journal American Veterinary Medical Association **169**, 915-919.

RIDDELL, C. and ATKINSON, D. (1981). Two cases of mycobacteriosis in psittacine birds. Canadian Veterinary Journal, **22**, 145-147.

SCHRÖDER, H. D. (1981). Tuberculosis prophylaxis in Zoo Birds. XXIII Internationales Symposium über die Erkrankungen der Zootiere, 1981. **23**,67-70. (In German).

STABLEFORTH, A. W. (1929). A bacteriological investigation of cases of tuberculosis in five cats, sixteen dogs, a parrot and a wallaby. Journal of Comparative Pathology and Therapeutics. XLII, 163-188.

WOERPEL, R. W. and ROSSKOPF, W. J. Jr. (1984). Retro-orbital *Mycobacterium tuberculosis* infection in a Yellow-naped Amazon Parrot. Avian/Exotic Practice **1**, 7-10.

PSEUDOTUBERCULOSIS

This infection is caused by *Yersinia* (previously *Pasteurella*) *pseudotuberculosis.* In common with *Mycobacterium* spp. the organism has a wide host range infecting mammals including man, birds and reptiles.

In psittacines the disease is relatively uncommon compared with many other species such as the canary and toucans which appear to be unusually susceptible (Arnall and Keymer, 1985); Borst *et al.* 1977). All aspects of the infection have been reviewed by Obwolo (1986). The closely related organism *Y. enterocolitica* is rarely recorded in birds but may have been overlooked. It has been described in budgerigars by Giles and Carter (1980).

CLINICAL SIGNS

Unlike tuberculosis this infection is an acute or subacute septicaemia. The incubation period varies from two days to about two weeks. Death may occur without any noticable signs or be preceded by a short period of depression, ruffled feathers, dyspnoea and diarrhoea, including watery, urate excretion. In more chronic infections there is also loss of weight and occasionally the excreta may become abnormally hard, (Arnall and Keymer, 1975). Losses in a collection of birds are often sporadic and unpredictable.

POST-MORTEM FINDINGS.

Septicaemia results in hepatomegaly and splenomegaly with generalised congestion of the internal organs. Multiple, usually minute creamy-white foci are found throughout the liver, spleen and less frequently the kidneys and gut. The lungs and other tissues are seldom affected, although the bacteria have been isolated from budgerigars with caseous necrotic lesions affecting the crop (Anon, 1985). Pseudotuberculosis, however, is not the usual cause of these lesions (Arnall and Keymer, 1975).

BACTERIOLOGICAL EXAMINATION

Examination of smears made from visceral lesions and stained with Ziehl-Neelsen is necessary to differentiate from tuberculosis. If Gram stain shows Gram negative, small, pleomorphic, non-sporing and non-capsulated coccobacilli then, pseudotuberculosis should be suspected. The organisms are aerobic and grow quite readily at $22^{\circ} - 37^{\circ}$ C in broth culture, and on MacConkey and blood agar without showing haemolysis. On MacConkey agar small, non-lactose fermenting colonies are produced. On blood agar they appear as small, yellowish-white granular colonies.

DIAGNOSIS

The infection can only be confirmed by necropsy and bacteriological examination.

EPIDEMOLOGY AND PREVENTION

The disease is spread by contamination of food by faeces, mainly of rodents and wild birds. Healthy rats and mice can be carriers of the bacteria. Packeted seed is therefore much less likely to be contaminated than bought loose. All seed should be stored in rodent proof containers. Greenfood should be washed prior to feeding and outdoor aviaries should be covered with solid roofing such as transparent plastic sheeting to mimimise contamination with wild bird's excreta.

There is some evidence that stress factors and malnutrition may be predisposing causes. The infection is most prevalent in the winter, and is mainly by the oral route.

TREATMENT

This is difficult due to the acute and sporadic nature of the disease and the fact that it can only be diagnosed by necropsy. However, in-contact birds can be given a course of broad spectrum antibiotics based on the results of sensitivity tests on the organisms. Owners should be warned that this is a zoonotic infection. No entirely satisfactory vaccine has been produced.

REFERENCES

ANON. (1985). Annual report. The West of Scotland Agricultural College, Veterinary Laboratory, Dumfries. p. 15.

ARNALL, L. and KEYMER, I. F. (1975) Bird Diseases. An Introduction to clinical diagnosis and treatment of diseases in birds other than poultry. Ballière Tindall, London and TFH Publications, Inc. Ltd., Neptune, New Jersey, U.S.A. 528 pp.

BORST, G. H. A., BUITELAR, M., POELMA, F. G., ZWART, P. and DORRESTEIN, G. M. (1977). Yersinia pseudotuberculosis in birds. Tijdschr. Diergeneesk, **102,** 81-85.

GILES, N. and CARTER, M. J. (1980). *Yersinia enterocolitica* in budgerigars. Veterinary Record, **107,** 362-363.

OBWOLO, M. J. (1976) A review of yersiniosis *(Yersinia pseudotuberculosis)* infection. The Veterinary Bulletin. **46,** 167-171.

Chapter 17

ESCHERICHIA COLI AND SALMONELLA SPP.

I. F. Keymer, Ph.D., F.R.C.Path., F.I.Biol., F.R.C.V.S.

ESCHERICHIA COLI INFECTIONS

These occur in a wide variety of birds. They give rise to diseases termed colibacillosis and *E.coli* septicaemia when there is a generalised infection and Hjärre's disease when the lesions are characterised by granulomata involving the gut wall, but also sometimes the liver and mesentery. *E.coli* organisms can also be associated with a variety of inflammatory lesions including pericarditis, peritonitis, omphalitis, salpingitis, air sacculitis, pneumonitis, sinusitis, panophthalmitis, blepharitis, rhinitis, and septic synovitis and arthritis. *E.coli,* however, is perhaps most frequently blamed for enteritis in a wide range of birds.

E.coli bacteria are generally secondary pathogens associated with other bacteria, fungi, some parasitic infestations or virus infections. They are frequent *post mortem* invaders and when isolated at necropsy great care is needed in assessing their pathogenic rôle. Providing there is minimal autolysis, interpretation requires histological examination.

The pathogenic rôle of *E.coli* in psittacines is much less clear than in the domestic fowl, although all the manifestations of the infection referred to above probably occur. However, there is much controversy regarding the rôle of *E.coli* in the gut of psittacines. Fiennes (1959, 1982) stated that in psittacines, Gram negative bacilli *(e.g. E.coli)* 'are absent from the normal gut' and the finding of *E.coli* in the droppings 'indicates the presence of a pathogen'. Beach (1962), Dolphin and Olsen (1977) and Graham and Graham (1978) appear to support this opinion. It is, however, questioned by Jones and Nisbet (1980) who in a survey of avian gut flora isolated *E.coli* from 25 of 54 apparently normal psittacines. They stress therefore 'that their presence may not necessarily suggest an impending clinical problem'. Nevertheless, it is possible that on occasion these bacteria may play at least a contributory rôle in enteritis of psittacines. Burr (1981) regarded *E.coli* as one of the causes of enteritis in parrots. More research, however, is needed including histological examination of the gut in all suspected cases of *E.coli* enteritis.

Bhambani and Krishna Murty (1963) attributed an outbreak of diarrhoel disease in budgerigars to *E.coli* probably of serotype 'O$_2$K$_1$' commonly associated with coli septicaemia in poultry. Although 'acute catarrhal enteritis' was noted at necropsy, clinical signs included greenish diarrhoea and re-gurgitation of food and greenish slimy fluid from the beak. The outbreak closely resembled the oesophageal and crop necrosis syndrome originally described by Keymer (1958) and illustrated and discussed further by Arnall and Keymer (1975). It is doubtful if *E.coli* is the primary cause of this syndrome, which is more likely to be multifactoral.

CLINICAL SIGNS

It will be obvious from the foregoing that these are extremely variable especially as *E.coli* is frequently merely a secondary invader. It can also attack a wide range of tissues. In psittacines it is, perhaps, mostly associated with rhinitis and supra or infraorbital sinusitis and blepharitis. It may also be found in association with other organisms such as *Staphylococcus* spp., *Pseudomonas aeruginosa, Proteus* spp. and *Aspergillus* spp. (Burr, 1982) or be secondary to hypovitaminosis A. Another common site for *E.coli* in psittacines is the lower respiratory tract, associated or unassociated with similar organisms, in which case dyspnoea may be present. *E.coli* also appears to play a secondary rôle in some cases of pedal synovitis and arthritis ('bumblefoot').

POST MORTEM FINDINGS

These are non-specific and include all the inflammatory lesions mentioned above.

BACTERIOLOGICAL EXAMINATION

The organisms are motile, Gram negative rods and grow readily on the usual nutrient media at 18°-44°C or lower. Colonies are smooth, shiny, large and pinkish. Most of the avian serotypes are pathogenic only for birds. Unlike poultry little is known about psittacine strains. The mould form of *E. coli* serotypes 08, 09 and 016 are responsible for the Hjärre's disease form (Gerlach, 1986).

DIAGNOSIS

The significance of *E. coli* isolations has to be carefully assessed in conjunction with the history, clinical signs and *post mortem* findings.

EPIDEMIOLOGY AND PREVENTION

As the organisms are prevalent in the environment of birds, strict attention to hygiene is essential together with high standards of nutrition. Good ventilation and freedom from unnecessary stress are also important. Oral is the usual route of infection, but the bacteria can also be transmitted aerogenically and via the egg (Gerlach, 1986).

TREATMENT

E. coli is sensitive to many antibiotics, although strains vary in this respect. Apart from taking suitable preventative measures it is important to have sensitivity tests carried out on organisms which have been isolated from lesions either during life or *post-mortem.* The primary cause of the disease, however, needs to be found and treated accordingly. With enteric forms of the disease, supportive treatments should be used as advised for Salmonellosis.

REFERENCES

ARNALL, L. and KEYMER, I. F. (1975). Bird Diseases. An Introduction to clinical diagnosis and treatment of diseases in birds other than poultry. Baillière Tindall, London and TFH Publications, Inc, Ltd., Neptune, New Jersey, U.S.A. 528 pp.

BEACH, J. E. (1962). Diseases of budgerigars and other cage birds — a survey of post-mortem findings. Veterinary record. **74**, 10-15.

BHAMBANI, B. D. and KRISHNA MURTY, D. (1963). An outbreak of diarrhoel disease among budgerigars *(Melopsittacus undulatus). Veterinary Record* **75**, 772-774.

BURR, E. W. (1982). Disease of Parrots. T.F.H. Publications, Inc. Ltd., Neptune, New Jersey, U.S.A. 318 pp.

DOLPHIN, R. E. and OLSEN, D. E. (1977). Fecal monitoring of caged birds. Veterinary Medicine and Small Animal Clinician. **72**, 1081-1085.

FIENNES, R. N. T.-W. (1959). Report of the Society's pathologist for the year 1957. Proceedings of the Zoological Society of London. **132, 129-146.**

FIENNES, R. N. T.-W. (1982). Diseases of bacterial origin, pp. 497-515. In: Diseases of Cage and Aviary Birds, 2nd Ed. M. L. Petrak, Lea and Febiger, Philadelphia, U.S.A.

GERLACH, H. (1986). **In** Bacterial Diseases, 434-453. Clinical Avian Medicine and Surgery. Eds. Harrison, G. J. and Harrison, L. R., W. B. Saunders Company, Philadelphia, U.S.A.

GRAHAM, C. L. and GRAHAM, D. L. (1978). Occurrence of *Escherichia coli* in faeces of Psittacine Birds. Avian Diseases **22**, 340-343.

JONES, D. M. and NISBET, D. J. (1980). The Gram negative bacterial flora of the avian gut. Avian Pathology, **9**, 33-38.

KEYMER, I. F. (1958). The Diagnosis and Treatment of Common Psittacine Diseases. Modern Veterinary Practice **39**, (21), 22-30.

SALMONELLA INFECTIONS

Salmonellosis in birds can be caused by many serotypes of *Salmonella*, but in psittacines *S. typhimurium* is usually the cause. The disease is often referred to as paratyphoid by bird keepers. *S. typhimurium* phage type U286 is particularly prevalent in African grey parrots *(Psittacine erithacus)* originating from West Africa (Edwards, 1981). Other species of *Salmonella* are rarely encountered, although Buxton (1957) recorded *S. thompson* and *S. pullorum* in budgerigars and Ehrsam (1985) also described pullorum disease *(S. pullorum* infection) in hawk-headed parrots *(Deroptyus accipitrinus)*. Keymer (1974) diagnosed salmonellosis *(S. enteritidis* infection) in an Amazon parrot *(Amazona ochrocephala)* and isolated *S. montevideo* from a budgerigar and *S. bareilly* from a cockatiel *(Nymphicus hollandicus)*. Panigrahy *et al.* (1984) recorded *S. arizonae* in a psittacine.

CLINICAL SIGNS

The usual signs are greenish diarrhoea, depression, ruffled feathers, polydipsia, anorexia, shivering and death. Sometimes, however, the disease is peracute and death occurs suddenly. Less acute and chronic forms with loss of weight will also occur. Partly recovered birds may remain carriers for a considerable time and excrete the organisms. Complete recovery is unusual and chronically affected birds slowly lose weight.

In some non-psittacines, apparently healthy carriers are a well recognised hazard to other members of a flock, because they may be intermittent excretors of the organisms. Fertility can be adversely affected, with poor hatchability of eggs as the result of retarded embryonic development or mortality. Chicks which do hatch may be stunted and fail to thrive (Arnall and Keymer, 1975). These signs, however, are less well documented in psittacines than in some birds such as the domestic fowl, other gallinaceous species and pigeons. Lories (Loridae) are stated by Gerlach (1986) to be extremely susceptible and develop a peracute disease with high mortality.

Salmonellosis in psittacines, as well as some other species, is sometimes associated with psittacosis especially in recently imported birds.

POST MORTEM FINDINGS

In acute cases there is typically a generalised congestion of the internal organs, hepatomegaly and splenomegaly. Petechial haemorrhages may be seen on the serosal surfaces of the small intestine. Sometimes, multiple, minute or occasionally larger creamy-white, granulomatous foci of necrosis may affect the liver and spleen. Panigrahy and Gilmore (1983) have also recorded chronic ulcerative enteritis and pyogranulomatous nephritis.

BACTERIOLOGICAL EXAMINATION

Salmonellae grow well on MacConkey media and are non-lactose fermenters. Deoxycholate citrate agar is often used because this inhibits or suppresses the growth of coliforms and Gram positive bacteria. Selenite broth is widely used, selective enrichment medium for avian isolates. Salmonellae are almost always motile except *S. pullorum* which is rare nowadays. *S. gallinarum* is also non-motile and rare but does not appear to infect psittacines.

DIAGNOSIS

The infection can only be confirmed by *post mortem* and bacteriological examinations. At necropsy the gross lesions can be easily confused with pseudotuberculosis.

EPIDEMIOLOGY AND PREVENTION

Rodents and wild birds are a potential source of infection. Salmonellae are transmitted via the egg and healthy carriers can also excrete the organisms intermittently. Once the infection becomes established in an aviary it can be extremely difficult to eradicate. Cleanliness and care in the choice and origin of foodstuffs is important. The infection is spread mainly by the oral route in a similar manner to pseudotuberculosis. Salmonellae can survive in dry excreta for eight months and in water for three weeks. (Gerlach 1986).

TREATMENT

No single antibiotic is entirely effective and the choice should be governed by the results of sensitivity tests. However, two of the more effective drugs are trimethoprim and furaltadone. Nevertheless, even repeated treatment may not eliminate the organism from infected birds. In spite of an apparent recovery they may remain carriers for long periods. Supportive treatments are also desirable using fluids, electrolytes, vitamin B complex, and *Lactobacillus* cultures to lower the pH of the intestinal tract either in the form of a commercial preparation or a sour milk product. No satisfactory vaccines have been developed.

REFERENCES

ARNALL, L. and KEYMER, I. F. (1975). Bird Diseases. An Introduction to clinical diagnosis and treatment of diseases in birds other than poultry. Baillière Tindall, London and TFH Publications, Inc. Ltd., Neptune, New Jersey, U.S.A. 528 pp.

BUXTON, A. (1957). Salmonellosis in Animals. A review. Commonwealth Agricultural Bureau, Farnham Royal, Bucks.

EDWARDS, W. A. (1981). Emergence of *Salmonella typhimurium* U286 in parrots. Veterinary Record. **109**, p313.

EHRSAM, H. (1985). Acute pullorum disease in hawk-headed parrots. (In German). Schweizer Archiv fur Tierheilkunde **127**, 397-400.

GERLACH, H. (1986) **In** Bacterial Diseases, 434-453. Clinical Avian Medicine and Surgery. Eds. Harrison, G. J. and Harrison, L. R., W. B. Saunders Company, Philadelphia, U.S.A.

KEYMER, I. F. (1974). Report of the Pathologist, 1971 p. 58. *In Scientific Report 1971-1973. The Zoological Society of London.* Journal of Zoology, London, **173**, 37-158.

PANIGRAHY B., and GILMORE, W. C. (1983). Systemic salmonellosis in an African grey parrot and salmonella osteoarthritis in canaries. Journal American Veterinary Medical Association. **183**, 699-700.

PANIGRAHY, B., GRIMES, J. E. and CLARK, F. D. (1984). Zoonoses in Psittacine Birds. Journal of Infectious Diseases, **149**, 123-124.

Chapter 18

NUTRITIONAL DISEASES

M.P.C. Lawton B.Vet.Med., Cert.V.Ophthal., M.R.C.V.S.

GENERAL DEFICIENCIES

Malnutrition is far too often the cause of disease in parrots. Jones (1979) considered that half of the clinical cases seen in psittacine birds involved nutritional deficiencies. This is not surprising, as deficient diets are commonly fed to parrots (Pitts 1983). The average diet consists mainly of seeds which contain low levels of calcium, vitamin A, lysine, methionine and tryptophan.

An uncomplicated deficiency of a single nutrient seldom, if ever, occurs (Tollefson 1982). Due to interaction of the nutrients of the diet, and the general deficiency of more than one nutrient in that diet, symptoms of more generalised non-specific malnutrition are more commonly seen. Specific nutritional deficiencies of parrots and their symptoms are not well reported in the literature; most descriptions are based on those known to occur in chickens, turkeys and domestic ducks.

In addition to deficiencies, nutritional diseases due to excess occur in sedentary or closely confined birds (Lowenstein 1986).

Nutritional disorders should always be suspected if a bird is emaciated or obese, or showing general ill health (the so called 'sick bird' syndrome). In the case of the 'sick bird' syndrome, nutritional deficiencies may only be one contributing factor to this multifactorial problem, though improving the diet will often help improve this condition.

NATURAL DIET (See also, chapter 21)

Diet is considered (Tollefson 1982) the single most important factor in ensuring a long, healthy life and complete physiological efficiency. An adequate diet is required for proper growth, reproduction and metabolism. An inadequate diet may result in problems with any or all of these.

The best way to avoid deficiencies is by mimicking the natural diet that the parrot would eat in the wild. From their digestive system, parrots are equipped to derive their nutrients principally from seeds and fruits. Refection, the eating of droppings to obtain nutrients, also takes place in parrots as in poultry (Smith 1979). Members of the parrot family in their natural habitat eat a wide variety of seeds, vegetables, fruits and insects. It has been observed (Long 1984) that some species may eat seeds of up to 52 species in 15 families of plants and six orders of insects. It is this wide variety of foods which enables a balanced diet. Although in the wild insects are often taken as a supplement to the diet of seed and fruit (Jones 1979), Long 1984), they are very rarely offered to the captive parrot.

Amino acids which can not be manufactured by the bird are termed essential amino acids, and these must be supplied in the food or deficiencies will result. Lysine, methionine and tryptophan tend only to be found in animal protein. Young growing birds, in particular, require a wide variety of protein sources other than just seeds. Almost all species ingest some animal protein in the wild (Jones 1979) but this is rarely offered to captive birds.

The diet of the average captive parrot consists predominantly of seeds, and usually a high proportion of these are sunflower seeds. Although sunflower seeds more than meet the parrot's needs for energy, protein and lipids, they are low in minerals and vitamins. It is for this reason that seeds should be restricted in their availability, especially because of their low calcium content. A more balanced diet including fruits, vegetables, insects and animal protein should be provided to prevent nutritional deficiencies. Furthermore, it is imperative that food is fresh as the nutritional value, and particularly the vitamin content, deteriorates rapidly with age.

FACTORS AFFECTING NUTRITIONAL REQUIREMENTS

The age, breeding state, moulting state and health of the parrot have a major effect on its nutritional requirements.

Young growing birds have a very much higher requirement for minerals, vitamins and proteins than adult birds. In smaller species there is a greater need for energy to maintain body heat; in larger species there is more of a requirement for the muscle and bone building elements of the diet.

A bird on a deficient diet may show no problems until it is stressed. For example, during egg laying there is an increased demand for calcium for the egg shell and vitamin A, fats and protein for the yolk. Moulting also stresses the bird and results in increased dietary requirements, especially of protein and lipids (Harrison & Harrison 1986).

Abnormalities of the beak and lesions of the tongue which result in prehension problems may result in an inadequate intake of nutrients. Vomiting and diarrhoea may result in the inability of the bird to absorb nutrients. All these conditions can result in deficiencies and a further worsening of the bird's condition.

FEATHER AND BEAK PROBLEMS CAUSED BY NUTRITIONAL DEFICIENCIES

Nutritional deficiencies have been implicated in the causation of malformed and curled feathers, stress marks, depigmentation and perpetual moult (Jones 1979, Tollefson 1982, Turner 1985, Harrison & Harrison 1986, Lowenstine 1986). They are considered more fully in Chapter 10. (See plate 18:1).

Harrison & Harrison (1986) also list extensive nail growth, dry flaky skin, a layered appearance of the beak, together with other beak abnormalities and the wearing of the plantar surface of the feet, so it is devoid of scale pattern, as all possible problems associated with malnutrition.

OBESITY AND ATHEROSCLEROSIS

Most owners of the single bird have a tendency to over feed (Jones 1979), especially if feeding is used as a boredom reliever. Furthermore, in such circumstances oilseeds are often a major component of the diet.

Obesity results in the dermal, subcutaneous and intra-abdominal storage of fat, as well as deposition of fat in the liver which may result in liver failure if severe enough (Jones 1979). The dermal and subcutaneous fat deposits may become lipomatous (Lowenstein 1986). A strict diet may reduce the size of the lipoma (Harrison & Harrison 1986) and is indicated prior to surgical removal (See Chapter 5).

High-fat diets, especially those rich in saturated fats and cholesterols may result in atherosclerosis, which is fairly common in older psittacine birds (Jones 1979, Lowebstein 1986). In atherosclerosis (Chapter 11) the affected vessels become rigid and thickened, due to the fatty and calcareous deposits and proliferation of fibrous tissue of the intima of the arteries. There are also yellowish opaque streaks and plaques which may even be radiopaque. Fatty infiltration of cardiac muscle with resultant heart failure is also considered a problem (Jones 1979).

High fat diets may also result in diarrhoea and secondary deficiencies in other nutrients.

Birds suffering with obesity should be placed on a strict low fat diet, which requires a restricted seed intake, especially sunflower seeds. There is often client and bird resentment of this advice, making this condition even more difficult to treat than a deficiency problem.

CALCIUM, PHOSPHORUS AND VITAMIN D$_3$

An imbalance in the absorption of calcium, phosphorus and vitamin D is common in parrots and results in a variety of disease conditions (Wallach & Flieg 1967, Wallach 1970, Jones 1979, Wallach 1979, Randell 1981, Tollefson 1982, Fowler 1986, Harrison & Harrison 1986). This problem arises as a result of their customary diet of high oil-bearing foods such as sunflower seed and peanuts.

The metabolic bone disease and their causation are considered in Chapter 12.

Calcium and phosphorus imbalance can also result in soft shelled eggs (Coles 1985), Harrison & Harrison 1986) or a cessation of egg laying altogether (Coles 1985). Egg binding may also be due to a calcium deficiency, as it appears to respond well to intramuscular injections of 10% calcium gluconate (Harrison & Harrison 1986), at a dose of 10 to 20 mls/Kg.

Hyperphosphataemia may induce polyuria so that the droppings appear loose.

Excessive amounts of Vitamin D_3 in the diet may also cause problems. The increased rate of calcium metabolism may result in mineralisation of soft tissues (Wallach 1970, Wallach 1979, Harrison & Harrison 1986), as well as increased bone resorption resulting in fragile and easily broken bones (Wallach & Flieg 1967).

IODINE DEFICIENCY

Although mainly seen in budgerigars (Blackmore 1963), it could occur in any pet bird which is kept on an iodine deficient diet (Jones 1979, Lothrop et al. 1986). Turner (1985) reports this condition as rarely seen today; this would be true if budgerigars were fed on packet seed, which is well supplemented, but unfortunately, cheaper loose seed is often used and this results in an iodine deficiency.

Iodine deficiency results in a decreased production of thyroid hormones, which stimulates an increased production of Thyroid Stimulating Hormone (TSH) by the adenohypophysis. TSH has a direct effect on the thyroid gland resulting in hyperplasia and dysplasia of the gland. It is usually not possible to palpate the goitre, as the paired thyroids lie along the trachea anterior to the syrinx and next to the common carotid arteries.

Although these hypothyroid budgerigars have a reduced metabolic rate and are prone to obesity, this is not diagnostic as ad lib. feeding often results in obesity in budgerigars. The presenting clinical signs are due to the mechanical effects of the enlarged thyroid pressing on other structures (Blackmore & Cooper 1982). Usually, the first sign noticed is loss of, or change of, voice. The pressure on the syrinx and the lower trachea results in a squeaking respiratory noise heard as a characteristic 'click'. The bird often adopts a sitting position with the head pointing upwards to help it breathe (See Plate 18:2).

Thyroid pressure on the lower oesophagus can prevent seed from passing into the proventriculus. The resulting dilation of the crop may be the reason for the bird to be presented. The inability of the crop to empty properly will also result in weight loss.

In very severe cases there may be cardiac embarrassment due to the pressure on the heart and blood vessels and this may result in convulsions and/or partial paralysis (Blackmore & Cooper 1982)

Diagnosis is suggested by the presenting clinical signs and dietry history but only really made on the response to treatment.

Treatment is by the addition of iodine into the drinking water and subsequently increasing the iodine content of the diet. A stock solution of iodine is made be adding 1 part of Lugol's iodine to 14 of water; one drop of this solution is then added to 30mls of drinking water daily for 3 weeks (Blackmore & Cooper 1982). Addition to the diet of ground oyster shell or cod liver oil are recommended (Altman 1986) as rich sources of iodine.

Although the larger parrots are often hypothyroid, it is not considered (Lothrop et al. 1986) necessary to treat them, as they rarely show clinical signs like their smaller relatives.

VITAMIN A DEFICIENCY

This is the commonest and best known deficiency of parrots, though Pitts (1983), after a search of the literature, found no reports of definitive Vitamin A levels or deficiency responses in any psittacine species. Most information is extrapolated from poultry. A diagnosis is made mainly on nutritional history, clinical signs and the bird's resonse to therapy (Harrison & Harrison 1986). A definitive diagnosis can be made on biopsy and histopathology. Blood levels require a large volume which would debilitate a live bird, other than a large Macaw. Most diagnoses are made retrospectively on response to treatment.

The majority of Vitamin A deficiencies are caused by inadequate diets (Pitts 1983, Harrison & Harrison 1986), particularly due to overfeeding of sunflower seeds.

Before dealing with the various possible problems associated with a Vitamin A deficiency, an understanding of the phisiology of Vitamin A is necessary. Pro-Vitamin A cartenoids, can be obtained from plants, especially the deep green and orange vegetables such as spinach, parsley, yams and carrots as well as egg yolk. In the intestinal mucosa these pro-Vitamin A carotenoids are converted into functional Vitamin A. This functional Vitamin A is stored in the liver until needed. The onset of signs of hypovitaminosis A thus not only depend on the dietary Vitamin A content, but also upon the stores of Vitamin A in the bird's liver at the onset of the deprivation (Lowenstine 1986).

Vitamin A is responsible for the maintenance of the mucous membranes in a moist and healthy condition. It also has a function in bone formation by participating in the formation of mucopolysaccharides (McDonald *et al.* 1973, Davies 1976).

Vitamin A aldehyde (cis-retinal) is a part of the visual pigment rhodopsin. In the normal functioning of this visual pigment due to its being bleached by light and then regenerating, there is some degradation of the Vitamin A. In the Vitamin A deficient bird there may not be enough Vitamin A for the regeneration of the rhodopsin and thus night blindness may result.

Vitamin A deficiency has been implicated in a wide range of conditions. Pitts (1983) suspects the reason for this is that most cases do not indicate a pure Vitamin A deficiency.

The earliest lesion of Vitamin A deficiency occur as a result of the changes in the mucus protection of the epithelium (Tollefson 1982, Pitts 1983, Harrison & Harrison 1986). These changes affect the epithelium in the respiratory, alimentary and reproductive tracts (Tollefson 1982). The lower level of mucus production reduces the resistance of the epithelial cells to the entrance of pathogenic organisms. This results in more severe secondary respiratory infections in Vitamin A deficient birds.

Later changes result in the thickening of the keratin layer of the epithelial surface (hyperkeratosis). Squamous metaplasia is the first change, usually of the oral mucosa, lacrimal and salivary glands, upper respiratory tract, renal tubules and collecting ducts of the urinary tract (Harrison & Harrison 1986, Lowenstein 1986).

The squamous metaplasia of the oral mucosa and, in particular, the glandular tissues result in keratin cysts which may become secondarily infected and be seen as pustules or abscesses. These are often accompanied by oral candidiasis and secondary bacterial infections. The lesions are seen on the tongue, around the choana in the pharynx (See Plate 18:3) and sometimes extending down into the oesaphagus (Jones 1979, Wallach 1979). Treatment is debridment under general anaesthesia, antibiosis where indicated and dietary change or Vitamin A supplementation.

Vitamin A deficiency is also a cause of multiple oral pustules in 10 day old chicks (Wallach 1970).

Most clinical cases are presented with respiratory disease or just the 'sick bird' syndrome of generalised unthriftness and lethargy (Pitts 1983). Respiratory signs may be sneezing, wheezing and dyspnoea, depending on the extent of the changes. There may be squamous cell metaplasia of the bronchi down to the syrinx (Harrison & Harrison 1986), or there may be nasal discharge or crusting of the nostrils (Pitts 1983). The sinuses may fill up with keratin and these can result in the blockage of the nares with material consisting of an amalgam of dust and keratin whorls referred to as rhinoliths (See Plate 18:4). Vitamin A deficiency should be considered if there is no response to antibiotic therapy, including treatment of mycoplasma. The rhinoliths should be removed surgically.

Vitamin A deficiency may result in squamous metaplasia of the ureteral epithelium (Lowenstine 1986). Chronic Vitamin A deficient cases may thus be presented suffering with gout due to this damage to the tubules of the kidneys.

There are also changes in the eye, which include xerophthalmia, conjunctivitis and swellings (Pitts 1983). The xerophthalmia is as a result of the squamous metaplasia of the lacrimal glands. There may also be associated swelling in the periocular region. (See Plate 18:5). These are usually abscesses which should be surgically removed, including the capsule, and sutured closed. Antibiotics are generally not necessary.

Vitamin A deficiency has also been implicated in French moult as a possible cause, together with poor hygiene and intense breeding, although viral infection is now considered the most likely cause. Other problems associated with Vitamin A deficiency include corns (Harrison & Harrison 1986), low hatchability and high mortality (Tollefson 1982).

Uncomplicated cases of Vitamin A deficiency usually respond to treatment with Vitamin A within 3 days. Therapeutic doses of 5 to 50 iu/gm daily for 2 to 4 weeks have been recommended. The maintenance dose is 0.25 to 1 iu/gm daily (Pitts 1983). ('ABiDEC' drops. 1 drop = 260iu Vitamin A).

The bird's diet should be changed to improve the Vitamin A status. Unfortunately most psittacines will readily eat an all seed diet but are unwilling to try anything new (Pitts 1983). Often patience and persistence are required in order to change the diet to a more balanced one. Dried chilli peppers are a good source of Vitamin A. Attempts should also be made to include spinach, parsley and carrots in the diet.

Hypervitaminosis A has not been described in psittacine birds, but it would seem prudent to avoid overdosage.

VITAMIN B COMPLEX

These vitamins act as coenzymes for several enzyme systems. Consequently, clinical signs associated with a deficiency will depend on which B vitamin is deficient, the system that is affected and the stage of growth of the bird.

There is little storage of thiamine (Vitamin B_1)in the body, necessitating regular intake from the diet. Cereal seeds are fairly good source of B vitamins. Thiamine deficiency is considered (Wallach 1979) to be a common problem but overlooked due to secondary bacterial and fungal infections masking the primary cause.

B Vitamin deficiencies have been associated with Central Nervous signs (Tollefson 1982, Coles 1985, Turner 1985). Thiamine is the vitamin usually associated with this, but a combination of other B vitamins may occur. The presenting sign may depend on the severity and the B vitamin deficient. Tollefson (1982) describes paresis or paralysis of the leg as the most common finding. Riboflavin (vitamin B_2) particularly has been implicated (Wallach 1979, Tollefson 1982, Lowenstine 1986) as a cause of curly toe paralysis, similar to that which is induced in birds kept on unsuitable surfaces. Perosis, the dislocation of the gastrocnemius tendon resulting in the deformity of the hock joint, has also been linked with many B vitamins (Tollefson 1982, Lowenstein 1986), including riboflavin (B_2), pantothenic acid, and niacin, biotin, folic acid and choline.

B vitamin deficiency may be involved in some cases of incoordination and tremor (Turner 1985) as response to thiamine therapy may be dramatic if treatment is instituted early enough.

In young birds a deficiency of B vitamins, such as folic acid, niacin, and pantothenic acid, may result in retarded growth, poor feathering, dermatitis or anaemia (Wallach 1979, Tollefson 1982).

Reproduction and hatchability may also be affected by B vitamin deficiencies (Wallach 1979, Tollefson 1982).

VITAMIN E DEFICIENCY

Vitamin E deficiencies in seed eating birds should be considered rare, as seed germs are generally very high in this vitamin. Vitamin E (alpha-tocopherol) is a fat soluble vitamin which acts as an antitoxidant in the cells and organelle membranes. Selenium has a synergistic effect in this process so that these two nutrients should be considered together.

Vitamin E is important in the raising of young psittacines. Schuppel (1979) has described the damage that occurs when raising young psittacines on a Vitamin E deficient diet, where a hepatodystrophy may occur. They are reported to be prone to this up to 6 months of age.

Vitamin E deficiency is characterised clinically in the older bird by central nervous signs (Coles 1985, Lowenstein 1986) in particular ataxia and torticollis. The basis of the lesion appears to be ischaemic necrosis with neuronal degeneration, demyelination and pronounced oedema (Lowenstine 1986). Muscular dystrophy or white muscle disease usually occurs in young birds. Muscles of the breast and heart and the smooth muscle of the gizzard have pale streaks or splotches when examined post mortem.

Cockatiels with varying degrees of paralysis have been found (Harrison & Harrison 1986) to respond to selenium/vitamin E supplementataion.

In chicks vitamin E deficiency may also result in encephalomalacia or so called Crazy Chick Disease (Tollefson 1982, Harrison & Harrison 1986).

VITAMIN K

Overuse of antibiotics is likely to be the only cause of a deficiency of this vitamin (Tollefson 1982). This is because the vitamin is synthesized by the microorganisms in the digestive tract.

Vitamin K is involved in the formation of prothrombin in the liver and consequently a deficiency of this vitamin may result in a prolonged bleeding time.

REFERENCES

ALTMAN, R. B. (1986). Noninfectious Diseases. In Zoo and Wild Animal Medicine. 2nd Edition edited by M. E. Fowler. Pub. W. B. Saunders Co.

BLACKMORE, D. K. (1963). The Incidence and Aetiology of Thyroid Dysplasia in Budgerigars (Melopsittacus undulatus). Vet. Rec. 75:1068-1072.

BLACKMORE, D. K. and COOPER, J. E. (1982). Diseases of the Endocrine System. In Diseases of cage and Aviary Birds. 2nd Edition edited by M. L. Petrak. Pub. Lea and Febiger.

COLES, B. H. (1985). Avian Medicine and Surgery. Pub. Blackwell Scientific Publications.

DAVIES, P. J. (1976). Animal Nutrition. In Primrose McConnell's The Agricultural Notebook edited by I. Moore. 16th Edition. Newnes-Butterworths.

FOWLER, M. E. (1986). Metabolic Bone Disease. In Zoo and Wild Animal Medicine. Edited by M. E. Fowler 2nd Edition. Pub. W. B. Saunders.

HARRISON, G. J. and HARRISON, L. R. (1986). Nutritional Diseases. In Clinical Avian Medicine and Surgery edited by G. J. Harrison and L. R. Harrison. Pub. W. B. Saunders Co.

JONES, D. M. (1979). The Nutrition of Parrots. In The Husbandry and Medicine of The Parrot Family Edited by A. G. Greenwood and J. E. Cooper. Proceedings of a BVZS/Parrot Society Meeting, Regent's Park, London.

LONG, J. L. (1984). The Diets of Three Species of Parrots in the South of Western Australia. Aust. Wildl. Res 11, 357-371.

LOTHROP, C., HARRISON, G. J., SCHULTZ, D. and UTTERIDGE, T. (1986). Miscellaneous Diseases. In Clinical Avian Medicine and Surgery edited by G. J. Harrison and L. R. Harrison. Pub. W. B. Saunders Co.

LOWENSTINE, L. J. (1986). Nutritional Disorders of Birds. In Zoo and Wild Animal Medicine, 2nd Edition, edited by M. E. Fowler. Pub. by W. B. Saunders Co.

McDONALD, P., EDWARDS, R. A. and GREENHALGH, J. F. D. (1973). Vitamins. In Animal Nutrition, edited by P. McDonald, R. A. Edwards and J. F. D. Greenhalgh, 2nd Edition. Longman.

PITTS, C. (1983). Hypovitaminosis A in Psittacines. In Current Veterinary Therapy VIII, Edited R. W. Kirk. Pub. W. B. Saunders Co.

RANDELL, M. G. (1981). Nutritionally induced Hypocalcaemic Tetany in an Amazon Parrot. J.A.V.M.A. 179 (11) 1277-1278.

SCHUPPEL, K. F. (1979). Vitamin E-Mangel Bei Der Aufzucht Von Psittaciden. Erkrankugen der Zootiere. Verhanlungsbericht des XXI. Internationalen Symposiums, vom 13. bias 17. Juni in Mulhouse.

SMITH, G. A. (1979). Parrot Disease as Encountered in a Veterinary Practice. In The Husbandry and Medicine of the Parrot Family Edited by A. G. Greenwood and J. E. Cooper. Proceedings of a BVZS/Parrot Society Meeting, Regent's Park, London.

TOLLEFSON, C. I. (1982). Nutrition. In Diseases of Cage and Aviary Birds. Editor M. L. Petrak. 2nd Edition. Pub. Lea and Febiger.

TURNER, T. (1985). Cagebirds. In Manual of Exotic Pets edited by J. E. Cooper, M. F. Hutchinson, O. F. Jackson and R. J. Maurice. Pub. B.S.A.V.A. Cheltenham.

WALLACH, J. D. (1970). Nutritional Diseases of Exotic Animals. J.A.V.M.A. 157: 583-599.

WALLACH, J. D. (1979). The Mechanics of Nutrition for Exotic Pets. In Non-Domestic Pet medicine. Editor W. J. Boever. The Veterinary Clinics of North America, Small Animal Practice, Vol 9/3 Aug. 1979. Pub W. B. Saunders Co.

WALLACH, J. D. and FLIEG, G. M. (1967). Nutritional Secondary Hyperparathyroidism in Captive Psittacine Birds. J.A.V.M.A. 151:7.

Chapter 19

BEHAVIOURAL PROBLEMS

M. P. C. Lawton B.Vet.Med., Cert.V.Ophthal., M.R.C.V.S.

Due to their intelligence, playfulness and ability of mimicry, psittacines are the most widely kept companion birds. In the wild, these birds are normally social, living with others. In captivity most are kept singularly in a cage. Keeping these birds away from others can have advantages and disadvantages. The main advantage is that they are more likely to become tame and develop their powers of mimicry of sounds, some becoming very good 'talkers'. The disadvantages will be covered in this chapter and are as varied as they are numerous and make up a large part of companion psittacine practice.

CHOICE OF SPECIES

Psittacine species differ not only in their size, dietary requirements and environmental needs, but also in their behavioural attributes. Before purchasing a pet bird, some thought should be given to the needs of the bird as well as what is required from it as a companion.

If the bird is required to be a talker then it should be obtained as young as possible. The younger the bird is, the easier it is to tame and the more agreeable it will usually become. This is due to imprinting, which in itself may result in behavioural problems.

Budgerigars *(Melopsittacus undulatus)* being small (and inexpensive) psittacines, are very popular. Their cage size need not dominate the room and their mess is correspondingly less than larger parrots. With time and patience they can become very tame and very good at mimicry. As companionship goes, there is very little that the larger parrots can offer that these birds cannot. Their main disadvantage is probably that they are considered less exotic than their larger (less common) relatives. Their behavioural problems include regurgitation in males and excessive egg laying in females.

Cockatiels *(Nymphicus hollandicus)* are very active birds but are not easy to tame or encourage to mimic. They, more so than most psittacines, prefer the company of their own kind rather than being a solitary pet. Boredom and feather plucking are the major problems encountered in this species.

African grey parrots *(psittacus erithacus)* are popular pets. These birds are shy and suspicious and consequently can be hard to tame. They are highly intelligent and inquisitive and thus, if enough time is spent with them, they can become excellent talkers. Their powers of mimicry and personalities are the main reason for their popularity. Their vices include biting and feather plucking.

Amazon parrots (*Amazona* spp.) are more colourful than African greys but can become aggressive when young (Davis 1987), usually from 4 to 9 months of age. It is essential that these head strong birds are controlled at this stage to prevent the development of dominance associated problems.

Cockatoos (*Cacatua* spp.) are very intelligent and very demanding requiring constant attention from their owners. They are more suitable for owners with a lot of time on their hands. They are generally not very good talkers being better at imitating other sounds than the human voice. They are lively birds which, if not given the attention they desire, are more likely to become screechers and suffer boredom related problems.

Macaws *(Ara* spp.) are the largest members of the parrot family. They are highly intelligent and easily imprinted towards their owner. They are very playful but can be mischievous, raucous and rowdy. Imprinting occurs readily in these birds, often resulting in them becoming aggressive towards strangers. Due to the size and strength of their beaks this can be a major disadvantage, and they have rightfully obtained the reputation of being nippy and unpredictable. One advantage is that they are less demanding on their owner's time than are cockatoos.

CAUSES OF BEHAVIOURAL PROBLEMS

The causes of behavioural problems are numerous and may be as odd as the behavioural problems they cause but usually they relate to either boredom or neurosis.

Boredom

Being intelligent, psittacine birds need to have variety and to be occupied or they become bored.

The following aspects of their lifestyle may lead to boredom: small cages, insufficient toys, same view, never being let out of the cage, incorrect perches, being alone for long periods and insufficient attention from owners.

Boredom may be a major contributory factor in any behavioural problem but especially screeching and self mutilation.

Neurosis

Neurosis is diagnosed in people who exhibit nonadaptive behaviour and attitudes or anxiety states in an attempt to come to terms with reality rather than to escape it. (Collocott 1971). The term Neurosis can thus also be applied to the behavioural traits seen in birds which are failing to adapt to their surroundings and way of life.

Birds are very sensitive animals and they can react to any change in the environment (Harrison 1984). Thus the causes of neurosis may be other birds, lack of other birds, the size or type of cage they are housed in, the quantity and type of toys and furniture, or even the owner. Disturbances at home may play an important part; a recent move, frequent visitors or constant arguments may induce neurosis. Some birds are left unattended for long periods; others are left with friends frequently while the owner goes away. Some birds become very neurotic about a pet of another species kept in the same house.

Keeping a bird in a cage is probably the greatest cause of neurosis, usually due to frustration associated with the size of the cage or due to attempts to escape from the cage. Dilger and Bell (1982) consider these unresolved frustrations responsible for many of the difficulties encountered in birds.

Some species, such as budgerigars and cockatiels, are highly social species and thus should not be isolated from their own kind or they may gradually decline in general health and may eventually die (Dilger and Bell 1982). Such birds may be isolated as individual pets, but they must not be in range of sight or hearing of other birds. If isolated birds can see each other, then neurosis will develop due to the frustration of trying to achieve physical contact. In larger psittacines, such as Amazons and African greys they may call out to each other continuously.

Periods of privacy are necessary for psittacine birds. A dark box should be provided as a 'hide' which the bird can enter and in which it feels secure.

Wild psittacines spend a large part of their waking time foraging for food in addition to other activities. The provision of food, usually *ad libitum*, allows more time on the parrots hands and this can result in neurosis or psychogenic overeating and obesity (see chapter 18). In order to relieve boredom and prevent this psychogenic overindulgence, it is a good idea to schedule specific feeding times.

Punishment by the owner may induce neurosis through fear, anger and/or resentment. The punishment is often carried out after the 'crime' has been committed and thus the bird is only confused by the punishment and is unable to relate it to its previous behaviour.

A neurotic and aggressive bird in a normal group of budgerigars can upset the whole of the flock (Coles 1985). In such a situation the identification and removal of that bird will often restore harmony in the flock.

Neurosis in its early stages may not be very noticeable; it may be shown as agitation in the bird, such as hopping from perch to perch or the continual shaking of the head in a figure eight on its side (Dilger and Bell 1982) or just a continuing dipping of the head from side to side.

Subsequently, the neurosis is shown as flighty and scatty birds and eventually, in extreme cases, may present as self-mutilation.

FEATHER PLUCKING

Self mutilation is the most commonly presented behavioural problem. Self mutilation includes nail biting, toe biting, feather chewing and feather plucking. In severe cases, birds may also go off their food and lose weight (Perry 1987).

Normal preening may develop into an exaggerated and aggressive chewing or pulling of the feathers in cases of neurosis (Galvin 1983), Harrison 1984). It has been suggested (Harrison 1984) that the bird may be chewing the feathers because it develops a taste for them.

The causes of feather plucking (in decreasing order of frequency) are:

1. Boredom and/or neurosis (Ensley 1979, Harrison 1984, Davis 1987). This is similar to the biting of finger nails seen in humans.

2. Poor quality feathers due to malnutrition, poor husbandry or hormonal imbalance are often plucked by birds and this may be the stimulus for further self mutilation.

3. Folliculitis due to bacterial or mycotic agents may result in feather plucking. A stained smear of the feather pulp from the follicles may yield useful information.

4. Feather mites are often thought to be the cause by the owner, but are rarely found (Galvin 1983).

When presented with a suspected feather plucker it is important to examine it properly to rule out infection or nutritional problems. A diagnosis is possible on the clinical history, cage size, social interactions and the presenting pattern of feather loss.

Self mutilated feathers, especially at the bottom of the cage, must be distinguished from the normal growing and feather sheath removal. If the feather plucking is psychological then the feathers are not deformed or discoloured and are lost from the areas that the bird is able to chew. Initially, flight and contour feathers are plucked (Perry 1987), but eventually the bird may be bald except for the head (Plate 19:1).

The use of an Elizabethan collar is often helpful, not only for treatment (see later), but also to assess feather follicle activity in cases of doubt.

Treatment

The suspected causes of the neurosis should be corrected. The aim should not be just to gain feather regrowth, but to prevent this behaviour from recurring or being replaced by another vice.

Treatment should include the following:

1. An Elizabethan collar should be fitted (Plate 19:2). This is often useful as a first approach as it prevents further mutilation while the original cause of the neurosis can be dealt with, as outlined below. The collar, ideally, should be clear so that the bird can see almost normally; it must also be large enough to prevent the bird from reaching the feathers. Psittacine birds do not like Elizabethan collars, but they work well. It is advisable that birds be initially hospitalised for a few days to allow them to adapt to the collars and ensure that they are able to feed normally. It is the author's experience that if this is not done, many owners remove the collar as soon as they get the birds home as they appear to upset the birds. However, if the birds have been given sufficient time to accept the collars and to learn to feed whilst wearing them, owners are much more likely to leave them on. Collars should be left in situ until feathers have regrown, which is usually about 2 months. Coles has recommended that in some cases the collar is better tolerated and more successful when fitted in the 'reversed' position as in Plate 19:3 (Coles, 1988). Other variations on the fitting of Elizabethan collars are described by Galvn (1983).

2. The plane of nutrition should be improved. Particular attention should be paid to the protein, calcium and energy levels to allow the replacement of the feathers.

3. The owner must try to give more attention to the bird, either directly or indirectly.

4. The environment should be changed frequently by moving the cage around the house or placing it in an area where there are distractions. Toys should be given to occupy the bird. A more suitable cage should be provided where necessary. The cage should be sufficient to allow exercise. Use of natural branches for perches allows something for them to peck at. If the bird is tame then it should be allowed out of the cage.

5. In order to give some privacy and security to the bird, a 'hide' should be provided. A dark box is suitable.

6. The photo period should be altered to a more normal level of 8 to 12 hours per day. Often birds are kept in the lounge and subjected to as much as 18 hours of light per day. Ensley (1979) recommends covering the cage at dusk and uncovering at sunrise.

7. Birds should be allowed to bathe or should be sprayed daily. This is especially important in African grey parrots which tend to get very dusty and often become overzealous groomers due to this.

8. If the above list does not eliminate the problem, then it may be necessary to attempt control by the use of drugs.

    Tranquillizers can be used to calm the state of neurosis. Diazepam (5mg/ml) at a dosage of 2 drops per 30 mls of drinking water or phenobarbitone oral suspension at a dosage of 0.003 mg/gm twice daily have been recommended (Galvin 1983).

    Empirical thyroid supplementation may be beneficial. Dosage should commence at the high or moult-inducing rate of 100mcg/kg thyroxine every other day for two weeks. This is achieved by suspending 1 x 100 mcg thyroxine tablet in 100 ml drinking water and offering on an every other day basis. This dosage should be continued for two weeks and then reduced to a quarter of the previous dose for a further four weeks (¼ tablet/100 ml drinking water).

    Galvin (1983) has recommended the use of megoestrol acetate at a dosage of 1.25 mg daily crushed in food for a 500 gm bird. After 7 − 10 days, this dosage is administered once or twice weekly. Alternatively, medroxyprogesterone acetate can be injected intramuscularly at a dosage of 0.07 mg/gm.

    Davis (1987) postulates that some feather pluckers may respond to sex hormones due to the neurosis being due to sexual frustrations.

9. Appropriate antibiotic therapy should be administered if bacterial folliculitis has been diagnosed.

10. Ensley (1979) states that sometimes the introduction of a cagemate helps but the author has found that this often results in the new parrot being shown how to feather pluck so that two bald birds are the result.

11. If the owner sees the bird plucking its feathers he should not run in and yell at the bird as this is often seen as a 'reward' by the bird, and thus just served to reinforce the negative behaviour. Often the bird is feather plucking because point 3. is not being provided, and by yelling at the bird, the owner is giving the attention the bird craves.

12. If a bird is seen feather plucking then punishment by placing in a dark cupboard or by covering the cage can be attempted. Initially, this should be for three minutes but subsequently the length of time can be increased up to 15 minutes (Harrison 1984). The use of a water pistol is also helpful. Use of high pitched alarms is not advised as it just serves to scare the bird and worsen the neurosis.

SEXUAL PROBLEMS
There are several problems that can be considered to be sexual in origin. These include:-

A. Regurgitation
Pair bonding is a strongly physiological factor in a bird's life. In the absence of another bird (of correct sex), there is often a pairing or imprinting on the owner, toys, mirrors or other objects. If the imprinting is abnormal then there may be sexual advances towards the owner or object upon which it has imprinted.

A common clinical presentation of this abnormal pair bonding is regurgitation. It is especially seen in male budgerigars but it can also occur in Amazons and macaws which have pair bonded with the owner (Harrison and Davis 1986). Usually the regurgitation is over the objects with which it has pair bonded, usually toys and mirrors (Harrison 1984). The owner often presents the bird as 'vomiting'. Diagnosis should be on the type of regurgitation and the site, i.e. the toys or mirror.

This problem can usually be prevented by the removal of the objects of the bird's affection. Initially this requires removal of all toys and mirrors in the cage. Later, a rotation of toys will allow the limited returning of some of the objects.

If regurgitation continues despite the removal of the toys and mirrors, or in the case where the owner is the object of the bonding an intramuscular injection of delmadinone (Tardak, Syntex) at a dosage of 1mg/Kg (0.02 ml/30g) may be administered. Coles (1985) also states that medroxyprogesterone (Promone E, Upjohn or Perlutex, Leo) can be used by intramuscular injection at a dosage of 30 mg/Kg.

B.   Persistent egg laying

This is a problem of a sole hen bird, which appears to continuously produce large numbers of eggs. This is often due to pair bonding with the owner. This is especially seen in cockatiels and budgerigars and may result in other problems due to the depletion of the body calcium stores.

The owner often removes each egg as it is produced, which stimulates the production of more eggs (Harrison and Davies 1986). It is often advisable to leave one egg, as then the bird is able to go through the brooding cycle, at the end of which the egg can be removed. The bird will then go a while before it lays again.

Egg laying in cockatiels can be controlled to some degree by lowering their calorific intake, by avoiding the owner stroking and handling the bird or by the use of hormones, similar to those for regurgitation. Ovarohysterectomy is the treatment of choice (Harrison and Davis 1986). (see Page 60)

C.   Brooding problems

Neurosis in birds can lead to desertion of eggs and abandoning of chicks or ceasing to feed at any stage of the brooding (Coles 1985).

Coles (1985) also describes egg eating as a vice which in the aviary situation can be copied by others.

DOMINANCE

The establishment of a pecking order is a normal behavioural feature of birds; it is essential for the establishment of a hierarchy. Usually, once the pecking order has been established it is unnecessary for the dominant bird to assert its dominance unless its place in the hierarchy is threatened.

Dominance becomes a behavioural problem once it is exhibited beyond the realms of the normal hierarchy. This can be divided into:-

A.   Dominance towards other birds.

In the case of two birds, even if they are of opposite sexes, incompatibility may lead to one becoming dominant over the other and actively bullying the submissive bird. This can lead to feather picking, usually off the head of the submissive bird. (See Plate 19:4). The aggression may be so severe as to result in the death of the submissive partner, or at best infertility due to stress. Treatment for such a situation is the separation of the two birds.

Parental dominance may be shown as aggression especially prior to and after fledging and thus it is best to separate the young after they are feeding independently. This is especially seen in Rosellas (*Platycercus* spp), Parakeets (*Psephotus* spp) and Lovebirds (*Agapornis* spp) (Alderton 1987). The cock bird especially appears to be aggressive and should be removed about one week before the expected fledgling time or the chicks should be hand reared (Alderton 1987).

B.   Dominance towards people

In a single pet bird, a hierarchy must still be established but between the bird and the owner. Problems arise when the bird becomes dominant over its owner and may even become aggressive towards him. This is particularly a problem in young Amazon parrots which have a reputation for being tyrants.

A bird can show it is dominant by being possessive over one person (to whom it is imprinted) and aggressive towards other people or other birds. This is particularly noted in the macaws. This behaviour is only really a problem in a family situation, where the bird is possessive over one member and aggressive towards the other members of the family. Treatment is difficult and relies upon other members of the family becoming more involved with the bird and the imprinted person less so, until the bird becomes a family pet once more.

A bird that is trying to become dominant over its owner is often skittish and untamable. Dominance is often shown by nipping at the owners fingers (see Biting, below), refusing to perform tricks and being difficult to handle. In extreme cases the bird may even attack the owner.

A bird whose head is much higher than the midchest of its owner may think it is the dominant household member (Davis 1987). When dealing with a dominant bird it is a good idea to lower the perches to below chest level. Harrison and Davis (1986) recommend waist level, to convey the dominance of the owner. If the bird is placed constantly below waist level then it becomes panicky and neurotic (Davis 1987).

The owner must also be assertive, but not aggressive or the bird may revert to being neurotic. If the parrot attacks, then the use of a water pistol helps fend off the bird. Food can also be used to reduce the dominance of the bird, especially if *ad libitum* feeding is stopped. Food can then be given by the owner after the bird has allowed the owner to stroke it, or has performed a trick.

BITING

Biting comes naturally to psittacine birds. With their large, powerful jaws they can inflict a lot of damage so this habit has to be curtailed at an early stage. Young birds need to be trained early not to use their beaks in playing or affection.

Most birds bite due to fear, especially on sudden or quick movements, or as a warning behaviour (Harrison and Davis 1986). Biting due to dominance occurs in Amazon parrots and especially in macaws, which Davis (1987) classes as nippers by nature.

In order to train a bird not to be a biter, the opportunities for it to do so must be avoided. If it is a dominance response, as in the tyrant Amazon parrot, then the dominance must be squashed (see above). Harrison and Davis (1986) recommend a verbal 'No' or punishment by isolation. This is achieved by placing the bird in a dark cupboard and cutting it out of contact for a set period, starting with three minutes and working up to a maximum of fifteen minutes for repeated offences.

Food may also be used as a training aid, similar to that for dominance. Hand feeding in itself is a good way of getting a nippy bird used to the hand that feeds it, and may go a long way to removing fear from the bird.

SCREECHING

Of all the behavioural problems, this is the most annoying, hardest to live with and most difficult to modify. It is mainly heard in cockatoos but also displayed by the Amazon parrots, African grey parrots and macaws.

Screechers can be classified according to the reason for screeching. This will also affect the prognosis for treatment of the problem.

A   Dawn and Dusk Screechers

Some parrots screech in the morning and/or at night. This is a common problem which is considered (Harrison and Davis 1986) similar to the crowing of the rooster, and thus natural.

This type of screeching often wakes the owner at the same time each morning as the parrot welcomes the dawn. Being a natural behaviour it is very difficult to modify. Attempts can be made to feed the parrot or occupy it prior to the expected screeching time. If this is attempted, it is very important that no reward is given once the screeching has begun or this will only serve to reinforce the negative behaviour.

B.   Attention Screechers

This type of screeching is mainly seen in cockatoos (Davis 1987) as they are so demanding of attention. It is essential that the owner does not give the bird the attention it is requesting during a screeching episode as this further reinforces the negative behaviour.

An attention screecher must be ignored, and attention only given once silence is obtained. Even shouting at the bird to be quiet, just serves to reward the screeching and should be avoided. The use of a thick cover to put the cage into darkness until the screeching stops is helpful. Once the screeching has stopped then the bird should receive attention as a reward for not screeching.

If ignoring or covering does not work, then squirting with a water pistol or placing in a different room or cupboard for a variable length of isolation (as previously described) may be useful.

C.   Happy Screechers

Some parrots start screeching as a welcome to the owner, especially on their return home. This type of behaviour is to be encouraged as it builds the bond between the bird and the owner. Any attempt at modification only results in other neurosis developing. In order to keep the screeching to a minimum, the owner should go straight to the bird and return the welcome.

Harrison and Davis (1986) state that good talkers are often noisier than are non-vocal birds, especially if there are other birds in the house and they can produce deafening noises calling out to each other. This type of screeching may be reduced by having the birds within sight of each other. If this is not desired for any reason (i.e. isolation of a sick or new bird), then a water pistol or thick dark cloth should be utilised.

D.   Unhappy Screechers

Some birds screech because they are discontent. This may be noticed after they have been placed in a new cage or moved from their normal site. If the reason is obvious then it should be corrected, such as returning the bird to its original site or cage.

Adult African greys, which have recently been purchased as pets, may develop their screeching powers as a protective and warning weapon. The owner must try to ignore this screeching when approaching the bird. If the owner retreats from the bird when it starts screeching, this just further convinces the bird that screeching works. Trying to hand feed the bird may help to calm it and with time the screeching should stop as people approach. Squirting such a bird with a water pistol just increases its neurosis. Patience and kindness are the only answers.

ANY TREATMENT BY THE OWNER

This is included here, as many owners are reluctant to comply with veterinary advice on treatment, especially medication, as they feel the bird will remember and hate them forever. Neurosis can be induced during treatment and certainly some birds will act differently to owners after administration of medication. So, to some extent, the owner's fear is justified.

Birds, however, are not able to recognise a 'changed' person (Harrison 1984), and this can be used to the owner's advantage during treatment. If a mask, hood or hat is used as a disguise during the capture and medication of their bird, the bird will not associate the owner with these 'dreadful' deeds.

Fear on behalf of the bird can sometimes be carried too far by the owners. This author has been presented with sick psittacines which he was not allowed to even take out of the cage for the fear that it might be 'upset'. Similarly some owners insist on leaving the room before the handling of a parrot for fear it will associate them with the action of capture and handling. This option should be routinely offered to all owners of single psittacine birds, as often the bird is easier to handle with an anxious owner out of sight.

REFERENCES

ALDERTON, D. (1987). Captive Breeding. In: 'Companion Bird Medicine'. Edited by E. W. Burr. Iowa State University Press.

COLLOCOTT, T. C. (1971). Editor of Dictionary of Science and Technology. W. & R. Chambers.

COLES, B. H. (1985). 'Avian Medicine and Surgery'. Blackwell Scientific Publications, Oxford.

COLES, B. H. (1988). Personal communication.

DAVIS, C. (1987). Avian Behaviour. In: 'Companion Bird Medicine'. Edited by E. W. Burr. Iowa State University Press.

DILGER, W. C. and BELL, J. (1982). Behavioural Aspects. In: 'Diseases of Cage and Aviary Birds'. Second edition, edited by M. L. Petrak. Lea and Febiger.

ENSLEY, P. (1979). Caged Bird Medicine and Husbandry. In: Non-Domestic Pet Medicine, the Veterinary Clinics of North America. Edited by W. J. Boever. Vol 9: No. 3. W. B. Saunders Co.

GALVIN, C. (1983). The Feather Picking Bird. Current Veterinary Therapy VIII. Edited by R. W. Kirk. W. B. Saunders Co.

HARRISON, G. J. (1984). Feather Disorders. In; The Veterinary Clinics of North America. Caged Bird Medicine Vol. 14: No. 2. Edited by G. J. Harrison. Pub W. B. Saunders Co.

HARRISON, G. J. and DAVIS, C. (1986). Captive Behaviour and its Modification. In: Clinical Avian Medicine and Surgery. Edited by G. J. Harrison and L. R. Harrison. W. B. Saunders Co.

PERRY, R. A. (1987). Avian Dermatology. In: 'Companion Bird Medicine'. Edited by E. W. Burr. Iowa State University Press.

Chapter 20

THERAPEUTICS

K. Lawrence B.V.Sc., F.R.C.V.S.

Medication may be administered to parrots by any of the following routes:-

    i.   Via a crop tube (gavage)

    ii.   In food

    iii.   In drinking water

    iv.   Parenterally

    v.   Nebulization and spraying

    vi.   Topically

Each has advantages and disadvantages that should be considered before a particular route is chosen.

i.   **Crop tube**

This is a particularly useful route of administration, allowing accurate dosing. However, the bird must be handled up to four times daily which may be detrimental because of the associated stress. Stress can be reduced by practice and experience. When dosing it should be ensured that everything is to hand before catching the bird.

A variety of oral antibiotic and anthelmintic suspensions and syrups are available. Some of the antibiotic preparations are very palatable having been developed for use in paediatric medicine.

The drug preparation is administered from a syringe via either a well lubricated metal catheter (for example, a Spreule's needle or an anal gland irrigating needle, Arnold's Ltd.) or cut down plastic urethral catheter. The bird's beak is eased open and the catheter is passed over the back of the tongue and gently inserted into the oesophagus. The neck is then gently straightened to allow the catheter to slide into the crop. The catheter should never be forced into the oesophagus. It is usual to allow the preparation to flow from the syringe by gravity. Too rapid an expulsion, using the plunger, may lead to regurgitation with the drug being inhaled or forced through the choana into the nasal passages during exhalation. Some oral preparations have been shown to cause damage to the nasal mucosa, although this should not be a problem with water-based products. Care should be taken not to administer so much fluid that the crop capacity is exceeded causing regurgitation. As a guide the following volumes should not be exceeded:-

Parakeet	1ml
Cockatiel	2-5 ml
Lovebird	1-6 ml
Small parrot	3-6 ml
Medium parrot	10-15 ml
Large parrot	15-20 ml

This route of administration is most useful for conditions affecting the gastro-intestinal tract but is not the route of choice for serious systemic illness as many drugs are poorly or unreliably absorbed from the intestinal tract.

ii.   In food

This is a very useful route for drug administration. Oral suspensions and syrups, crushed tablets and the contents of capsules can be coated onto, or hidden in fruit. They can also be mixed with cooked maize, brown rice, dehusked seed or nectar. This route is, obviously, unsatisfactory if the bird is anorectic and is most useful for prophylaxis, follow-up treatment or the treatment of a gut-associated condition.

Calculation of the drug inclusion rate in the food can pose some problems. As a guide, a daily dose calculated on a mg/kg bodyweight basis is mixed with the only source of food. A 500 gramme bird consumes approximately 90 to 100 grammes food daily with a 50 gramme budgerigar eating relatively more — 15-20 grammes. A fresh mixture should be prepared each day as some products are unstable.

iii.   In drinking water

In many ways this is the least suitable route for the administration of therapeutic preparations to birds. Too often in the past, however, this has been the chosen route for administering antibiotics, such as tetracyclines, which were dispensed as a substitute for a clinical examination and a diagnosis. This route should never be used to treat systemic bacterial infections. Intake and absorption of antibiotics, especially in xerophilic species of parakeets, when administered in drinking water are too erratic and unreliable to be the basis of such a treatment regimen. Significant harm may be done by adding foul tasting medicaments to the bird's sole source of drinking water. An already stressed bird may refuse to drink the medicated water and thus precipitate hypovolaemic shock, with fatal consequences. Alternatively, polydipsic birds may also be compromised because of an excessive intake of drug. A similar problem may arise when breeding pairs are medicated with the male drinking large quantities of water in order to provide for the sitting female. This may result in a drug overdose in the male bird and under dosage of the female. The only benefit of including antibiotics in the drinking water is perhaps to reduce bacterial contamination of the water and prevent lateral spread of disease to other birds sharing the accommodation.

Water medication, although unreliable, may be the only possible route when medicating large flocks or wild birds. To avoid some of the problems discussed and to ensure a reasonable water intake, attempts should be made to disguise the foul taste of many of the antibiotics. Sugar, sodium saccharin and aspartame have all been suggested as sweeteners to mask the taste of the antibiotic in the water. However, this approach is not without its risks as a sugar solution may promote bacterial growth in the water bowl.

iv.   Parenterally

This route is the only reliable way to treat systemic disease in birds. Many antibiotics (e.g., aminoglycosides) are not absorbed from the intestine whereas the absorption of penicillins and tetracyclines is at best erratic. The most common route of administration is by intramuscular injection into either the pectoral or quadriceps group of muscles. It is relatively common for birds to show discomfort following the injection, be it lameness or wing droop. Repeated injections, especially of some of the more irritant preparations, can lead to permanent muscle atrophy. Cooper (1983) has described the pathological changes seen in bird muscle associated with injection sites. As birds have a renal portal system it is possible that the pharmacokinetics of antibiotics excreted primarily by the kidneys may be altered, after injection into the quadriceps group of muscles. However, there is little evidence to support this possibility.

Intravenous injections can be used to deliver a bolus dose of drug. The most useful veins in birds are the brachial and the right jugular vein. However, because they are thin walled and fragile, they cannot be used for continuous infusions. In the larger parrots these veins are readily accessible and drug administration is easy using a 25 gauge needle.

In the larger parrots antibiotics can be injected directly into the infraorbital sinus, to treat localized sinusitis. This treatment is often a follow-up to sinus irrigation.

v. Nebulization and spraying

Nebulization offers a route of drug administration that allows penetration into the air sacs. The air sacs can be the site of a number of significant infections, including *Mycoplasma, Esherichia coli* and *Aspergillus.* Because the air sacs are relatively avascular, many parenterally administered therapies are ineffective.

For nebulization to be effective the equipment must deliver particles in the size range 0.5 to 6 microns. Any larger and the particles will not penetrate into the air sacs. Disposable plastic nebulizers, designed for use in man, are available from medical supply firms. Bottled oxygen or air delivered via a reducing valve i.e. an anaesthetic machine being the most convenient delivery vehicle. The major expense in nebulization is the construction of the cabinet to hold the bird during treatment.

The major advantage of nebulization is that effective treatment can be undertaken with little stress and drugs can be delivered directly to the site of infection, even those that would prove toxic if administered via other routes.

Antibiotics are usually dissolved in normal saline for nebulization but some such as tylosin (Tylan soluble, Elanco Products Ltd) produce higher tissue levels if dissolved in dimethyl sulphoxide (DMSO). Levamisole (Nilverm, Coopers Animal Health) may be added to nebulizing solutions in an attempt to enhance the bird's immune response.

It takes time and experience to discover the right combination of air or oxygen flow rate, duration and frequency of treatment, temperature of nebulizing fluid and drugs. Therefore, initially, nebulization should be seen as an adjunct to the more conventional routes of administration.

In some relatively uncomplicated cases of upper respiratory tract disease in parrots an antibiotic aerosol has proved effective. This technique is often particularly useful in flock situations because handling of the birds is minimised.

vi. Topical

Topical application of creams and ointments can cause clogging of the feathers. This will lead, especially in small birds, to a loss of insulation. The bird's attention may also be drawn to the area under treatment leading to self-mutilation. Powder in-aerosol preparations, such as Polybactrin spray (Calmic Medical Division) has no such disadvantages.

Ear and eye drops may prove useful in treating rhinitis by instillation of the external nares. This route may also be effective in treating pharyngitis.

SUPPORTIVE THERAPY

Many birds presented for treatment will only recover if adequate supportive therapy is provided. Indeed, the efficacy of the treatment of systemic disease is often dependent on adequate tissue perfusion. This is rarely sufficient in sick birds and in most cases fluid therapy is essential (Redig 1984). Alone, fluid therapy may not provide the complete answer and heat and tender loving care are always useful adjuncts.

In severely ill birds the initial administration of fluid should be by the intravenous route, as a bolus. In smaller birds the right jugular vein can be used, in larger birds the brachial vein is an alternative. Redig (1984) has suggested that lactated Ringer's solution is the fluid of choice and Harrison (1986a) tabulated the volume of the initial intravenous injection in various sizes of bird.

Volume of initial injection of Ringer's solution.

Budgerigar	1 ml
Cockatiel	2 ml
Conure	6 ml
Amazon	8 ml
Cockatoo/Macaw	12-14 ml

Additional fluid may have to be administered either by the intravenous, subcutaneous or oral route, the minimum daily requirement being in the region of 50 ml/kg bodyweight. If energy requirements are also to be met, Redig (1984) suggests that the lactated Ringer's solution be diluted 1:1 with a 5 per cent dextrose solution. Fluids should never be administered by intramuscular injection (Harrison 1986a).

The replacement fluid must be warm (30-35°C) and administered via a fine needle (26-30 gauge). It is important to minimise haematoma formation at intravenous injection sites by pushing the skin overlying the vein away from the site before puncturing the vein. After the injection the tensed skin is allowed to roll back and firm but gentle pressure is applied to the injection site using a swab. A vein may have to be used on a number of occasions; seriously compromised birds may need up to six injections in the first 24 hours after admission.

Until recently, the provision of heat was an unquestioned adjunct to fluid therapy. However, Redig (1984) has cautioned that warming a seriously ill bird before re-establishing adequate tissue perfusion may cause the bird to deteriorate as peripheral vasodilatation may increase metabolic acidosis. With this proviso, sick birds should be maintained in an environment heated to 28-30° C. If the warmth is being provided by a heat lamp it must be ensured that the bird is strong enough to move. Otherwise, it may become overheated as the spot temperature under such a lamp may exceed 50° C.

The use of parenteral vitamins and minerals has a place in supportive therapy. Their use alone, however, is negligent. Vitamins A, D_3 and E (Jectadine, Beecham Animal Health. Dose 1-2 ml/kg) as well as C and B complex (Parentrovite, Beecham Animal Health. Dose 0.5-0.75 ml/kg bodyweight) may prove useful. The concurrent use of iron dextrans (Imposil - 100 mg iron/ml, Fisons plc. Dose 0.1 ml/kg) should be considered in anaemic individuals.

NOTE

Supportive therapy is an essential adjunct to all other treatments in a sick bird. Redig (1984) should be consulted for a detailed consideration; although most of his work was with raptors, the techniques are equally applicable to psittacines.

ANTIMICROBIALS

a   ANTIBACTERIALS

Dorrestein et al (1984) and Clark (1986) have reviewed the pharmacokinetics of antibiotics in birds. However, little of the data was derived from antibiotic use in parotts and, in spite of the known difficulties, many dosage suggestions are extrapolated from other groups of birds and mammals. This section will only deal with a limited number of antibiotics that have proved most useful in practice. The source of the dose rate will be quoted where possible. The following antibiotics will be considered:-

i.	Ampicillin and amoxycillin	vi.	Chlortetracycline
ii.	Carbenicillin	vii.	Oxytetracycline
iii.	Cephalexin	viii.	Vibramycin
iv.	Gentamicin	ix.	Tylosin
v.	Tobramycin	x.	Metronidazole

i)   Ampicillin and amoxycillin

These are semi-synthetic broad spectrum bactericidal antibiotics, with useful activity against non Beta-lactamase producing *Staphylococci* and other Gram-positive bacteria and some Gram-negative bacteria including many of the Enterobacteriaceae and *Pasteurella*. As with many penicillins they are also effective against most anaerobic bacteria with the exception of *Bacteroides fragilis*. They have no activity against *Mycoplasma*, *Chlamydia* or *Pseudomonas*.

Both ampicillin and amoxycillin are acid-stable penicillins and are active when administered orally as well as parenterally.

Penicillins are widely distributed in the body and reach therapeutic concentrations in the liver, lung, muscles, kidney and intestine. There are usually no detectable levels in tears, saliva or the CSF.

Ampicillin is poorly and erratically absorbed after oral administration in birds. Single oral doses in the range 150 to 175 mg/kg bodyweight failed to produce blood levels that would be effective in treating anything other than the most sensitive organisms, in seven out of nine parrots (Ensley and Janssen 1981). Even repeated daily oral dosing of ampicillin for up to four days failed to produce a steady state level of >1 mcg/ml in chickens (Ziv et al 1979). Therefore, oral administration of ampicillin can not be used to treat a systemic illness in a parrot. The reason for the low blood levels was poor absorption with only between 5 and 17 per cent of an oral dose being systemically available. Ensley and Janssen (1981) also investigated the parenteral use of ampicillin in parrots. They showed that a single dose of 100 mg/kg bodyweight produced peak blood levels in excess of 60 mcg/ml but therapeutic levels persisted for only four hours. It is evident that the excretion rate of ampicillin in birds greatly exceeds that in domestic mammals. It has been suggested that ampicillin is not only excreted via the kidneys as in mammals but via the bile and across the intestinal wall into the gut lumen (Clark 1986).

Suggested dose rates for ampicillin
Ampicillin (Penbritin soluble powder, Beecham Animal Health) 100 mg/kg bodyweight by gavage, three times daily. For localised gut infections only. Ampicillin (Penbritin injection, Beecham Animal Health) 100 mg/kg bodyweight by intramuscular injection, three times daily. Ampicillin (Amfipen L/A, Gist-brocade Animal Health) 150 mg/kg by intramuscular injection, daily.

[Ensley and Janssen (1981) Blue-naped parrots *(Tanygnathus lucionesis)* and Amazons (*Amazona* spp.)]

Amoxycillin has few features that differentiate it from ampicillin. However, oral availability may be much greater (20-60 per cent of a single oral dose), but again absorption is erratic and systemic therapeutic levels may not be reached in all birds. Dorrestein *et al.* (1981) showed that in-feed (500 mg/kg food) and water medication (300 mg/l) in canaries produced mean blood levels in the range 1 to 2 mcg/ml. Intramuscular administration of amoxycillin produced higher blood levels which persisted for only four hours (Dorrestein *et al.* 1984).

The Beta-lactamase stability of amoxycillin has been improved by the addition of clavulanic acid. This has increased the range of sensitive bacteria to include Beta-lactamase producing strains of *Staphylococci, Esherichia coli* and *Salmonella.*

Suggested dose rates for amoxycillin
Amoxycillin (Clamoxyl Palatable Drops 50 mg/ml suspension, Beecham Animal Health). 2 ml/kg bodyweight by gavage, three times daily. For localized gut infections only.
Amoxycillin (Clamoxyl LA Long Acting Injection, Beecham Animal Health). 250 mg/kg bodyweight by intra muscular injection, daily.

Clavulanate-potentiated amoxycillin (Synulox Palatable Drops 50 mg/ml suspension, Beecham Animal Health) 2.5 ml/kg bodyweight by gavage, twice daily. For localized gut infections only.
[Dorrestein *et al.* (1981) Canary *(Serinus canaria)*
Dorrestein *et al.* (1984) Pigeon *(Columba livia)*
Cooper (1985) Pigeon *(Columba livia)].*

Ziv et al. (1979) showed that if probenicid (Benemid, Merk Sharp and Dohme Ltd.) was administered at the rate of 200 mg/kg bodyweight, at the same time as ampicillin, peak blood levels could be trebled and their persistence doubled, in poultry. This combination therapy may have practical use in parrots to reduce the frequency of administration.

Safety
Both ampicillin and amoxycillin have a very wide safety margin and there are no reports of adverse reactions in birds in the literature. Cooper (1985) showed that clavulanate-potentiated amoxycillin (Synulox, Beecham Animal Health) was safe in pigeons when administered for 7 days at a dose rate of 125 mg/bird.

ii) **Carbenicillin**
Carbenicillin is a bactericidal, semi-synthetic penicillin with a broad spectrum of activity. The spectrum of activity is similar to ampicillin but carbenicillin has an enhanced activity against *Pseudomonas.* Carbenicillin is rapidly destroyed by Beta-lactamases produced by some strains of *Pseudomonas* or *Staphylococcus.* However, as it has been used only infrequently in avian medicine resistant strains are rarely isolated.

Carbenicillin is destroyed by stomach acid and is therefore unstable when administered orally. The usual route of administration is by intra-muscular injection. It is widely distributed in the body, probably in a similar way to ampicillin.

The main indication for the use of carbenicillin in parrots is the treatment of serious systemic infections involving *Pseudomonas, Proteus* and *Aeromonas.* Its use is particularly indicated in dehydrated birds or those suspected of having damaged kidneys. Carbenicillin is not nephrotoxic as is the alternate treatment, gentamicin.

Suggested dose rate for carbenicillin

The suggested dose rates are based on extrapolation from recommended mammalian doses. They have proved effective in clinical usage. There are no reported studies of blood or tissue levels associated with these suggested doses.

Carbenicillin (Pyopen injection 1 g, Beecham Research Laboratories), 100 to 200 mg/kg bodyweight by intramuscular injection, twice daily.
[Lawrence (1986) and Clubb (1986)].

Safety

No adverse effects have been reported in parrots, but pain on injection has been described in man (Kucers and Bennett 1979) and in reptiles (Lawrence *et al.* 1984)

Carfecillin (Uticillin tablets, Beecham Research Laboratories) is an orally active ester of carbenicillin. The ester being broken down in the intestine by hydrolysis to release the active form of the antibiotic. A suggested dose rate of 60 mg/kg bodyweight three times daily proved clinically effective in the treatment of a bacterial *(Pseudomas aeruginosa)* overgrowth in the intestine of an African Grey parrot *(Psittacus erithacus)*

iii. **Cephalexin**

Cephalexin is a semi-synthetic cephalosporin antibiotic with the major advantage over the penicillins so far described that it is stable in the presence of Staphylococci- and *E. coli*-derived Beta-lactamases. The spectrum of activity otherwise differs little from that of ampicillin.

Cephalexin is acid-stable and is administered orally. It is widely distributed in the body. Cephalexin, unlike the other antibiotics so far discussed, is readily absorbed from the avian intestine after oral administration. If given by gavage, absorption is nearly complete (Bush *et al.* 1981a), with peak blood levels reached within an hour. Administration of the drug with food may delay absorption and depress peak blood levels. Cephalexin is available as a sweetened suspension which many birds take readily.

Suggested dose rate for cephalexin

Cephalexin (Ceporex Oral Drops, Glaxovet Ltd.) 50 mg/kg bodyweight by gavage, four times daily for birds weighing over 500 grammes. 30 mg/kg bodyweight by gavage, eight times daily for birds weighing less than 500 grammes. These dose rates would maintain cephalexin blood levels >2 mcg/ml, which would be effective for the treatment of systemic disease.

[Bush *et al.* (1981a) Eastern bobwhite quail *(Colinus virginianus,* Pigeons *(Columba livia),* Rosybill ducks *Netta* sp), *Sandhill cranes (Grus canadensis tabida),* Emu *(Dromiceius novaehollandiae)*].

iv. **Gentamicin**

Gentamicin is an aminoglycoside antibiotic which is recovered from the fungus *Micromonospora.* This explains the spelling of -micin, the root -mycin is reserved for aminoglycosides recovered from *Streptomycetes.* It is a broad spectrum antibiotic being active against many strains of Gram positive and negative aerobic bacteria. It has no activity against anaerobes, *Mycoplasma* or fungi. Gentamicin is particularly active against *Pseudomonas aeruginosa, Proteus* and *Aeromonas.*

Gentamicin cannot be administered orally for the treatment of systemic disease in birds as it is not absorbed from the intestine.

The distribution of gentamicin in the bird's body, after parenteral administration, follows the pattern described in mammals, except for the low levels of gentamicin found in avian muscle tissue (Dorrestein *et al.* 1984). Therapeutic levels may be reached in heart, liver, kidney and interstitial fluids. However, it may prove impractical to maintain therapeutic levels in the bird because of the binding of gentamicin to renal cortical tissue, leading to nephrotoxicity. Gentamicin levels in renal tissue at least 100 times higher than serum have been demonstrated in man (Schentag and Jusko 1977). Delayed clearance of gentamicin from renal tissue has also been reported in chicks (Spreat and Beckford, 1977) and exotic birds (Bush *et al.*, 1981b). Bush *et al.* (1981b) also showed an accumulation of the drug in the liver.

Gentamicin should be administered by intramuscular injection for the treatment of systemic disease. It is not absorbed from the intestine after gavage or from lung tissue after nebulization. Because of the known risks of nephrotoxicity, the use of gentamicin should be limited to birds with serious septicaemic conditions associated with *Pseudomonas.* It should not be used in birds with known or suspected kidney pathology or dehydrated individuals. It is not uncommon even in healthy birds for a reversible polydipsia and polyuria to develop during treatment.

Suggested dose rate for gentamicin

Gentamicin (Genticin Paediatric Injection, Nicholas Laboratories Ltd.) 5 mg/kg bodyweight by intramuscular injection twice daily.

Gentamicin (Genticin Paediatric Injection, Nicholas Laboratories Ltd). 200 mg in 15 ml saline, for use in a nebulizer.

[Bush *et al.* (1981b) Sandhill cranes *(Grus canadensis tabida).* Rosybill duck (*Netta* sp), Wood duck *(Aix sponsa).*

Clark (1986) Blue and Gold macaw *(Ara ararauna).*

Steiner and Davis (1981) Report of nebulization.]

Safety

Nephrotoxicity, vestibular damage and neuromuscular blockade have all been described in birds after gentamicin therapy. In general these signs have been reported when daily doses of 20-40 mg/kg bodyweight have been administered. Clark (1986) considers that the maximum daily dose of gentamicin in birds should not exceed 10 mg/kg bodyweight.

v. **Tobramycin**

Tobramycin is closely related to gentamicin and the spectrum of activity and distribution in the body are similar. However, tobramycin has two advantages over gentamicin. Firstly, it has a greater activity against *Pseudomonas* and, secondly, it is less likely to be nephrotoxic. This has been demonstrated in animal studies (Wick and Welles 1968; Whelton *et al.* 1978; Gilbert *et al.* 1978) and is associated with a marked reduction in the levels of renal accumulation. This relationship has also been demonstrated in raptors (Clark, 1986) with up to a 65 per cent reduction in renal cortical binding.

Even though there are legitimate reasons to consider tobramycin the expense of the product may limit its use.

Suggested dose rate for tobramycin

Tobramycin (Nebcin, Eli Lilly and Co Ltd) 2 mg/kg bodyweight by intramuscular injection, twice daily.

[Kaplan *et al.* (1973). Dose extrapolated from paediatric recommendations.]

vi. **Chlortetracycline (CTC)**

Chlortetracycline (CTC) is a bacteriostatic broad spectrum antibiotic of the tetracycline group. It is therapeutically useful against aerobic and anaerobic Gram positive and negative bacteria, *Mycoplasma, Chlamydia* and *Rickettsia.*

CTC can be effective in treating systemic illness when administered orally even though as little as 0.3-0.5 per cent of an oral dose is absorbed.

CTC penetrates well into body fluids and can be detected in therapeutic levels in all the major organs except the kidney. CTC may be detected in nasal secretions, but not in tears.

Because CTC is so poorly absorbed from the intestine and it has a foul taste, it cannot be effectively administered in drinking water. Indeed, Dorrestein *et al.* (1986) showed that CTC was unpalatable in pigeons' drinking water at concentrations greater than 1 gramme/litre. Only by incorporation in food at rates between 500 ppm (0.05%) and 17,500 ppm (1.75%) can therapeutic blood levels be reached [Landgraf *et al.* (1982); Luthgen *et al.* (1973)]. The lower inclusion levels may only be effective in the prophylactic therapy of *Chlamydia* and the treatment of localized gut infections whereas the high inclusion levels are required for the treatment of *E. coli* and *Salmonella* septicaemia.

Absorption of tetracyclines is decreased because of complexation with metallic cations such as magnesium and calcium. This effect can be reduced and absorption increased by the concurrent administration of citric acid in the drinking water (500 mg/100 ml) (Pollet *et al.* 1983).

Chlortetracycline (Aureomycin Soluble Powder, Cyanamid of Great Britain)

500 mg/kg food for prophylaxis

5000 mg/kg food for systemic therapy.

[Gylstorff *et al.* (1984). Red-crowned parrots *(Amazona viridigenalis)*.

Landgraf *et al.* (1982). Yellow-crowned amazons *(Amazona ochrocephala)*.

Luthgen *et al.* (1973). Budgerigar *(Melopsittacus undulatus)*.

Schachter *et al.* (1984) *(Neophema* sp)

Safety

There are no reports of direct toxicity from these levels of feed inclusion. However, long-term therapy may lead to disturbances in the intestinal flora and fungal superinfections.

vii. **Oxytetracycline**

The spectrum of activity and distribution within the bird's body are similar to CTC. However, the absorption from the intestine is enhanced, being up to twice as available. Even so, this suggests that only one per cent of an oral dose is systemically available. Drinking water is therefore unlikely to prove an effective vehicle for the treatment of disease in birds. Even when administered at feed inclusion levels, in poultry, as high as 500 mg/kg food the lung levels remained low (Black 1977). Only in liver and kidney were persistent therapeutic levels reported (Black, 1977; Yoshida, 1975).

The most effective route of administration is via an intramuscular injection using a long acting formulation. Studies in Amazon parrots *(Amazona* sp) by Teare *et al.* (1985) have shown that a dose of 58 mg/kg bodyweight (0.3 ml/kg bodyweight) daily will provide a minimum trough level of 5 mcg/ml, a level which should prove effective against most infections. This formulation and route of administration has many major advantages over other treatment regimens.

Oxytetracycline (Terramycin Feed Supplements, Pfizer Ltd) 500 mg/kg feed.

Oxytetracycline (Terramycin/LA injectable solution — 200 mg/ml, Pfizer Ltd) 58 mg/kg bodyweight daily by intramuscular injection.

[Black (1977). Domestic Fowl *(Gallus domesticus)*.

Yoshida *et al.* (1975). Domestic Fowl *(Gallus domesticus)*.

Teare *et al.* (1985). Orange-winged Amazon *(Amazona amazonica)*.

Blue-fronted Amazon *(Amazona aestiva)*, Mexican red-headed Parrot *(Amazona viridigenalis)*].

The concurrent use of bromhexine (Bisolvon, Boehringer Ingelheim Ltd) at a dose of 1.5 mg/kg bodyweight intramuscularly, will not only loosen respiratory mucus, but will also increase the oxytetracycline levels in it.

viii. **Doxycycline**

Doxycycline has a spectrum of activity and distribution pattern similar to CTC. However, there is a much greater degree of absorption from the intestine and it is twice as active as CTC. There are adequate tissue levels in kidney and lung in poultry after oral administration. Unlike mammals, where doxycycline is excreted via the liver and through the intestinal wall, the primary route of excretion in birds is via the kidney. The major advantage of doxycycline is its long half-life in birds in comparison with the previously discussed tetracyclines.

Doxycycline has proved effective in the treatment of psittacocis when administered in the drinking water, mixed with the food or administered by gavage (Jakoby and Gylstorff, 1983; Gylstorff *et al.* 1984). However, Dorrestein *et al.* (1986) showed that doxycycline was unpalatable to pigeons when added to drinking water at the rate of 250 mg/litre. Although an injectable formulation is not available in the United Kingdom, German reports (Luthgen *et al.* 1979; Gylstorff *et al.* 1984) indicate that the parenteral route is most effective and because of the prolonged half-life, dosage is infrequent.

Suggested dose rates for doxycycline

Doxycycline (Vibramycin dispersible tablets, Pfizer Ltd)
    500 mg/litre in sole source of drinking water. Change solution daily.
Doxycycline (Vibramycin syrup, Pfizer Ltd) 10 mg/kg bodyweight by gavage, daily.
Doxycycline (Avicake, Lafeber Co). 300 mg/kg food. ONLY AVAILABLE IN THE U.S.A.
Doxycycline (Vibravenos, Pfizer — West Germany)
    100 mg/kg bodyweight every five days. ONLY AVAILABLE ON THE CONTINENT OF EUROPE.
[Archimbault *et al.* (1983). Domestic fowl *(Gallus domesticus).*
Clubb (1986). Report of commercially available food containing Doxycycline.
Luthgen *et al.* (1979) Three species of Cockatoos *(Cacatua* spp).
Jakoby and Gylstorff (1983) Blunt-tailed parrot.
Gylstorff *et al.* (1984) Red-crowned parrots *(Amazona viridigenalis)].*

Safety

The oral LD50 of Doxycycline in poultry was determined at 2,500 mg/kg bodyweight.

ix. **Tylosin**

Tylosin is a macrolide antibiotic with a wide spectrum of activity against Gram positive bacteria, some Gram negative bacteria such as *Pasteurella, Morexella, Campylobacter* and *Fusiformis, Mycoplasma* and *Chlamydia.*

It is well absorbed from the intestine and is found in high concentrations in the liver and particularly the lungs. The levels in the lung may be many times greater than serum levels and they persist even after tylosin has apparently disappeared from the serum. Therapeutically useful levels of tylosin are also found in tears.

Tylosin is licensed for use in poultry, including turkeys, by administration in the drinking water (500 mg/litre for up to five days). Intramuscular therapy has been studied by Locke *et al.* (1982) in a variety of exotic birds, but not in parrots. They showed that the size of the bird to be treated affected the dose rate.

Tylosin has also proved useful in a nebulizer (Locke and Bush, 1984) or as an ocular spray in sinusitis (Clubb, 1986).

Suggested dose rates for tylosin

Tylosin (Tylan soluble, Elanco Products Ltd)
        500 mg/litre in sole source of drinking water.
Tylosin (Tylan 50 injections, Elanco Products Ltd)
        60 mg/kg bodyweight by intramuscular injection
        three times daily — Parrots weighing 50 to 250 grammes.
        25 mg/kg bodyweight by intramuscular injection
        three times daily — Parrots weighing 250 to 1000 grammes.
        15 mg/kg bodyweight by intramuscular injection
        three times daily — Parrots weighing over 1000 grammes.

Tylosin (Tylan soluble, Elanco Products Ltd) 1 gramme/50 ml Dimethyl sulphoxide (DMSO) for use in a nebulizer.

Tylosin (Tylan soluble, Elanco Products Ltd). Dilute the powder one part with ten of water. Ocular spray for use up to four times daily.

[Locke and Bush (1984). Pigeon *(Columba livea)*. Bobwhite quail *Colinus virginianus*).

Lawrence (1986) Budgerigar (Melopsittacus undulatus).

Locke *et al.* (1982). Bobwhite quail *(Colinus virginianus,* Pigeon *(Columba livea),* Sandhill crane *(Grus canadensis tabida),* Emu *(Dromaius novaehollandiae).*

Clubb (1986). Report of use as ocular spray.]

Safety
There are no reports in the literature of adverse reactions in exotic birds.

x. **Metronidazole**

Metronidazole is a member of the nitroimidazole group of antimicrobials. It only has significant activity against anaerobic protozoan and bacteria. Susceptible organisms include the protozoan parasites *Trichomonas, Entamoeba, Giardia* and *Balantidium* and such bacteria as *Bacteroides,* some *Campylobacter, Clostridia* and the anaerobic cocci.

Metronidazole is well absorbed from the intestine but an injectable solution is available which can also be used for local irrigation.

The main indication for the use of metronidazole is in the treatment of *Trichomonas* (Woerpel and Rosskopf, 1981). However, it is unlikely to be effective when administered in the drinking water. Scholtens *et al.* (1982) showed that its inclusion at 20 mg/litre reduced water intake by 60 per cent. Gavage is probably the most effective administration route, although the parenteral route is now an option. Metronidazole was shown to be ineffective, even when administered by gavage, in the therapy of *Giardia* in psittacines (Panigrahy *et al.* (1981); Scholtens *et al.* (1982). The treatment of choice being a related compound dimetridazole (Emtryl, May and Baker) — 50 mg/kg bodyweight by gavage, three doses at twelve hourly intervals.

The role of anaerobic bacteria in bird disease is poorly understood (Needham 1981) but metronidazole has proved a useful adjunct to antibiotic therapy in some severe systemic conditions. Carwardine (1984) reported that anaerobic bacteria inhibit the phagocytosis of *Proteus:* killing the anaerobes restores the phagocytes to normal activity. Metronidazole may also enhance the efficiency of penicillins by eliminating Beta-lactamase producing anaerobes.

Suggested dose rate for metronidazole
Metronidazole (Flagyl, May and Baker) 50 mg/kg by gavage, daily for seven days.

Metronidazole (Torgyl, May and Baker) 5 mg/kg by intramuscular injection, twice daily.

[Woerpel and Rosskepf (1981). Extrapolation from mammallian dose rate.]

Safety
Toxicity has been reported in finches (Harrison 1986b) after oral administration, but Metronidazole appears to be safe in psittacines at suggested dose rates.

B. **ANTIFUNGAL THERAPY**

There are two common fungal infections in birds:-

1. Candidiasis
2. Aspergillosis

1. **Candidiasis**

Candida albicans is a yeast that may be a normal inhabitant of the bird's intestine (Keymer 1982); however, disease is likely if it overgrows the bacteria present. This may occur as a consequence of long-term tetracycline therapy, vitamin A deficiency, crop impaction or the feeding of spoiled grain. The infection is usually limited to the intestine, therefore the antifungal preparations prescribed should remain in the intestine and be poorly absorbed. If the lesions of candidiasis are in the mouth the bird should be dosed by gavage. The recommended therapies are only active if in direct contact with the lesions.

For the routine therapy of candidiasis the most effective compound is nystatin. However, the suggested dose rates are very variable and seem to depend on the severity of the condition. If therapy proves ineffective, the use of amphoteracin B should be considered.

Nystatin (Nystan Oral Suspension — 100,000 units nystatin/ml. E.R. Squibb and Sons Ltd). 3 to 6 ml/kg bodyweight orally from one to three times daily for 7-14 days.

[Flammer (undated); Clubb (1986); Steiner and Davis (1981)].

Safety

There are no reports of toxicity in psittacines.

2. **Aspergillosis**

Aspergillosis poses a much greater problem, with therapy often proving disappointing. As aspergillosis is a systemic disease primarily affecting the relatively avuscular air sac, the major problem is to achieve therapeutic levels at the site of the infection. Therapeutic regimens are based on orally absorbed antifungal preparations, parenterally administered formulations and often, as a concurrent medication, nebulization. These products may have to be delivered directly into the respiratory tract by intratracheal injection or directly into the air sac by injection or nebulization (Redig 1978).

Many of the therapeutic regimens have been developed in the turkey, which was used as an experimental model for raptors (Redig and Duke, 1985). Few of the data considered in the determination of dose rates for parrots have been derived directly in psittacines.

Supportive therapy is important when considering the outcome of treatment for aspergillosis. This includes fluid therapy and the use of levamisole (Nilverm, Coopers Animal Health) as an immunostimulant at a dose rate of 2 mg/kg bodyweight (3 injections at intervals of 4 days).

Suggested dose rates for amphoteracin B

Amphoteracin B (Fungizone Intravenous — 50 mg per vial, E. R. Squibb and Sons Ltd). 1.5 mg/kg bodyweight intravenously, three times daily for three days.

Amphoteracin B (Fungizone Intravenous — 50 mg per vial, E. R. Squibb and Sons Ltd). 1 mg/kg bodyweight by intratracheal injection, three times daily for three days.

Amphoteracin B (Fungizone Intravenous — 50 mg per vial, E. R. Squibb and Sons Ltd). Dose rates range from 15 mg in 15 ml saline via a nebulizer for 15 minutes twice daily *to* 100 mg in 15 ml saline via a nebulizer for 4 hours daily.

Amphoteracin (Fungilin Suspension or Fungilin in Orobase, E. R. Squibb and Sons Ltd). Topically on oral *Candida* lesions especially those found to be refractory to nystatin therapy.

[Steiner and Davis (1981); Redig (1978); Clubb (1986)].

Suggested dose rate for miconazole

Miconazole (Daktarin Intravenous Solution — 200 mg in 20 ml, Janssen Pharmaceutical Ltd) 10 mg/kg by intramuscular injection, daily. This dose rate may not prove effective in parrots (Lawrence 1983a).

[Furley and Greenwood (1982)].

Suggested dose rate for ketoconazole

Ketoconazole (Nizoral tablets, Janssen Pharmaceutical Ltd). 10 mg/kg bodyweight by gavage, twice daily for 14 days.

Ketoconazole and amphoteracin B should initially be administered together because of the time lag before ketoconazole starts to work (5 to 10 days).

Amphoteracin B has a more immediate effect, bonding directly to the membrane ergestrols of the *Aspergillus*.

[Moriello (1986) for discussion of dose rates in a variety of species.]

Safety

These compounds are all likely to be toxic, with hepatotoxicity being most common. However, *Aspergillus* will inevitably kill the bird if treatment is not attempted.

ANTIPARASITIC THERAPY

A. ANTHELMINTICS

There is little published data on the efficacy and safety of anthelmintics in psittacines. Lawrence (1983b) reviewed the efficacy of fenbendazole in 22 species of parrots, while Harrison (1986b) has tabulated the reported adverse reactions to a number of different anthelmintics in birds. A wide range of anthelmintics have been employed in birds (Arnall and Keymer, 1975; Cooper, 1978; Greve, 1978) with most dose rates being extrapolated from those proving effective in poultry and other domestic animals. All suggested dose rates are referenced and the species of birds involved in an investigation are listed.

There are four main groups of anthelmintics suggested for use in psittacines:-

 i. Imidazothiazoles
 ii. Benzimidazoles
 iii. Avermectins
 iv. Pyrazinoisoquinalines

i. Imidazothiozoles

The most commonly prescribed compound in this group is levamisole or the racemic mixture of the two optical isomers, tetramisole. Since their introduction in the late 1960s they have been widely used in poultry as a water medication. It is recommended that the calculated dose of levamisole be dissolved in the amount of water drunk by the birds in six to eight hours.

Overnight withdrawal of water is advisable to ensure that the birds are sufficiently thirsty to drink the medicated water the following day. Such a potentially stressful regimen is necessary to ensure an adequate intake, over a short period of time, of a foul tasting medicine. Indeed, many parrot species refuse to take the medicated drinking water which poses the problem of deciding how long birds should be left if they refuse to drink. Twenty four hours is probably safe if they are in good health but if they have a nematode associated diarrhoea this length of time could prove fatal.

Parenteral administration of levamisole by subcutaneous or intramuscular injection has proved effective.

Levamisole is a useful product for flock medication via the drinking water. It is effective against mature and immature *Ascaridia, Capillaria* and *Syngamus.* Acanthocephalids (Thorny-headed worms) seem relatively resistant to the effects of levamisole. The parenteral or gavage route in psittacines has little to recommend it as more effective products are available for the treatment of individual birds.

Suggested dose rate of levamisole

Levamisole (Nemecide Injection — 7.5% solution, Coopers Animal Health). 1 ml/3kg bodyweight orally in drinking water. Dissolve in the quantity of water consumed in six to eight hours.

Overnight withdrawal of drinking water may be necessary. No other source of unmedicated water should be available. This includes fruits and moist foods.

Treatment may have to be repeated in aviary birds at four weekly intervals to prevent re-infestation.

Safety

Parenteral administration of levamisole has been associated with reports of adverse reactions. These include depression, ataxia, regurgitation, paralysis, hepatotoxicity and death. The dose rates involved vary between 25 and 66 mg/kg bodyweight. The use of parenteral levamisole is definitely contra-indicated in debilitated birds and lories (Loriidae).

ii. Benzimidazoles

The first product to be launched in this group was thiabendazole. Since then a series of related compounds have been synthesised which have a broader spectrum of activity and a greater efficacy at a reduced dose rate. The newer benzimidazoles such as fenbendazole also have an increased safety margin, although this is not necessarily true of all analogues in parrots. While a single oral dose of fenbendazole has proved effective in the treatment of *Ascaridia*, a smaller repeated dose has been found to be more effective against *Capillaria* (Lawrence, 1983b; Santiago *et al.,* 1985). Fenbendazole can be administered by crop tube or, as it is tasteless, it is well accepted coated onto or mixed with food.

The benzimidazoles are not only effective against mature and immature nematodes but also tapeworms and fluke. However, only albendazole and fenbendazole are likely to prove effective against *Syngamus.*

Suggested dose rates for fenbendazole

Fenbendazole (Panacur 10% Suspension, Hoechst UK Ltd). For *Ascaridia.* 50-100 mg/kg bodyweight by gavage as a single dose.

For *Capillaria* and *Syngamus:* 25-30 mg/kg bodyweight by gavage, daily for five days. An equivalent dose can be incorporated in to the bird's food.

Treatment may have to be repeated monthly in aviary birds to prevent re-infestation.

[Lawrence (1983b) Parakeets *(Myiopsitta, Neophema, Nymphicus, Platycercus, Psittacula),* macaws *(Ara)*, amazons *(Amazona, Pionus)* and lovebirds *(Agapornis).* Santiago *et al. (1985)* Red-tailed hawk *(Buteo jamaicensis).]*

Safety

Fenbendazole has a very wide safety margin in psittacines. Frank and Reichel (1977) have reported the use of a dose of 30 mg/kg bodyweight for 14 days in zoo birds with no ill effects.

However, the benzimidazole group as a whole is not free from side-effects in parrots. Mebendazole is contra-indicated in parrots since its use in two major zoological collections was associated with deaths.

All benzimidazole anthelmintics should be used with care in birds 'in the moult' as feather stunting and abnormalities have been reported (Devriese, 1983). Albendazole, parbendazole and cambendazole have all been shown to be teratogenic during the first month of pregnancy in sheep. Until this situation has been clarified in birds these products should not be used in breeding pairs.

iii. Avermectins

Avermectin B1, known as ivermectin, is an antibiotic with potent antiparasitic activity. Both endo- and ectoparasites have proved susceptible to very low doses of this compound, given orally or parenterally. However, as the solution is made up in propylene glycol it can not be used to medicate drinking water. The only licensed injectible formulation in the UK is designed for use in large animals (1% solution), with 1 ml being the effective dose for a 50 kg individual. For use in birds it requires to be diluted with propylene glycol.

Ivermectin is effective against mature and immature nematodes, microfilaria, lice and mites. Its effect is prolonged, a single dose often proving effective for many weeks (Drummond, 1985).

Suggested dose rate for ivermectin

Ivermectin (Ivomec Injection — 1% solution, MSD Agvet). Dilute 1 ml Ivomec with 4 ml propylene glycol. The dilute solution is then administered at the rate of 0.1 ml/kg bodyweight either orally or by intramuscular injection. This is equivalent to a dose rate of 200 mcg/kg bodyweight. [Clubb (1986).]

Safety

The use of ivermectin at normal suggested dose rates has been associated with deaths in budgerigars (Harrison 1986b). Ivermectin Oral Paste (Eqvalan paste — 1.87% paste, MSD Agvet) may also have caused deaths in treated birds. However, it would appear that the deaths were not associated with the active ingredient but possibly a stabilizer in the paste.

iv. **Pyrazinoisoquinalones**

Praziquantel is a highly effective, well tolerated, anthelmintic with marked activity against parasitic trematodes and cestodes. Andrews *et al.* (1983) reported its use in a variety of avian species. All the reported dose rates were effective in eliminating adult cestodes. Intestinal trematodes have also been successfully treated in birds (Kumar, 1980).

Praziquantel is available either as a tablet or an injectible formulation.

Suggested dose rates for praziquantel

Praziquantel (Droncit tablets, Bayer UK Ltd). 10 mg/kg bodyweight by gavage as a single dose. Repeat after two to four weeks.

Praziquantel (Droncit injection, Bayer UK Ltd) 7.5 mg/kg bodyweight by intramuscular injection as a single dose. Repeat after two to four weeks.
[Andrews *et al.* (1983). Domestic goose *(Anser),* Duck *(Anas platyrhynchos),* Pigeon *(Columba livia)* Domestic fowl *(Gallus domesticus).*]

Safety

Toxicity has been reported in Society finches or Bengalese *(Lonchura domestica)* after parenteral adminstration of praziquantel. The symptoms described were depresssion, collapse and death. This report is hardly surprising as a dose rate of 100-250 mg/kg bodyweight was administered i.e. 10 to 25 times suggested levels. Doses up to 90 mg/kg were well tolerated in domestic fowls and pigeons (Bauditz, 1978).

B. ECTOPARASITICIDES

Bromocyclen (Alugan, Hoechst UK Ltd) has proved effective in cage birds. For the treatment of *Cnemidocoptes* infestations of the face or legs, a 0.2% suspension (Alugan Concentrate Powder, Hoechst UK Ltd) can be painted on to the affected area weekly. Alugan Dusting Powder (Hoechst UK Ltd.) can be applied into the feathers every 7-10 days for the control of other ectoparasites. Alugan Aerosol Spray (Hoechst UK Ltd.) should not be used on birds (Turner, 1985). If red poultry mite infests the nesting boxes in an aviary or bird room, topical treatment of the bird will be ineffective, but the use of the spray or a 0.5% suspension of concentrate powder can be used to treat the environment. Bromocyclen should not be used in breeding birds as residues can be detected in eggs.

Cnemidocoptes pilae infestation of the face (Scaly face) or legs (Scaly legs) can also be treated using a topically applied 10% emulsion of benzyl benzoate, at weekly intervals. This is the preferred treatment in advanced cases.

Some aviculturists permanently suspend a dichlorvos-impregnated strip (Vapona, Shellstar) in the bird room to reduce the risk of ectoparasitic infestation. These strips must be used with care as they can prove toxic and Turner (1985) has suggested that they should only be used for three days at a time, being removed at night.

REFERENCES.

ANDREWS, P., THOMAS, H., POHLKE, R. and SEUBERT, J. (1983). Praziquantel. Medical Research Reviews. **3**; 147-200.

ARCHIMBAULT, P., AMBROGG, G. and JOINEAUD, J. (1983). Doxycyline in poultry: bioavailability and transfer to eggs. Veterinary Medical Reviews. **134**; 291-295.

ARNALL, L. and KEYMER, I. F. (1985). Bird Diseases. T.F.H. Publications. Neptune NJ, USA. pp 492-495.

BLACK, W. D. (1977). A study of the pharmacodynamics of oxytetracycline in the chicken. Poultry Science. **56**; 1430-1434.

BUSH, M., LOCKE, D., NEAL, L. A. and CARPENTER, J. W. (1981a). Pharmacokinetics of cephalothin and cephalexin in selected avian species. American Journal of Veterinary Research. **42**; 1014-1017.

BUSH, M., LOCKE, D., NEAL, L. A. and CARPENTER, J. W. (1981b). Genetamicin tissue concentrations in various avian species following recommended dosage therapy. American Journal of Veterinary Research. **42**; 2114-2116.

BAUDITZ, R. (1978). Bayer AG Internal Report. Quoted in Andrews et al. (1983). Praziquantel. Medical Research Reviews. **3**; 193.

CARWARDINE, P. (1984), Clinical Trials with metronidazole. Paper, with accompanying fact sheet, presented at the BVA Congress, Stirling. (Available from May and Baker Ltd., Dagenham, Essex, RM10 7XS)

CLARK, C. H. (1986). Pharmacology of Antibiotics. In: Clinical Avian Medicine and Surgery. Editors G. J. Harrison and L. R. Harrison. Saunders Philadelphia USA. pp 319-326.

CLUBB, S. L. (1986). Therapeutics: Individual and flock treatment regimens. In: Clinical Avian Medicine and Surgery. Editors G. J. Harrison and L. R. Harrison. Saunders Philadelphia, USA. pp 327-355.

COOPER, J. E. (1978). Parasites. In: Veterinary Aspects of Captive Birds of Prey. pp 82-96.

COOPER, J. E. (1983). Pathological studies on the effects of intramuscular injections in the Starling (Sturnus vulgaris). Sonderdruck aus Verhandlungsbericht des 25th Internationalen Symposiums uber Erkrankungen der Zootiere, Wien 1983. pp 61-65.

COOPER, J. E. (1985). Safety and efficacy of clavulanate-potentiated amoxycillin in pigeons (Columba livia). Research in Veterinary Science. **39**; 87-89.

DEVRIESE, L. A. (1983). Fenbendazole treatment of nematodes in birds. Veterinary Record. **112**; 509.

DORRESTEIN, G. M., BUITELAAR, M. N. and WIGGELINKHUIZEN, J. M. (1981). Pharmakokinetische aspekten von antibiotika bei Volierevogeln und tauben. Proceedings IId. Symposium on 'Krankheiten der Vogel', Munchen 1981.

DORRESTEIN, G. M., van GOGH, H. and RINZEMA, J. D. (1984). Pharmacokinetic aspects of penicillins, aminoglycosides and chloramphenicol in birds compared to mammals. A review. The Veterinary Quarterly. **6**; 216-224.

DORRESTEIN, G. M., van GOGH, H. and de WIT, P. (1986). Blood levels of certain drugs administered via drinking water to homing pigeons (Columba livea). In: V. Tagung uber Vogelkrankheiten Munchen, 6. und 7. Marz 1986. pp 73-89.

DRUMMOND, R. O. (1985). Effectiveness of ivermectin for control of arthropod pests of livestock. Southwestern Entomologist. Supplement 7; 34-42.

ENSLEY, P. K. and JANSSEN, D. L. (1981). A preliminary study comparing the pharmacokinetics of ampicillin given orally and intramuscularly to psittacines. Journal of Zoo Animal Medicine. **12**; 42-47.

FLAMMER, K. (undated). Personal communication. Quoted in: Woerpel, R. W. and Rosskopf, W. J. (1981). Avian Therapeutics. Modern Veterinary Practice. **62**; 949.

FRANK, W. and REICHEL, K. (1977). Erfahrungen bei der Bekampfung von Nematoden und Cestoden bei Reptilien und Amphibien. Verhandlungsbericht des XIX. Internationalen Symposiums uber die Erkrankung der Zootiere, Poznan 1977, Akademie-Verlag Berlin. pp 107-114.

FURLEY, C. W. and GREENWOOD, A. G. (1982). The treatment of aspergillosis in raptors with miconazole. Veterinary Record. **111**; 584-585.

GILBERT, D. N., PLAMP, C., STARR, P., BENNETT, W. M., HOUGHTON, D. C. and PORTER, G. (1978). Comparative nephrotoxicity of gentamicin and tobramycin in rats. Antimicrobial Agents and Chemotherapy. **13**; 34-39.

GREVE, J. H. (1978). Parasitic Diseases. In: Zoo and Wild Animal Medicine. Editor M. E. Fowler. Saunders Philadelphia USA. pp 374-384.

GYLSTORFF, I., JAKOBY, J. R. and GERBERMANN, H. (1984). Comparative studies on psittacosis control by drugs. II. Testing the efficacy of different drugs in various formulations in experimentally infected red-crowned parrots (*Amazona viridigenalis*) Berliner und Munchener Tierarztliche Wochenschrift. **97**; 91-99.

HARRISON, G. J. (1986a). What to do until a diagnosis is made. In: Clinical Avian Medicine and Surgery. Editors G. J. Harrison and L. R. Harrison. Saunders Philadelphia USA. pp 356-361.

HARRISON, G. J. (1986b). Toxicology. In: Clinical Avian Medicine and Surgery. Editors G. J. Harrison and L. R. Harrison. Saunders Philadelphia USA. pp 491-499.

JAKOBY, J. R. and GYLSTORFF, J. (1983). Comparative investigations on chemotherapeutic psittacosis control. I. Blood levels in blunt-tailed parrots following oral application of different medicated foods and parenteral application of doxycycline in an import station. Berliner und Munchener Tierarztliche Wochenschrift. **96**; 261-264.

KAPLAN, J. M., McCRACKEN, G H., THOMAS, M.L., HORTON, L. J. and DAVIS, N. (1973). Clinical pharmacology of tobramycin in newborns. American Journal of Diseases in Children. **125**; 656-661.

KEYMER. I. F. (1982). Mycoses. In: Diseases of Cage and Aviary Birds. Editor M. L. Petrak. Lea and Febiger Philadelphia USA. pp 599-605.

KUCERS, A. and BENNETT, N. McK. (1979). Carbenicillin, Indanyl carbenicillin and carfecillin. In: The Use of Antibiotics, 3rd Edition. Heinemann London. pp 149-169.

KUMAR, V. (1980). Personal communication. Quoted in: Andrews *et al.* (1983). Praziquantel. Medical Research Reviews. **3**; 147-200.

LANDGRAF, W. W., ROSS, P. F. and CASSIDY, D. R. (1982). Concentration of chlortetracycline in the blood of Yellow-crowned parrots fed medicated pelleted feeds. Avian Diseases. **26**; 14-17.

LAWRENCE, K. (1983a). Treatment of aspergillosis in raptors. Veterinary Record. **112**; 88.

LAWRENCE, K. (1983b). Efficacy of fenbendazole against nematodes of captive birds. Veterinary Record. **112**; 433-434.

LAWRENCE, K. (1986). Facts and data to help the treatment of smaller domestic pets. In: The Henston Veterinary Vade Mecum. Editor J. Evans. Henston London.

LAWRENCE, K., NEEDHAM, J. R., PALMER, G. H. and LEWIS, J. C. (1984). A preliminary study on the use of carbenicillin in snakes. Journal of Veterinary Pharmacology and Therapeutics. **7**; 119-124.

LOCKE, D. and BUSH, M. (1984), Tylosin aerosol therapy in quail and pigeons. Journal of Zoo Animal Medicine. **15**; 67-72.

LOCKE, D., BUSH, M. and CARPENTER, J. W. (1982). Pharmacokinetics and tissue concentrations of tylosin in selected avian species. American Journal of Veterinary Research. **43**; 1807-1810.

LUTHGEN, W., SCHULZ, W. and HAUSER, K. W. (1979). Parenteral administration of doxycycline to cockatoos, with reference to prevention and treatment of psittacosis. Praktische Tierarzt. **60**; 233-236.

LUTHGEN, W., WACHENDORFER, G. and SCHULZ, W. (1973). Relationships between dosage with chlortetracycline, its concentration in the blood and excretion in the faeces in budgerigars *(Melopsittacus undulatus).* Berliner und Munchener Tierarztliche Wochenschrift. **86**; 454-457.

MORIELLO, K. A. (1986). Ketoconazole: Clinical pharmacology and therapeutic recommendations. Journal of American Veterinary Medical Association. **188**; 303-306.

NEEDHAM, J. R. (1981). Bacterial flora of birds of prey. In: Recent advances in the study of raptor diseases. Editors J. E. Cooper and A. G. Greenwood. Chiron Publications Ltd. West Yorkshire, England. pp 3-9.

PANIGRAHY, B., MATHEWSON, J. J., HALL, C. F. and GRUMBLES, L. C. (1981). Unusual disease conditions in pet and aviary birds. Journal of the American Veterinary Medical Association. **178**; 394-395.

POLLET, R. A., GLATZ, C. E., DYER, D. C. and BARNES, H. J. (1983). Pharmacokinetics of chlortetracycline potentiation with citric acid in the chicken. American Journal of Veterinary Research. **44**; 1718-1721.

REDIG, P. T. (1978). Mycotic infections of birds of prey. In: Zoo and Wild Animal Medicine. Editor M. E. Fowler. Saunders Philadelphia USA. pp 273-290.

REDIG, P. T. (1984). Fluid therapy and acid base balance in the critically ill avian patient. International Conference on Avian Medicine, Toronto, Canada. pp 59-73.

REDIG, P. T. and DUKE, G. E. (1985). Comparative pharmacokinetics of antifungal drugs in domestic turkeys, Red-tailed hawks, Broad-winged hawks and Great-horned owls. Avian Diseases. **29**; 649-661.

SANTIAGO, C., MILLS, P. A. and KIRKPATRICK, C. E. (1985). Oral capillariasis in a red-tailed hawk: Treatment with fenbendazole. Journal of the American Veterinary Medical Association. **11**; 1205-1206.

SCHACHTER, J., BANKOWSKI, R. A., SUNG, M. L. MIERS, L. and STRASSBURGER, M. (1984). Measurement of tetracycline levels in parakeets. Avian Diseases. **28**; 295-302.

SCHENTAG, J. J. and JUSKO, W. J. (1977). Gentamicin persistence in the body. Lancet. **1**; 486-489.

SCHOLTENS, R. G., NEW, J. C. and JOHNSON, S. (1982). The nature and treatment of giardiasis in parakeets. Journal of the American Veterinary Medical Association. **180**; 170-173.

SPREAT, S. R. and BECKFORD, S. M. (1977). Pharmacodynamics of gentamicin in day-old chicks. Proceedings of the 26th Western Poultry Disease Conference. pp 101-107.

STEINER, C. V. and DAVIS, R. B. (1981). Cage Bird Medicine: Selected topics. Iowa State University Press Ames, Iowa USA.

TEARE, J. A., SCHWARK, W. S., SHIN, S. J. & GRAHAM, D. L. (1985). Pharmacokinetics of a long-acting oxytetracycline preparation in ring-necked pheasants, great horned owls and Amazon parrots. American Journal of Veterinary Research. **46**; 2639-2643.

TURNER, T. (1985). Cagebirds. In: Manual of Exotic Pets. Editors J. E. Cooper, M. F. Hutchinson, O. F. Jackson & R. J. Maurice. BSAVA Cheltenham UK. pp 106-123.

WHELTON, A., CARTER, G. G., CRAIG, T. J., BRYANT, H. H. HERBST, D. V. & WALKER, W. (1978). Comparison of the intrarenal disposition of tobramycin and gentamicin: Therapeutic and toxicological answers. Journal of Antimicrobial Chemotherapy. Supplement. **4**; 13-19.

WICK, W. E. & WELLS, J. S. (1968). Nebramycin, a new broad-spectrum antibiotic complex. IV. *In vitro* and *in vivo* laboratory evaluation. Antimicrobial Agent and Chemotherapy. -1967; 341-349.

WOERPEL, R. W. & ROSSKOPF, W. J. (1981). Avian therapeutics. Modern Veterinary Practice. **62**; 947-949.

YOSHIDA, M., HOSHII, H., YONEZAWA, S., NOGAWA, H., YOSHIMURA, H. & ITO, O. (1975). Residue and disappearance of dietary oxytetracycline in the blood, muscle, liver and bile of growing chicks. Japanese Poultry Science. **12**; 181-187.

ZIV, G., NEUMANN, J., FRIDMAN, J., ZIV, E., SINGER, N. & MESHORER, A. (1979). Effects of probenecid on blood levels and tissue distribution of ampicillin in fowls and turkeys. Avian Diseases. **23**; 927-939

Chapter 21   # FEEDING, HOUSING AND BREEDING

A. A. J. Stoodley, I. M. Hadgkiss and L. A. Rance

FEEDING

The dietary requirements of the parrot family are varied and, in some species, complex. Many are seed eaters; others, like the brush-tongued, feed mainly on nectar, while there are those that feed on grain, nuts, fruit, berries, buds, insects, grubs and legumes. Some find what they need in the canopy of the forest, while others keep to low scrub land, or the savanna.

In the main the majority of captive parrots can be divided into 3 groups: seed eaters, nectar feeders and those that need a bulky diet containing vegetable matter. Whilst it is interesting to study parrots in their natural habitat to learn about their individual food preferences, it is generally not practical to maintain the same diet in captivity. There must be compromise and, because of this, only parrots that take a varied diet should be considered as aviary subjects. Those that have a restricted diet, some feeding on the seed or flesh of a single plant for instance, cannot be considered since, obviously, the food they require would not be readily available.

Not only must the food provided be acceptable to the captive parrot, but it must also meet its dietary requirements, containing all the nutrients to maintain good health both for the cage pet and those that are kept for breeding purposes.

Some parrots will be affected by change of environment and it is therefore important, when a new bird is introduced, to know its previous diet and how the food was given e.g. clip-on pots at eye level, a dish or a tray, or perhaps a plastic food dispenser. Until new arrivals are well established it is best to continue feeding their accustomed diet, whether or not it is adequately balanced. If it is inadequate, a more balanced food can be made available at the same time, and as interest is shown, the accustomed poor diet can be gradually withdrawn. The continuation of the accustomed diet is especially important to birds that are hospitalised and undergoing treatment to avoid the added stress of being given unfamiliar food.

To help eliminate boredom cage parrots can be fed several times a day. Those that take seed, nuts, pulses and vegetables can be given chopped fruit and vegetables as the first food of the day, and the allowance of seed, nuts and pulses can be divided into two feeds, with fresh green plant food and live branches to hold their attention.

In a large establishment where the feed is taken in bulk, an inexpensive parrot is sometimes kept as a 'Guinea pig'. This bird receives samples of all new batches of food to test for any poisonous substance. Even in a small collection it is advisable to feed new batches of food to only one of the collection as a precaution to prove it safe.

SEED MIXTURE

It is essential that seed is obtained from a reputable supplier. Most breeders prefer to prepare their own mix but standard mixtures are available.

Seeds commonly fed are wheat, oats, canary seed, millet (Panicum, Dakota red, Japanese, Pearl white), buckwheat, nigre and groats.

Seed mixtures should also contain some oil seeds but they must be carefully rationed to prevent obesity. A higher percentage of oil seed may be fed during the cold months than during the summer. Commonly fed oil seeds are sunflower seed, linseed, rape seed and hemp seed.

SOAKED SEED

During the breeding season soaked seed can play a significant part in producing good breeding results. All the seeds mentioned are suitable for soaking except linseed which tends to give an oily texture if soaked in conjunction with the other seeds. However, the ones that appear to both germinate quickly and appeal most to the birds are sunflower, hemp, niger, mungbeans and wheat.

The seeds should be soaked for a period of twenty four hours and washed under running water in a sieve several times during this part of the process. Then the soaked seed should be spread on shallow trays which are then placed in a warm room. Once again the seeds should be washed at regular intervals. After approximately twenty four to thirty six hours in the trays the white tips of germination should be visible. It is at this stage that the vitamin content is at its highest and therefore is of most benefit to the birds.

This is best fed three times a day in small quantities when the birds have chicks in the nestbox.

SOFTFOOD

Several softfoods are commercially available and are suitable for feeding to the smaller psittacine birds particularly during the breeding season. They should be fed in small amounts, several times a day.

FRUIT

Many fruits can be fed to psittacine birds but some are more readily accepted than others. Fruits that can be tried are apples, plums, raspberries, blackberries, pears, peaches, grapes and oranges.

VEGETABLES

Carrots and celery are often very popular especially if grated.

PULSES

Harricot beans, soya beans, green peas, mung beans, chick peas, maple beans, black-eyed beans and other whole pulses are available from Health Food Shops. They are particularly valuable for the larger psittacine birds as they have a high protein and low fat content but, of course, will not be eaten by seed eaters. They are usually soaked before feeding as for seeds.

GREENFOOD

Alfalfa, watercress and lettuce are the most popular greenfoods. Young plants of chickweed, groundsel and dandelion may also be eaten and the young heads of plantains and dock are enjoyed by some birds. Care must be taken to ensure the absence of chemical sprays if wild plants are used.

PEANUTS

Peanuts must be obtained from a reputable source and be fit for human consumption. They should only be a minor constituent of the diet to avoid obesity.

SUPPLEMENTS

Supplements such as Vionate (Ciba-Geigy Agrochemicals) and SA37 (Intervet) can be sprinkled onto fruit, soaked seed and softfood.

MILLET SPRAYS

These can be an extremely useful addition to the seed part of the diet. Birds will often eat millet spray in preference to other seeds, particularly during the moult when appetite appears to be much reduced. When young birds leave the nestbox it is important that they discover a source of food, other than from the parents, as soon as possible. By hanging millet sprays at the perch ends they will be encouraged to eat far more quickly than if they are left to find the food bowls. This approach will often encourage a sick bird to eat when all other seeds are rejected.

GRIT

Various grades of grit are commercially available and should be made available to birds in a shallow tray.

BONES

A meaty bone will be enjoyed by many of the larger species but it must be lean and fresh and removed once it has been discarded.

CUTTLEFISH BONE

Cuttlefish bone is often given to captive birds as a source of calcium. Some birds will devour it avidly while others will ignore it completely. It should be available all the year round as requirements may be seasonal and unpredictable.

BRANCHES

The larger species enjoy whittling a hard wood log. The branches of young non-poisonous trees give great pleasure to some of the smaller species, especially lovebirds, which strip the bark, eat the pith and use the more fibrous matter to add to their nesting material.

WATER

Water should be available at all times even for nectar feeders, many of which bath once or twice daily. Water pots must be kept scrupulously clean as parrots are usually most particular that the water they bathe in is clean, but they are less particular over drinking water.

REQUIREMENTS OF INDIVIDUAL SPECIES.

COCKATIELS — Genus *Nymphicus*

Cockatiels should be fed a good mixture containing canary seed, millet, hemp seed, linseed, niger seed, sunflower seed, safflower seed, groats and wheat. They also enjoy apple, lettuce or chickweed.

KAKARIKIS — Genus *Cyanoranphus*

A good seed mixture should be fed although some kakarikis will eat only the sunflower seeds. These birds are extremely fond of greenfoods and particularly enjoy a turf of grass. The roots and the blades are eaten as well as any insects which may be present.

Fruit may be eaten by these birds and apples, pears, grapes, strawberries and red currants should be offered.

The diet should be supplemented with soaked seeds when rearing young.

BUDGERIGARS — Genus *Melopsittacus*

Budgerigars should be fed a reputable proprietary seed mix to ensure adequate levels of vitamins and minerals (particularly iodine). Birds will also enjoy some greenfoods particularly watercress, lettuce, chickweed, groundsel and dandelions. Fruit should also be provided and most birds will enjoy nibbling cuttlefish bone.

LOVE BIRDS — Genus *Agapornis*

These small parrots make delightful cage pets and are interesting aviary subjects, too. They are best maintained on a good canary mixture. In addition, those kept in a garden aviary with room for flying can be given wheat, rice, kibbled maize, sunflower seed and pine nuts. The lovebird enjoys stripping bark from the branches of young non-poisonous trees, eating much of the pith and using the more fibrous matter to add to its nesting material. Berries in season are enjoyed, especially hawthorn. Every effort should be made to encourage this group to take green plant food, fruit and vegetables as part of the daily diet. It is difficult to supply the leaf buds, blossoms and fruit taken by the wild lovebird, and many captive birds will not accept much other than sweet apple and carrot, so becoming almost totally seed eaters. When there are young in the nest, the parent birds should be encouraged to feed plenty of green plant food such as land cress or alfalfa. There should also be soft food available, which can be a porage of cereal with egg and milk or a mash of cooked pulses.

RING NECK PARROTS — Genus *Psittacula*

This group also includes the slaty headed, plum headed, blossom headed, moustached, Derbyan parrots and several others. Both cage pets and aviary birds of this group can be offered a parakeet seed mixture which includes safflower, oats, wheat and hemp. Black, white and striped sunflower seed, pine nuts, buckwheat, canary seed and mixed millets should also be given. Sweet apple, soft fruits and salad type greens are taken, also tomatoes, carrot and beetroot. Some of the Psittacula group need a nectar food as part of their diet.

COCKATOO — Genus *Cacatua*

All too often the cockatoo in captivity is regarded as a seed eater when in point of fact its diet should be varied to include root vegetables, green leafy plant food, nuts (including acorns and sweet chestnuts — preferably germinating), fruit, pulses, (again germinating), parrot seed mix and live non-poisonous tree wood. This group of parrots will, like most of the parrot-like birds, enjoy leaf buds and live pith under the bark, but it also has a great need to whittle on wood. Those that have access to grass or earth will spend much time rooting for grubs and growing shoots. Soft food such as rusk soaked in milk is enjoyed but should be restricted to aviary kept birds since cage pets, if over fed, become obese.

CONURES — Genus *Aratinga, Nandayus, Leptosittaca, Ognorhynchus* and *Cyanoliseus*

These are birds of the New World which cover a very large group, and many are commonly kept as cage pets. In the wild they take berries, seed, fruit, blossoms and some take nuts of the Araucaria tree. In captivity the smaller conures do well on canary and budgerigar seed, while larger conures take parrot seed mixture. Rice, oats, pine nuts, wheat and buckwheat can also be included in the seed diet. Whilst most conures will readily take germinated seed some are reluctant to eat pulses or vegetables. A little sweet apple and fleshy green plant food is perhaps all that will be readily taken. Those kept in large aviaries can be offered soft food especially when there are young in the nest.

AUSTRALIAN PARROTS — Genus *Alisterus, Apromictus, Polytelis, Purpureicephalus, Barnardius, Platycercus, Psephotus* and *Neophema*.

Most of these birds are well known in aviculture, and few make good cage pets. Because they are so active and need room to fly, they are better kept as aviary subjects. In the wild they feed on seeds, berries, blossoms, fruit, sometimes nectar and leaf buds. In captivity they can be maintained on canary and budgerigar seed mixtures, parakeet mixture, buckwheat, hemp, wheat, oats and pine nuts. The smaller birds are more interested in smaller seed. Green plant food, fruit and sprouted pulses are enjoyed by this group. Soft food including those containing egg or insects are taken by many, especially those with young in the nest.

BRUSH TONGUED PARROTS — the Loriidae family

Commonly known as lories and lorikeets, these feed on pollen and nectar, while some will take fruit and a little seed. In captivity this genus can be fed on a commercial marketed formula, but many keeping the brush tongued parrot make up a nectar, each person using slightly different specifications. It is therefore advantageous when purchasing birds from a breeder to ask for a little of the nectar used and to ask for the recipe, so that the bird can continue on the same diet. Most nectar diets contain protein and some carbohydrate, and are made by adding to a pint of water, sugar to sweeten (never molasses), one teaspoon of vegetable powder formulated for infants, and one teaspoon of cereal powder, again formulated for infants. Some brush tongued parrots will take liquidised sweet soft fruit mixed up with the nectar, others will eat chopped fruit and some seed. Most keepers use vitamin additives to compensate for the inadequacies of the diet. Some nectar feeders need a thicker food, therefore less water can be used to make up the nectar. The nectar is quick to sour and, if fruit is used, quick to ferment. It must be given freshly made several times a day, and the food pots kept clean.

MACAWS

The small macaws can be given a diet similar to that of the larger conures which contains sunflower seed, pine nuts, maize, oats, wheat, buckwheat, rice and small seed. Many will take soft food, peanuts, fruit, some vegetables and mixed germinated pulses. The larger macaws can be fed the same diet as the small macaw, but will also take nuts in the shell and flesh. Many parrots enjoy a little animal protein from time to time, but the macaw will take meat as part of its diet if it is made available regularly. Soft food and plenty of corn on the cob should be made available when there are young in the nest. Some parrots, especially the large macaw, are known to fast and will take only perhaps one kind of nut or seed. If this is allowed to happen the health of the parrot will be affected. It is best to withdraw the favoured food completely from the diet until the bird is again eating a wide variety of balanced ingredients.

AMAZON and PIONUS PARROTS

These are New World parrots of medium size. Like many cage or aviary kept birds they can become seed eaters. If these birds are to be kept for breeding they need a good balanced diet containing vegetable matter and plenty of fresh greens and fruit. Parrot mixture should only be a very small part of their diet since both the amazon and the pionus are inclined to overeat. A high percentage are too fat, and do much better on a diet of sprouted pulses, chopped fruit and vegetables, fresh greens and very little wheat, maize, oats, buckwheat and sunflower seed.

ECLECTUS PARROTS — Genus *Eclectus*

These parrots are all too often maintained on a seed diet, and many often look in poor condition. In the wild their diet is much like the largest of the bush tongued parrots — nectar and blossoms, with fruits, especially figs, leaf buds, berries, but very little seed. In captivity the eclectus will take boiled, polished rice (long grain), chopped salad, soft fruit, chopped vegetables, sweetcorn, soaked dried fruit including figs, sultanas and raisins, pine nuts, nectar, small amounts of sunflower seed and meat (cooked). The nectar can be given daily in a separate pot, but the remainder of the diet can be chopped and added to the rice. A tea cup would be plenty for one pair of birds but more would be taken if there were young in the nest.

FIG PARROTS — Genus *Opopsitta, Psittaculirostris*

Seeds especially of figs, fruit, blossoms and nectar, some insects and their larva, all form part of the wild bird's diet. In captivity fig parrots can be encouraged to feed if millet seed is fed in a paste of fresh or dried figs. Once they become accustomed to taking millet seed any scarcity of fresh figs will not prove a disaster. Some will eat sunflower seed but soft sweet fruit should always be available as part of their diet. A sweet nectar is enjoyed by some.

HOUSING

This chapter will only consider housing suitable for birds kept in the United Kingdom.

GARDEN AVIARY

Site

The aviary should be sited in a quiet, secluded situation so that the breeding birds will not be disturbed by passers by. In exposed sites, protection from wind should be provided by a hedge and the aviary should be positioned to face the sun.

Pairing

Ideally parrots should be kept in breeding pairs. Most species will live happily together in this way all the year round.

The Flight

The minimum dimensions for a flight housing a pair of birds should be 6 feet long by 6 feet high by 3 feet wide. Such accommodation would be suitable for lovebirds and some of the Australian grass parakeets such as Bourke's, Splendid and Elegant. At 9 feet long the flight can accommodate a much wider range of species including cockatiels, the smaller South American concures, Australian red-rumped, many-coloured and Swift parakeets, and the turquoisine and blue-winged grass parakeets.

With the larger species, the length of flight should increase. The minimum width required can be calculated by at least doubling the wing span of the species being kept. This will allow sufficient width for the birds to pass one another in flight.

The higher flights are built the less threatened the occupants will feel. As small birds seem to prefer to roost at the highest points, they will naturally go to that end of the aviary at night and consequently be under the roof. In this location they will be safe fom cats, foxes and owls.

Galvanised welded mesh should be used to wire the flight and 16 gauge 1'' x ½'' is suitable for all the smaller parrotlike species. Nothing finer than 10 gauge should be considered for macaws, with a spacing of 1'' x 1''. Amazons and medium size parrots with heavy bills need 12 gauge, and smaller parrots 14 gauge. Double wiring between flights is essential to prevent a parrot from biting its neighbour's feet.

Underwiring of the flights is an essential contribution to vermin control if there is an earth base but, as is explained later, this is undesirable.

The wooden framework should be at least 1 ½'' x 1 ½'' and preferably 2'' x 2''. This should be pre-treated with Cuprinol or creosote and allowed to dry completely before use. Concrete footings are necessary. For larger species a metal framework is essential.

Approximately one third of the length of the flight should be covered by a roof of clear perspex or glass. The same material can be used to provide protection at the sides of the flight, again covering approximately one third of the length.

Shelter

A frost proof shelter must be provided. This may be constructed of thermal blocks or wood, the latter being unsuitable for large species. Also wood offers less protection against rats than thermal blocks.

A shelter at least 7 feet high and incorporating a service passage is ideal. Food then can be given in the shelters leaving the flights free of unsightly debris, and the nest box hung just outside the shelters for easy access.

Small shelters are often built to accommodate the smaller parrots and parakeets. In general the box-like structure occupies the top half of the back section of the flight. Access to the shelter should be inviting, especially if this is where the food is given; many a new parrot in a collection has been lost simply because it failed to enter the shelter to feed. New arrivals need dishes of food clipped on the panelling at perch level, and perhaps a dish or two at ground level, just until they settle,

To encourage parrots to sleep inside the shelter safe from frost and predators the perches should be higher than those in the flights. Those reluctant to sleep inside can have the perches in flights lowered overnight until they become accustomed to sleeping inside.

Perches

The siting of perches in both the flight and the shelter is most important. The smaller parrotlike species will favour the highest perch and this is particularly so in relation to roosting. Two perches are sufficient for the flight and should be situated towards either end. A single perch in the inside shelter should be at a level above the highest perch in the flight to encourage the birds to roost in the most protected part of the aviary.

The thickness of the perches should directly relate to the species being housed. Each perch should allow the bird's feet to grip it but it should not be so thin that the toes overlap. Firm perching is very important during mating. Perches should be changed frequently or scrubbed regularly as they quickly become soiled.

Branches of most deciduous trees are suitable, willow and fruit trees being commonly used. Yew, laburnum, juniper, rhododendron and exotic shrubs should *not* be used.

Floor

Flights should never have soil floors. Concrete is ideal but shingle is acceptable.

Pea shingle should be at least 2 inches deep and raked regularly and ideally paving slabs should be sited beneath perches to permit daily removal of droppings; it must be changed frequently and, at least, annually.

The floor of the inside shelter should be covered in fine sand and changed at regular intervals.

Lighting

Birds only eat during daylight so that during the short winter days their food intake would be reduced.

The solution to this problem is to extend the feeding period by controlled lighting. Approximately twelve hours light should be provided each day by providing artificial light preferably in the morning. If artificial lighting is provided in the evening a dimming system is sometimes used to avoid the panicking which can occur when lights are turned straight off.

Bathing

Birds kept in fully enclosed aviaries (i.e., those with both glazed fronts and roofs) will need access to bathing water. The small parakeet will bath well enough in a dish of water. The larger parrots, however, like to leaf-bath and since the aviary is not a planted one then a mist spray can be provided from an overhead spraying system. A run of small-bore copper pipe *outside* the roofing wire with a fine spray nozzle, one to each pen, is ideal.

Vermin

Mice are a common problem in aviaries. Not only do they over winter in nest boxes and prevent hens from nesting but they can also contaminate food. Their activity at night disrupts the harmony of the entire collection.

The common rat can be an even more serious problem. When immature it can enter through the wire and then grow too large to escape. Under such circumstances it becomes carnivorous, killing parrots up to the size of the Amazon.

Once established, rodents can prove difficult to eradicate since the usual baits are dangerous to use within the aviary. Even if bait is securely covered and out of reach of the parrot, rodents can carry traces on their feet to food dishes and water pots. Bait is best used well away from the aviaries and kept covered against small wild birds, since after taking bait these small birds will perch on the aviary structure to clean their beaks and leave traces of poison within reach of the aviary birds. A variety of traps, baited and unbaited, are available for controlling mice and are much safer than poisons but probably the safest method of control is rat varnish. Ideally a varnish-covered piece of glass is placed in a receptacle such as a biscuit tin in which an entrance hole has been made. The hole is placed nearest the wall and a heavy weight prevents the parrot gaining access to the varnish. To attract the rodent on to the varnish a piece of chocolate is placed at the centre.

Cats can present a problem that is not easy to deal with as their presence on the aviary roof, especially at night, can result in sufficient panic to cause fatalities.

Sparrowhawks can also be a nuisance as they attack birds when they are hanging on the wire. Such an attack can only be prevented by double-wiring.

MULTIPLE UNITS

If a number of species are to be kept, the multiple unit system is the best way of housing them. This system consists of a row of flights built off one or both sides of a central building. If both sides of the building are to be utilised, a well sheltered part of the garden must be chosen as the flights will face opposite points of the compass. There are many advantages to this system not least of which is security. The door into the building is placed at the end and the doors into the flights in the passageway. Therefore, once the door into the building is secure, with no exterior access into the flights, escapes are totally ruled out. The inside shelter part of the aviary can be incorporated into the building so that the servicing of food and water can be undertaken from the central passageway.

The area under the inside shelter should be part of the flight, with the entrance door to the flight flush with the inside shelter. This is where bowls should be positioned so that they can be changed without physically entering the flight. As, obviously, there is no perch over this area there will be no fouling of the water from droppings.

Double wiring between the flights is essential to prevent the problem of pairs fighting. Even with 1'' x ½'' mesh the damage inflicted to beak and claws can be severe. The birds most at risk are young ones during the first few days after leaving the nestbox. They are prone to hang on the wire and can be fatally injured by the birds in the adjoining flight. Inside shelters must also be double wired.

BIRD HALLS

Bird halls may be built of brick with a thermal insulation filled cavity, or thermal blocks can be used. The length of the building is determined by the number of hung flights to be accommodated, and the height of the building will be influenced by the height of the flights. Natural daylight enters the building from a run of plate glass above the flights, in such a way that the birds can perch beneath the solid roof or the glass according to their preference. Heating should be provided to keep the air temperature a few degrees above freezing in winter and ventilation is provided by extractor fans.

The birds are housed in flights constructed of 1'' x 1½'' wire of 14 gauge for birds up to Amazon size; larger cockatoos and macaws will need 10 gauge with 1'' x 1'' spacing. The flights are suspended from the ceiling. Service doors are best cut in the sides of the flights so that the food and water pots can be placed in the centre. Perches are positioned towards either end of the flight.

Nest boxes can be hung on the outside of the flights, preferably at the outer wall end where the wall will give security, and the monitoring of the nests will be uncomplicated.

Since parrots housed in indoor flights have no access to rain-water a mist spray, as used in garden aviaries, is essential. It will serve to keep birds in good feather, as even those that shy away from direct contact with water will benefit from the moisture in the air.

Lighting in the halls should, as in the garden aviary, be programmed to come on in the early morning and, to be of benefit to the parrots it is hoped to breed from, it must be sufficiently bright. In the wild state the parrot will have a day and night of approximately 12 hours each throughout the year; in captivity, if the daylight can be extended to about 15 hours, it does help bring both males and females into breeding condition earlier.

MIXED COLLECTIONS

In some situations, it is desirable to house a large mixed collection as an attraction. To carry this out effectively the subjects must be chosen with the utmost care. Nothing is more distressing than a group of parrots put on display in a too-small aviary where the dominant birds fight and the subordinate ones live in obvious terror. In a collection of non-breeding birds it is best to have birds all of the same sex, as this will eliminate much of the fighting over mates.

New additions to a mixed collection should not be turned loose in the aviary at the mercy of the resident birds. After a new bird has undergone a period of quarantine, its cage can be set up in the aviary for a few days in order to get to know the inmates, learn the pecking order and become accustomed to its new surroundings. When there is a problem of fighting in mixed collection, rather than permanently removing those that have been attacked, the problem is usually overcome if the aggressor is rehoused. It is advisable to have several feeding points to enable shy birds to try again if driven from the food by bolder ones. Irregularly shaped aviaries will give shy birds some measure of security since they are not compelled to perch where eye contact with an aggressive bird is unavoidable.

HOUSE PETS

Parrots that are kept as house pets also need an area of territory and even those that have the run of the house will want a place they can return to, to rest or feed. This home base can be a single cage or one of the more elaborate indoor aviaries. If a cage is used then it should be large enough to allow two or more perches. There must be room for the parrot to beat its outstretched wings and to stand tall on the perches. Whether a cage or an indoor aviary is used to house a pet parrot, it must be kept very clean and be placed in a good light away from strong sunlight and draughts.

It was not uncommon at one time to see large macaws and cockatoos permanently chained by the leg to a perch or a stand. In these more enlightened days house pets can expect to receive more humane care. They will not be happy if left alone for long hours at a time as they need constant companionship, either from their owner or from other pet parrots.

BREEDING

Where there are only a few pairs of parrots kept the exercise is usually very much in the form of a hobby, and the number of young raised each season is not of paramount importance. Similarly, parrots that are kept primarily as show or display birds are not always housed in a good enough environment to encourage them to breed well. Most of the commonly kept parrots will readily go to nest if given the opportunity — indeed, in commercial units most pairs double clutch.

One of the major reasons for parrots being unsuccessful in producing young is that the pair are of the same gender. Two males or two females can live together happily, forming a close bond, one often being the dominant partner. Hens kept together will produce eggs, sometimes sharing the one nest box; they can be observed going through a form of copulation as will two male birds. The dominant male often drives the weaker one into the nest box where it can be held for long periods and become weak from lack of food. Closely bonded parrots of the same sex kept together will vent preen, stoop to be mated, feed partners with regurgitated food, drive other birds away from the mate and will try to copulate.

When the sex of each of these closely bonded pairs has been positively identified it is often difficult to rematch them. Many of the larger parrots are life-long mates and it is therefore difficult to break up closely wedded couples within the unit, since even out of each other's sight they will call to each other and ignore or attack any new partner selected for them. It is often better to place one of the couple in another collection.

Many of the smaller parrots and parakeets are not as difficult, and do not pair for life. These can be given new partners should their breeding results be disappointing. Couples that are to be split up are best moved soon after they moult out; they will have recovered from their lowest ebb but they will not be in breeding condition and will have several months to become close to their new partner. Only if they mate can eggs be fertile. An aggressive hen can scare away her new mate, and a dominant male may find his partner takes refuge in the nest box hiding away from his advances. She may even lay a few eggs and, if permitted, sit on them until the male loses interest in breeding.

Breeding pairs that have been well cared for during the winter months will not have lost too much condition. Not only must they have sufficient food in the coldest part of the winter, but they must also be properly cared for during the short, dull days. This is the time of the year when losses occur, especially in collections where the treatment for round worms is inadequate. If birds can be over-wintered comfortably they will be quicker to come into the peak of condition needed for breeding.

As the daylight becomes stronger and days lengthen so the breeding males become more vocal and feather colour improves, becoming intense in some parrots. Some males and occasionally females that are over-keen to mate will harass their partner, driving them from perch to perch. If chivvying becomes too persistent and the bird pursued is exhausted then some of the flight feathers on one wing of the aggressor can be cut to slow the bird in flight. Appetites will be sharpened and a courtship will begin. In some birds this may be more demonstrative than in others, with much dilating of pupils (especially in the males), arching of bodies, extending of necks and exaggerated wing displays. Some parrots will jump from the perch, turning somersaults. Single males without hens to feed may try to feed objects in their cage with regurgitated food and will try to copulate with food pots, toys or even their owner.

NEST BOXES

In the aviaries, nest boxes should be in place before birds come into breeding condition. Those that are left in situation all year for birds that use them for sleeping can be cleaned out of old nesting material. Clean peat and sand can replace the old, or soft wood chippings can be used instead. Sometimes a combination of peat and wood chippings is used. Nest boxes are mostly constructed out of stout wood and are rectangular in shape. The base should be large enough to hold the hen comfortably without her feeling she is in a great void, but there must be room to house a brood of chicks that will each be as large as the parent birds before they leave the nest. If the nest box is too small then there can be trouble later when the male helps with the feeding of the young, sometimes ending in fatality if the male is overcrowded by demanding chicks.

The height can be two or three times the width of the base. A nest box that is too shallow will allow too much penetration of light; equally, one that is too deep and over-dark will not be inviting. The hen must feel safe and secure, otherwise she will not sit tight on the eggs. An inspection door is set to one side just above the level of the nesting material. If it is cut too close to the base, then nesting material will be disturbed when it is opened to inspect eggs or young.

An entrance hole is cut a few inches from the top of the nest box. A suitable perch needs to be fixed at the entrance to allow easy access. Inside the nest box a metal ladder should be provided taking care to avoid sharp edges. If wood is used the hen may whittle it away to add to her nesting material and so trap herself and later her young. Strips of green wood can be fixed inside the nest box which the hen will break down for added nesting material. Parrots that are destructive may need the outside corners of their nest box edged with metal strips. Cockatoos are especially destructive, some needing their nest box to be completely covered outside in metal or wire netting and a concrete skin.

As the female comes into lay, she may fuss over her nest, scratching and digging in the nesting material, chewing about the entrance hole. Some parrots will enlarge the entrance hole to such an extent that they are insecure and will not deposit eggs in the nest. Often a strip of wood nailed over the entrance, almost sealing it, will provide the stimulus a hen needs.

PERCHES

Perches are of great importance, too. If they are too large or too small in circumference the breeding birds will not find the hold they need during copulation — both the male and female need a good footing.

COPULATION

Copulation will take place while the birds are on the perch, on the ground, or on top of the nest box. The pair may back on to each-other, or the male place one foot on the hen, or he may stand on the hen's back. Mating can be observed several times a day with some pairs; others may not be seen to mate or have any close contact with each other and yet babies are hatched.

INCUBATION

Macaws and many of the smaller parrots lay up to four eggs, while large cockatoos often produce only two eggs. It is not always easy to note the exact day the hen starts to set the eggs. Some hens will sit tight on the second egg, others on the third. It cannot be assumed that because the hen keeps to her nest after the laying of the first egg that she is sitting tight and incubation has begun. Eggs may be warmed and cooled several times as subsequent eggs are laid. When incubation has properly begun then the eggs must not chill. Many male birds will feed the sitting hen, calling her to the entrance hole or entering the nest box himself to regurgitate food. The hen may only leave her eggs once or twice a day to defecate and perhaps take water. If she is disturbed unnecessarily and is quick to come off her eggs the embryos will weaken and may later die.

Everything possible should be done to help flighty hens. The nest box should not only be sighted out of direct sunlight and rain, it should be placed away from passing people and away from neighbouring birds. There can be few things more distracting for a sitting hen than a neighbouring pair perching close to her box, albeit on the other side of a wire partition, and, for nest boxes hung on the wire, a constant vibration as the male climbs along the wire partition.

Some male parrots will take part in the incubation of eggs and the brooding of the chicks. In particular, the cockatiel and some cockatoos.

CANDLING

Although sitting hens should have all the security required, it is of great advantage to candle eggs. These days the eggs need not be taken from the nest, as a portable transilluminator can be used. It is possible to identify a fertile egg within 30 hours of incubation; however, most breeders prefer to candle parrot eggs after they have been incubated for 7 days. At this stage, a pattern of blood vessels can be seen in the yolk. The shell of the parrot egg is white. They have no need of camouflage since most parrots nest in holes or deep clefts in trees, these originally made by some other bird or animal.

If on candling the eggs they are found to be fertile, then the hen need not be disturbed again. If at 7 days of incubation they are clear, then they should be removed in the hope the hen will lay again, possibly three weeks from the taking of her clear eggs.

NESTLINGS

When there are chicks in the nest, food consumption will be greatly increased. For the first few days, perhaps even for the first two weeks, the male will collect food and call the hen to the nest box entrance to be fed. She will take all the food he brings and will hold it within her crop until it is at the right stage for regurgitation. Newly hatched chicks are fed a thin liquid containing bacterial crop flora. After a few days a thicker soup-like liquid is given until, at about a week or so, the chicks are fed quite lumpy food. As they demand more food the male will help in the feeding, coming into the nest box and regurgitating food into the open beaks of his chicks.

The rôle played by the captive male parent is very artificial. In the wild the parent birds are at all times alert to danger. They often must fight to gain possession of the nesting site and then must hold it against all comers, driving off other house hunting birds and animals, and in their turn must avoid predators. Food is often some way from the nesting site, and it has to be gathered and taken to the ever hungry youngsters. When the young leave the nest they must be constantly called to keep them together as a group. They need to be taught to find food and to feed themselves, and they must learn to survive. The parents are fully occupied until the young become independent. Captive birds become lax, they have no need to keep one eye cocked to the sky for birds of prey, food is always to hand, and there is no competition within the aviary. Such an artificial existence can bring about problems within the nest. One or both parents can become aggressive — perhaps the chicks are too demanding and the male feels threatened or maybe the chicks are not taking all the food the parent birds bring to the nest thereby frustrating the adults. For whatever reason, very occasionally chicks are killed in the nest; injuries include the pulling off of the mandible and the feet — the body, too, can be badly bitten. When this happens within a nest it does not necessarily mean the parent bird will always kill its young. In most cases it never occurs again.

The plucking of youngsters is another problem that sometimes occurs; the parents can be anxious to go to nest again and will pluck the heads of their young in an endeavour to have them vacate the nest. Some parrots especially the larger species will pluck young that are flighted. Obviously it is best to remove these youngsters.

Food made available for parent-raised chicks is usually that which is found suitable for adults, but many breeders put out an abundance of green plant food and soft food for the parents to feed their chicks. Many pairs will welcome soft food which can be rusk, monkey chow, cooked rice, or one of the breakfast cereals softened with fruit juice or perhaps milk and hard boiled egg.

When the young leave the nest box they will not be as skilled as their parents in controlling their wings. They need practice, and must learn the confines of the aviary. If alarmed, small parakeets can take off at speed. Therefore, in addition to putting up more perches before they leave the nest box, a back drop in the form of leafy branches can be attached to the outside of the wire panelling. This will check flighty youngsters who may otherwise fly blindly into the wire. Once flighted, few youngsters will return to the nest box to sleep, only those whose parents normally use a sleeping box will endeavour to do so.

The first few nights newly flighted youngsters go to roost is usually an anxious time for the breeder, since they will seldom perch with the adults. They hang on the wire in the most exposed place with little protection from weather and predators. An unfamiliar object such as a sack can be placed on the panelling just before dark to discourage youngsters from perching in places other than where they will be safe. The practice can be repeated for a few nights, removing the sack each morning.

Most parents will continue to feed their flighted young. The family group may be happy to stay together for some weeks, but inevitably the pattern is broken. The parents may want to go to nest again or the male may object to the rivalry of the young males and will attack them.

FOSTERING

Not all chicks are raised without problems. If the male becomes ill or dies while there are eggs in the nest the hen can usually cope. Food can be placed within easy reach, and when the chicks hatch and later become too demanding some can be fostered, as would be the case if the hen was lost and the male unable to care for the chicks.

Most parrots will accept one or two extra babies, and if they can be fostered out then the keeper will be saved a lot of work. Baby chicks to be fostered are best introduced into a nest of similar sized chicks. If the other chicks are too big then they will be overlooked at feeding time; equally if large chicks are placed in a nest of tiny ones then the smaller will not survive.

The diet must also be similar. For instance, brush tongued parrot chicks would not survive if placed in a nest containing seed eating parrot chicks. When a nest has been selected to receive chicks it is best to introduce them while the hen is absent. If she can be kept off her nest for several minutes her foster chicks will have become part of her brood, and indistinguishable. The best time of day to introduce chicks is in the early part of the day. The nest can then be inspected later to make sure the chicks are being fed.

MECHANICAL INCUBATORS

Whilst raising young in the natural nest is a joy, there are other ways which are usually adopted by large commercial and non-commercial units. One of these methods is to mechanically incubate eggs.

There are many good incubators available on the market, many costing less than a common pet parrot. Those contemplating using an incubator to hatch parrot eggs would be well advised to gain the fundamental basic knowledge by practising with fertile chicken eggs first. Incubators are usually cabinets containing a thermostat or other means of heat control. Those commonly used are either still air or forced air machines.

There must be water within the unit, and a simple means of obtaining humidity readings is to place a cotton wick at least 3cm (1 ¼ '') over a mercury bulb. The other end of the wick is immersed in distilled water. There has to be air intake and exhaust. Distilled water is preferable to tap water to avoid the build up of mineral deposits in the water bowl.

With few exceptions parrot eggs require a temperature of 98.5°F in the incubator with a wet bulb reading of 84°F (28.8°C) which will give a relative humidity of 53%. Incubators are often influenced by the surrounding temperature and atmosphere. A unit sited in an unheated cold building will be asking too much of the heating components — the constant making and breaking will reduce its working life. Whereas an incubator sited in a room kept at a constant 70°F will run more efficiently. Humidity is not always constant, either. A dry atmosphere outside the incubator may necessitate an increase of surface area of water for evaporation; too humid an atmosphere will mean less surface water needed within the unit.

Eggs placed in the incubator will need to be turned several times a day. This can be accomplished by hand if the unit does not have an automatic turner. The incubation period differs between species. Eggs of some small parrots and parakeets take from 18 days, whereas the Amazon eggs take 24 — 26 days and the large macaws 28 days. During the incubation period an egg should lose between 15% and 16% of its new laid weight. A graph kept on each egg will ensure it keeps on course, and should it fail to lose enough weight the surface water within the incubator can be reduced. Similarly, eggs that lose too much weight will need more humidity within the incubator.

BROODERS

Once hatched, chicks are taken from the incubator and kept in a brooder at a comfortable temperature, which for most parrots is 97°F (36.1°C) for the first few days. Over the next three weeks, the temperature can be lowered to 90°F (32.3°C) but at all times chicks should be comfortable. Chicks that are kept in groups of 3 or 4 should form a huddle in the container, and if they are warm enough they will be content, active when fed, and their crops will empty. Those that are too warm will break the huddle, lying apart.

Brooders and incubators must be thoroughly cleaned and disinfected daily to prevent a build-up of bacteria, especially pseudomonas. 1% Teego (Goldsmidt) is ideal.

HAND FEEDING

Newly hatched babies should feed well. Tiny ones can be fed by means of a paint brush dipped into the formula; with the head of the baby steadied in an upright position, the liquid is allowed to trickle into the open beak. Larger, newly hatched chicks can receive their first few days feed from a pipette.

Breeders have different views regarding feeding formula. With the exclusion of the brush tongued parrots, most newly hatched parrot chicks are fed a formula which contains infant foods, especially jars of fruit puree which is made very liquid with the addition of water. The mixture is fed warmed to body temperature. Within a few days, chicks should be ready for a little cereal, such as baby breakfast cereals, added to their feed and the extracted liquid from dark green plant food (not cabbage). As they progress a more bulky food is required and many breeders find powdered vegetable or fruit formulae marketed for infants are ideal since they contain a little cereal and skimmed milk powder and also all the vitamins and minerals the baby chick needs.

In commercial units breeding for the pet market, a cheaper food is required. This often contains cooked rice, monkey chow, hulled sunflower seed and nuts which are all finely ground to a powder and made into a gruel with water.

Once chicks are feeding well, something larger than a pipette is required, and many breeders find a small spoon with the sides of the bowl drawn together makes a satisfactory feeding tool. Others use a plastic syringe — it is all a matter of personal choice. As the chicks progress they will need to be moved into larger containers and whereas tiny chicks can be kept on absorbent tissue which is renewed at each feed, larger chicks can be kept on dry moss peat or white wood chippings.

By the time the chicks are in pin feather they will need to be kept at a room temperature of 70 — 75°F until they are fully feathered and no longer needing to be hand fed. A small group of chicks in pin feather can be accommodated in a heated, wire-fronted box, but for large numbers it is often easier to heat a room and hold the birds in plastic tubs until they are flighted.

UNEMPTIED CROPS

Unemptied crops in chicks are often a concern to the inexperienced and the causes are numerous. They include chicks suffering from diseases, including candidiasis, and in need of urgent veterinary treatment; those that are losing strength and fading; those that are cold and kept at too low a temperature. If the problem is dietary the chicks, even very young ones, can be given a starchy liquid made by overboiling round grain rice in water. The strained liquid can be given without any other food or additions for several days. Food should clear from the crop within 24 hours and there should be no need to flush out the crop. However, if the content is material other than food, such as peat or wood chippings, it can often be removed by passing a soft rubber tube attached to a syringe into the oesophagus and so into the crop. The crop can be flushed with warm water, and this is then gently extracted bringing with it the contents of the crop. The procedure can be repeated until all foreign matter is brought out. In some cases it may be necessary to operate to remove larger pieces from the crop.

Diets that contain high amounts of fibre are especially unsuitable for young chicks, as the liquid is extracted and the fibrous matter remains in the crop. Should this occur it is important to give liquids, otherwise the chick will dehydrate. A rice water diet for a day or two is usually necessary, and once the crop has emptied and the chick is ready to take food again a less fibrous diet can be given.

WEANING

Parent-raised chicks leave the nest once they have flight feathers and these youngsters keep together as a family group. They will learn from the adults how to feed from the food pots etc., but hand raised chicks lack these teachers. They need to be taught to feed themselves, and this can be achieved by hanging up soft ripe apple, pear, peach, banana, pawpaw and cobs of corn in the tubs of chicks just past the pin feather stage. The food may be ignored for many days, and it may seem a chore to keep replacing it with fresh fruit. Once a start has been made, however, a little food such as the parent birds eat can be placed near the fruit. As more interest is shown in self feeding, less hand feeding will be necessary. A feed can be offered in the morning and again at night. The morning feed can later be withdrawn, and when the young are feeding well the night feed can be stopped.

Youngsters that are being weaned need to be watched carefully, as there are often setbacks. Those that have been feeding well may suddenly start begging to be hand fed again, refusing self feed. These youngsters do better if the food pots are at the end of the perches where they cannot help but notice them. One or two greedy parrots of about the same age and size housed with a difficult one will sometimes help it to regain an interest in self feeding. It may be necessary to hand feed such a bird at night. The crop can be felt, and if it is empty then the bird can be given all that it can take. If it is offered more than the night feed it may become lazy and refuse to feed itself. Every effort should be made to avoid this situation. Youngsters that have been self feeding for two weeks can be considered fully weaned, but they need to be watched for a further two weeks in case of set backs.

INDEX